RELIGION, PSYCHOPATHOLOGY AND COPING

D1475832

Edited by

Halina Grzymała-Moszczynska
and Benjamin Beit-Hallahmi

∞ The paper on which this book is printed meets the requirements of "ISO 9706:1994, Information and documentation - Paper for documents - Requirements for permanence".

CIP-GEGEVENS KONINKLIJKE BIBLIOTHEEK, DEN HAAG

Religion

Religion, psychopathology and coping / ed. by Halina
Grzymała-Moszczyńska and Benjamin Beit-Hallahmi. —
Amsterdam - Atlanta, GA 1996 : Rodopi. — (International series
in the psychology of religion, ISSN 0925-4153 ; 4)
ISBN: 90-5183-626-0
Trefw.: godsdienstpsychologie.

©Editions Rodopi B.V., Amsterdam - Atlanta, GA 1996
Printed in The Netherlands

POPE PIUS XII LIBRARY, ST. JOSEPH COL.
3 2528 07527 4136

RELIGION, PSYCHOPATHOLO

INTERNATIONAL SERIES IN THE PSYCHOLOGY OF RELIGION

4

Edited by

J.A. van Belzen and J.M. van der Lans

Consulting Editors

B. Beit-Hallahmi (Haifa)
L.B. Brown (Kensington, N.S.W.)
D.S. Browning (Chicago)
D.E. Capps (Princeton)
J.P. Deconchy (Villiers-le-Bel)
A. Godin (Bruxelles)
H. Grzymała-Moszczyńska (Cracow)
H.G. Heimbrock (Frankfurt)
N.G. Holm (Åbo)
D. Hutsebaut (Leuven)
J.M. Jaspard (Louvain-la-Neuve)
W.W. Meissner (New Haven)
H. Müller-Pozzi (Zürich)
H. Newton Malony (Pasadena)
J. Scharfenberg (Kiel)
A. Uleyn (Molenhoek)
A. Vergote (Leuven)
O. Wikström (Uppsala)

Amsterdam - Atlanta, GA 1996

TABLE OF CONTENTS

SECTION 2. THEORY-GUIDED RESEARCH

SECTION 3. CLINICAL RESEARCH

SECTION 4. CASE STUDIES

INTRODUCTION

The relationship between religion and mental health has received a substantial amount of attention from psychologists in the last decades. Over the course of this time researchers have become interested in both aspects of the relationship: theoretical analysis and empirical research. This approach becomes convincingly demonstrated by Schumaker in his introductory overview in "Religion and Mental Health" (Schumaker, 1992).

We can trace certain lines of development concerning research and theoretical reflection on this topic. Up to the beginning of the 1960s, the research and theoretical analysis were dispersed and treated separately in the literature. One of the first attempts to integrate them was organized along various measures of mental health, i.e., personal adequacy, ability to adjust to life crises, suicide potential, alcohol use/abuse, crime and delinquency (Argyle, Beit-Hallahmi, 1975). Sometimes analyses of the research were conducted concerning various dimensions of religion, i.e., beliefs, practices, emotions, knowledge of doctrine and consequential aspects of religious convictions (Becker, 1971).

Correlations between religiosity and mental health served also as a basis for grouping results. Results were selected depending on positive, negative or zero correlation between religion and mental health (Sanua, 1969). One highly successful attempt to overcome partly confusing results of previous summaries was undertaken by Batson, Schoenrade, and Ventis (1993). They employed a meta-theoretical method of analysis in which they specified "background" definitions of religion and mental health to which various authors contributed. Batson and his colleagues catalogued results according to explicit or implicit definitions of both terms. Their analysis revealed a quite coherent pattern according to which the correlation between religion and mental health variables depends conjointly on the way of being religious and the adopted normative pattern of mental health, rather than on only one of those factors considered separately.

Another important contribution towards clarification of the relationship between an individual's religiosity and his/her mental health was achieved through recognition and analysis of certain methodological inadequacies present in some published research (Lea, 1982). Among the major errors noted were the following: certain research studies had been based on samples of convenience, lack of control of basic demographic variables, correlational character of research procedures followed by overinterpretation of results as connected by cause-effect relationship.

The relationship between religion and psychopathology has gained a new dimension by the employment of the coping perspective. It stresses a cognitive approach to the analysis of the influence of religion on the mental health of individuals. It also provides possible background for cross-cultural and inter-religious analysis of the relationship between religion and psychopathology. The coping perspective emphasizes a more active role for religion in human life. The operating element of the coping perspective can be understood in this way. People not only "have" their religion because they inherited it during socialization or because they converted to it. People also quite actively "use" their religion in facing the important and challenging situations of everyday life. Choices in such situations will be co-shaped by culture, religion and personality. Not only major life stresses (death, heavy injury, fatal illness) require coping efforts. Otherwise, more trivial moments in a person's life demand such efforts due to the importance of such for the individual.

A second element of the coping process concerns evaluation of the reasons attributed to the situation by an individual. Religion plays a vital role in determining this causality in two ways. First, each religious tradition contains a coding system for human behaviour and its consequences. Second, individual religiosity contributes towards the attribution of causes to the situation: irrevocable fate, Gods' anger, invasion by demons, one's moral failure, or trespasses by another from the same tribe.

Coping activities (the next part of coping process) undertaken by individuals are significantly informed by their religion. Individuals might engage in any of the following: a passive acceptance of God's will or in an attempt to calm God's anger by various sorts of offering and cleansing ceremonies or in mental exercises, designed towards a changing of perception concerning the current situation, or in consulting religious specialists and their remedies.

A coping process employing one's religion can be based on various strategies to alleviate the problem. Redefinition of one's situation could be considered the most universal: to be stigmatized by a difficult situation means that God (gods) is assessing one's capacity for a special mission. The situation therefore might be redefined as a chance for improving one's character through suffering in order to receive eternal life, or it might be considered as one's karma (irrevocable sequence of events based on deeds in previous life). Among the most powerful resources to cope with such a situation is to disperse the responsibility for such to other members of the community and to reformulate one's role as causal agent suffering for the misdeeds of someone else from the tribe.

Results of the coping process employing religious perspective might be manifold. Some might be of clear benefit for the person in question. Beneficial effects of religious practices like prayer, meditation, exorcism, trance induction ceremonies, are some examples. Another effect might lead to the alleviation of the stress connected to the challenging situation through the process stepping into the role of a divine messenger. Finally, employing a religious perspective might attribute to the degradation of a person through an accumulation of feelings associated with living under God's wrath or a conviction that one is being selected for suffering and annihilation by an angry god.

The coping perspective employing the relationship between religion and mental health has proved promising in one more area. It has created not only opportunity for integrating research results from various cultures and different religious traditions without losing their culture-specific and religion-specific orientation but also opportunity to analyze the preventive and health promoting role of religion.

This second opportunity has been undertaken and the results amply documented in the recent book by Pargament, Maton, and Hess, "Religion and Prevention in Mental Health: Research, Vision and Action" (1992). Their research documents how religious coping can be helpful in preventing stress stemming from expected life demands. As the coping strategies are of a preventive character they stress learning how to actively avoid a stressful situation, how to promote non-threatening appraisals of that situation, how to increase the level of one's competence to deal with such a situation, and how to mobilize resources for a successful outcome.

Our book grew out of a conference on religion, mental health, and psychopathology, sponsored by the Institute for the Science of Religion, Cracow University, and held in December 1990 in Mogilany, Poland. The conference hosted numerous participants representing a spectrum of approaches, cultures, theories, clinical experience and scholarship. In this volume the reader will find variety, debates, some new ideas, and a variety of settings, clinical and academic. If one is looking for uniformity and agreement, he or she will not find them here, while finding a wealth of findings and ideas.

The coverage is comprehensive, up to date, and eclectic, sometimes even contradictory.

The eclectic orientation of this volume is reflected in its division into four sections:

1. theoretical overviews

2. theory-guided research
3. clinical research
4. case studies

The book deals with the consequential aspect of religion, or more precisely, with the consequences that religion has for the mental health of individual. Because of the fact that historical developments in the field exercise important influence on today's theorizing and research, the volume starts from a historical overview of differentiation between psychic vs. somatic and natural vs. supernatural causes attributed to mental illnesses during the course of human history from biblical times to the present. Jaap A. Belzen presents a ramification of the relationship between religion and mental health also within a context of different theoretical traditions: psychoanalytic, phenomenological and historical-cultural.

Marinus H.F. van Uden and Jan Z.T. Pieper's paper offers an interesting review of research mostly not available to the broader public because it was originally published in Dutch. The authors structure their presentation according to the Spilka, Hood and Gorsuch schema specifying possible relations between religion and mental health (positive influence of religion on mental health, suppression of deviant behavior by religion, religion as haven, religion as an outlet for pathology, religion as a hazard for mental health).

Jozef Corveleyn presents a critical review of the psychological research on coping with death. This research is dominated by the functional explanation of religion promoted by Freud: religion as a wish-fulfilling response to the tragedy of death. It is astonishing how much influence this schematic idea has had on the empirical research into attitudes towards, and strategies of coping with, death. Corveleyn demonstrated that this functional approach is in many research projects more of a self-fulfilling prophecy than a means of clarifying the complex psychological meaning of death.

The next two authors explore new theoretical paths for approaching the relationship between religion and mental pathology. Analyzing the affinities between religion and mental pathology, Benjamin Beit-Hallahmi maintains that they occupy the same continuum. Differences between them are more a question of the quantity rather than the quality of symptoms. Similar content and mechanisms could be detected in both religion and pathology. There is, however, a very important difference between them: mental pathology does not allow an individual temporary regression in cognitive and emotional processes, regression in service of the ego. Religion contains sources and potentials for pathology, which under particular historical conditions (as a political crisis causing stress and distress among members of the society) have a very good chance to present themselves as deviant mental states. The paper presents a continuation of the author's search for suitable metaphors helpful for understanding psychological mechanisms of religion. The author uses pathology as a metaphor in the same way he was using art in previous publications.

The next author, Halina Grzymala-Moszczyńska, also stresses similarities between mechanisms involved in religion and mental pathology. She tries to analyze both of them from the cognitive point of view represented by the theory of transgression. Both religion and mental pathology create an attempt to cross individual limitations and broken life space by means of creating an alternative image of the world. Different forms of heterostatic motivation stimulating efforts to enlarge and re-create an individual's life also play an important role in the adopting of particular religious orientations (means, end or quest).

Mental health and its connection to religion is the topic of main interest for the last two authors in the first section. Jan van der Lans analyses the influence of the meaning-giving function of religion for mental health, operationalized as the psychological well being of the individual. Religion provides people with an enormously rich source of life purposes, cognitive orientations and evaluations of the life situation. The author presents a model that helps to predict when religion can and when it cannot fulfill this role.

Specification of the positive influence of religion is the focus of James T. Richardson's overview of research on the mental health of NRM members. The author expresses the conviction, based on presented research that membership in NRM's positively influences the mental health of the members. Because of that, the negative attitudes of representatives of legal professions towards membership in NRM's, which are mainly based on the conviction that the mental health of members is harmed by the influence of the religious group, seem to lack any sound basis.

The second section of the book consists of papers focused on the analysis of the influence of religion on mental health in the light of various psychological theories. Paweł Socha tests various models of religious development and its consequences for mental health understood as a capacity for further social and individual growth of the human being. He places various religious orientations along a life-span developmental continuum. Extrinsic, indiscriminately positive, intrinsic and quest orientations are just steps interwoven in the developmental dynamic of the individual.

Cognitive concepts of coping have gradually become more conspicuous within research on individual religiosity. Lawrence B. Brown and Kenneth I. Pargament are using them to analyse how religion helps individuals to understand and to deal with significant and difficult moments in their lives. Pargament specifies criteria for dentifying effective religious coping. Brown presents research results concerning coping strategies chosen by religious and nonreligious subjects in health risk situations.

A cognitive approach, combined with ego psychology, has been adopted by Antoon Geels to create a scheme for interpreting the healing role of mystical experiences for contemporary persons in difficult, stressful situations. The experiences are treated as a way of regaining mental balance after severe stress. Experienced crisis creates a most important motivational basis for religious visions. The particular lines of analysis trace out the influence of mystical experiences on the emotional, communicative and perceptual styles of experiencing persons.

Neurotic patients and their religiosity are the subjects of the papers in the third section of the book. In the first two papers, Eystein Kaldestad, Hans Stifoss-Hanssen, and K. Gunnar Götestam analyse the connection between particular religious orientations and mental pathology. A strong point of the research is the use of control groups consisting of non psychiatric patients, staff members and clergy.

The authors of the third paper in this section Dorota Kubacka-Jasiecka, Małgorzata Opoczyńska and Roman Dorczak, present research on neurotic patients in clinical context. They try to answer questions regarding the influence of religious values on the process of coping and the position of religious values in individual value systems of neurotics. Religious values in the group of neurotics turned out to be of declarative character, and quite often play an instrumental role by providing a person with feeling of security and a feeling of support. There is also an analysis of influences of religious values on emotional and social maturity of individual and his or her mental health.

H. Newton Malony's essay discusses the spiritual dimensions of counseling. The possibility of clients including increased spirituality among their goals is considered. The Religious Status Interview and the Religious Status Inventory are described as examples of one way of determining how well persons within a given spiritual tradition are appropriating the resources of their faith in daily living. A possible relationship between spirituality and mental health is proposed. The paper also introduces specific directions for how counselors can take advantage of uniquely transforming moments in helping people grow in their faith or become more spiritual.

The last section of the book concentrates on the role of religion in the lives of psychotic patients. Religion among psychotics plays the role of an alternative ordering of the world, which helps to restore a broken life space. It seems to create a confirmation for understanding religion and pathology within transgression theory presented in first section by Grzymala-Moszczyńska paper.

Nils G. Holm and Pertti Jarvinen analyze the influence of religious roles concentrated in religious tradition. Roles help individuals to find new identities patterned on personages within religious tradition.

Krzysztof Cieslak stresses the similarly beneficial effects of introducing the psychotic patient into a religious community. This arrangement helps not only to change the patient is frame of reference for interpretating previous experiences but also provides the person with the positive relationships that are vital for recovery. Depression might, however, lead to negative changes in religiosity. The patient might abandon faith in God or lose the feeling of contact with God or the presence of God. This could be interpreted as a temporary defense maneuver, which helps a patient to avoid feelings of anger or hated directed towards God.

Whatever difficulties the international nature of our team may present, the combining of different cultures and experiences is the source of considerable benefits. It is with the spirit of the new Europe and the new world moving into the 21st century that this book was created.

REFERENCES

Argyle, M., Beit-Hallahmi, B. (1975). *The Social Psychology of Religion*. London: Routledge and Kegan Paul.

Batson, C.D., Schoenrade P., Ventis, W.L. (1993). Religion and the Individual: A Social-Psychological Perspective. New York: Oxford University Press.

Becker, R.J. (1971), Religion and Psychological Health. In M.P. Strommen (ed.), *Research on Religious Development*. New York: Hawthorn Books. (pp. 391-421).

Lea, G. (1982). Religion, Mental Health and Clinical Issues. *Journal of Religion and Health*, 21, 336-351.

Pargament, K.I., Maton, K.I., Hess, R.E. (Eds.). (1992). *Religion and Prevention in Mental Health: Research, Vision, and Action*. New York: The Haworth Press.

Sanua, V.D. (1969). Religion, Mental Health and Personality: A Review of Empirical Studies. *American Journal of Psychiatry*, 125, 1203-1213.

Schumaker, J.F. (Ed.). (1992). *Religion and Mental Health*. New York, Oxford: Oxford University Press.

Contributors:

Benjamin Beit-Hallahmi
University of Haifa
Haifa 31905
ISRAEL

Jaap A. Belzen
University van Amsterdam
THE NETHERLANDS

Lawrence B. Brown
The Alister Hardy Research Centre
Westminster College, Oxford, OX2 9AT
Great Britain

Krzysztof Ciesłak, Ph.D. (died 1993)
Institute of Psychology
Jagiellonian University
ul. Piłsudskiego 13, 31-110 Krakow
POLAND

Jozef Corveleyn
Faculteit der Psychologie en Pedagogische Wetenschappen
Katholieke Universiteit Leuven
Tiensestraat 102, 3000 Leuven
BELGIUM

Roman Dorczak
Institute of Psychology,
Department of Developmental and Educational Psychology
Jagiellonian University
ul. Piłsudskiego 13, 31-110 Kraków
POLAND

Antoon Geels
Department of Religious Studies
Allhelgona Kyrkogata 8, S-223 62 Lund
SWEDEN

Halina Grzymala-Moszczyńska
Institute for the Science of Religion

Jagiellonian University
Rynek Glowny 34, 31-010 Krakow
POLAND

K. Gunnar Götestam
University of Trondheim
The Medical Faculty
Department of Psychiatry and Behavioural Medicine
Östmarka Hospital
P.O. Box 3008 Lade
7002 Trondheim
NORWAY

Nils G.Holm
Department of Comparative Religion
Abo Akademi
Bishopsgatan 10, SF-20 500 Abo
FINLAND

Pertti Jarvinen
Department of Comparative Religion
Abo Akademi
Bishopsgatan 10, SF-20 500 Abo
FINLAND

Eystein Kaldestad
Research Institute of Modum Bads Nervesanatorium
N-3371 Vikersund
NORWAY

Dorota Kubacka-Jasiecka
Institute of Psychology, Department of Clinical Psychology
Jagiellonian University
ul. Pilsudskiego 13, Krakow
POLAND

Jan van der Lans
Psychological Laboratory
Catholic University Nijmegen
Montessorilaan 3, 6525 HE Nijmegen
THE NETHERLANDS

H. Newton Malony
Graduate School of Psychology
Fuller Theological Seminary
Pasadena, California 91182
USA

Kenneth I. Pargament
Department of Psychology
Bowling Green State University
Bowling Green, Ohio 43403-0228
USA

James T. Richardson
Department of Sociology
University of Nevada
Reno, Nevada 89557
USA

Malgorzata Opoczynska
Institute of Psychology, Department of Clinical Psychology
Jagiellonian University
ul.PiŁsudskiego 13, 31-110 Krakow
POLAND

Jan Z.T. Pieper
University of Nijmegen
Facultu of Theology, UTP
Postbus 4406
6401 CX Heerlen
The Netherlands

Gustaf Stahlberg
Institute of Theology
University of Uppsala
Slottsgrand 3, S-751 46 Uppsala
SWEDEN

Hans Stifoss-Hanssen
University of Trondheim
The Medical Faculty
Department of Psychiatry and Behavioural Medicine
Östmarka Hospital

P.O. Box 3008 Lade
7002 Trondheim
NORWAY

Paweł Socha
Institute for the Science of Religion
ul. Karmelicka 34, 31-128 Kraków
POLAND

Marinus H.F. van Uden
University of Nijmegen
Faculty of Theology, UTP
Postbus 4406
6401 CX Heerlen
THE NETHERLANDS

SECTION 1. THEORETICAL OVERVIEWS

CHAPTER 1
METHODOLOGICAL PERSPECTIVES ON PSYCHOPATHOLOGY AND RELIGION: A HISTORICAL REVIEW

J.A. Belzen

Well nigh inextricably found in every human culture, religion has woven itself into the existence of humanity, and a culture theory can only abstractly distinguish it as an "ideological system" from techno-economics, social structure and personality (Kaplan & Manners, 1972). Religion has inspired the highest and the best. On our voyages we admire temples and cathedrals; in concert halls we enjoy the compositions of religious themes and in museums we devote ourselves to so-called 'religious art'. On the other hand, however, the history of religion is a tale of the menschliches allzu menschliches (Nietzsche), and sometimes of even worse than that: religion has constituted, legitimized and confirmed itself to unworthy relations in the spheres of labour and of society. As on the one hand religion formed people and inspired them to highest service to others, on the other hand she deformed people, oppressed, persecuted and burnt other believers and non-believers.

Leafing through modern handbooks, one will very soon be led to the conclusion that also with regard to the psychopathology of religion, nearly every possibility exists: often religion has nothing to do with mental illness, sometimes, however, it is a pathogenic factor. In some cases religion functions as a 'prophylactic' against mental illness, in other cases she has to be unmasked as one of its symptoms. To make any justifiable and worthwhile statement in this field, it is strictly necessary to study carefully concrete cases to detect what this particular religious form means with this particular patient having this particular illness. The last formulation should not —or at least not just— be judged as an empty, evasive or even pusillanimous manoeuvre to avoid taking a stand. When the formulation does imply ignorance with regard to the question 'what exactly is the relation between religion and mental illness', it nevertheless implies a docta ignorantia and was reached only after a long history during which every other possible position has had its defenders.

1. The Questions

The history of the relations between religion, mental illness and psychiatry certainly would be a voluminous part of a long series of books telling the history of humanity and religion. Exciting and bizarre stories could be told about many individual forms of religious mania (an out-dated term, by the way), of religiously coloured 'psychic epidemics' (for example the well known flagellants in the late Middle Ages: religious groups that beat themselves to the point of bleeding during pilgrimages). A separate chapter in this history has to do with the religious care for the insane, with its counterpart of exorcism, witch-hunting and other now abhorred practices. All this, however, will not be our topic. We shall concentrate on the scientific enterprise called 'psychopathology of religion', and shall review briefly the different viewpoints which have led the 'experts', physicians, psychiatrists and psychologists in their dealing with what they perceived to be pathological forms of religiosity. The scope has to be restricted even more, however, as 'psychopathology of religion' can be understood in several ways.

Different methodological viewpoints lead to different conceptions of the (sub)discipline. In this chapter, however, we shall deal neither with religious examples of different psychopathological diseases (one of the most current understandings of the term), nor with (seemingly) pathological examples of religious behaviour, as for example the experience of being possessed, glossolalia, visions, stigmata (another way in which 'psychopathology of religion' is often understood). This chapter will focus on one of the fundamental methodological viewpoints: the methodical dualism with regard to the genesis of religious psychopathology. We shall treat this topic from a somewhat historicizing perspective. This is not done in order to suggest that unilinear progress has been made in the history of the psychopathology of religion, on the contrary. However, there have been some developments and there has been a succession of dominant viewpoints which can be historically situated. A last preliminary note: with regard to the present, we should realize that every one of the reviewed standpoints still plays a role.

2. Through Antiquity and the Middle Ages

Contrary to popular opinion, the dualism which was alluded to above is certainly not an achievement of modernity. In nearly all cultures, whether historic or contemporary, one finds, with different emphasis, two different explanations for remarkable or deviant psychic phenomena and also for illness in general: natural and supernatural ones. In classic texts as the Bible one finds on the one hand knowledge about somatic determinants of psychic phenomena (for example, dreams), on the other hand however one reads that the condition of the Old Testament king Saul was interpreted as being the work of an non-human, evil spirit, external to Saul. Also in Greek mythology psychic disturbance was seen as something coming from outside the individual, caused by gods.

In the history of medicine it is generally accepted that the Corpus Hippocraticum was a first scientific milestone. Hippocrates tried to explain states of mind and even psychological types by means of variations in the mixture of bodily fluids (blood, phlegm, yellow bile and black bile). He discerned choleric and phlegmatic constitutional types, a later generation added to these types the melancholic and the sanguine. Hippocrates is highly appreciated because he finished with all kinds of 'obscure' causes of illness. In his thought, illness was interpreted strictly somatically, deviations were explained by processes in the body. More 'psychological' approaches still resembled 'demonological' interpretations: illness as the result of something that works from outside on man, on his body, on his soul. Illness then was seen as something that exists independent of the human being, alien to the essence of human nature, something that comes over man and that could be thought of as a demon or as the result of demonic influences. In Aristotle's writings this dualism is also found in strictly somatic interpretations of mental disorders on the one hand and in interpretations in terms of psychic influences on the other hand.

In the European Middle Ages the demonological interpretation gained the field again, due to the influence of Christianity. The works of Albertus Magnus, for example, dealt with the classic hippocratic approach as well as with the possibility of demonic causes of mental illness. Natural, somatic, psychological and supernatural interpretations interfered without problems. P.E. Huston tells of a diagnostic 'trick' that was used to differentiate epileptic attacks caused by demonic influences from those due to natural causes. Words from the Bible were whispered into the ear of the victim: if the attack stopped, it was considered to be a case for the clergyman, for the devil cannot bear hearing these words and leaves the body. If the attack did not stop, the patient had to be treated by a physician (Siegler & Osmond, 1974).

3. Modernity: Psychic versus Somatic.

Two, not independent, developments have been responsible for the new points of view that came up in the psychopathology of religion: the introduction of the experiment in medical science and the Enlightenment. Due to the use of the experiments, medical knowledge progressed enormously in those domains which were accessible to experimental research and to the natural sciences. At the same time, other approaches and viewpoints were discredited as less or even as non-scientific. The Enlightenment had as one of its consequences an emphasis on the transcendental nature of the deity and the divine sphere, which led, among others, to positions like deism. For scientific inquiry the consequences were that one did not have to deny God and his activity, but that it was no longer necessary to take these as a variable in empirical research. God exists, demons too perhaps, but —so reasoning goes— (mental) illnes is not caused by super- or extra-natural influences. This became an important point of view.

As could be expected, before this consensus was reached, the scientific debate or fight (which it actually was) heated up. As the discussion was fought out primarily in German-speaking countries, it is known under the name of the fight between Psychiker (psyschicists) and Somatiker (somaticists). These groups held opposing anthropological presuppositions. The psychicists emphasized the unity of body and soul. In their opinion only the soul is independent and the body is the instrument of the soul. Mental illness provoked by the body is impossible in this view. The body could, if defective, only hinder the correct activity or manifestation of the soul. Only something 'psychic' could be the cause of the disturbances of the soul.

The somaticists on the other hand, defended a dualism of soul and body. In their opinion, illness is never a matter of just the soul or of just the body, but is always an effect of the animated body. The 'soul' can not be ill. Mental illness is a disturbance of the form of the (animated) body, as is implied in the Aristotelian hylomorphism which is underlying their position. For the praxis of scientific research and treatment of the patient this meant that one had to search for the still unknown but presupposed somatic correlate of the psychic symptoms. However, it also meant that in the end these dualists would adopt a methodological monistic materialism, i.e., biologism. Next to the notion of the 'animated body' they did use the concept of the 'soul', but to them this was the object of religion and of metaphysics (eventually inclusive of psychology), not of scientific psychiatry and psychopathology (Verwey, 1985). Thus, they severely criticized J.C.A. Heinroth, the best known representative of the psychicists. Heinroth defined the nature of mental illness as unfreedom, as a consequence of sin or guilt. According to the somaticists he mixed up irresponsibly psychiatric and moral-religious categories in this way.

It would take us too far to discuss the whole controversy. It suffices to know these points of departure and the end of the debate: the somaticists won. The methodological priority that in research they gave to the body, would later be expressed in the adage by Wilhelm Griesinger (1817-1868): 'Geisteskrankheiten sind Gehirnkrankheiten' (1844, p. 96), diseases of the mind are diseases of the brain. Psychiatry at universities (which Karl Jaspers strictly discerned from the psychiatry in asylums) developed ever more in materialistic direction, understood science according to the Galilean tradition and wished psychiatry a share in the prestige of the natural sciences.

4. Fin de Siècle: The Victory of Somatically Oriented Psychiatry

At the end of the 19th century the praises of these developments are generally sung in the leading German handbooks of the time. When for example Von Krafft Ebing reviews the history of psychiatry, he describes how only the conception of psychiatry as a natural science, and as a medical discipline brought liberation from the 'one-sided metaphysical and psychological school', which descended from the Middle Ages. As most important representatives of this 'mystical-pious school' he mentiones Heinroth and Ideler. Von Krafft Ebing found that psychiatry at last 'after a severe struggle gained her rightful place among the natural sciences and purified herself from the last philosophical and metaphysical slags', thanks to the work of men from 'natural science who fought this spiritualistic, ethical and psychological school' (p. 46-7). As the object of psychiatric research he determines: 'the conditions and phenomena, under which the psychic functions deviate from the norm, as well as the assessment of the ways in which the functions can be brought back to the norms'. A psychiatric disease in his opinion is: an 'element of the diseases of the brain and the nerves'.

This somatically oriented school clearly was a reaction to the preceding psychical and ethical schools. There were extreme representatives as T. Meynert (1833-1892) in Vienna (one of Freud's teachers, by the way). Meynert was opposed even to using the word 'psychiatry', because in this science one should deal with the 'soma', not with the 'psyche' (Zilboorg 1941). Thus a somatic reductionism came up in psychiatry. No scientific attention was left for more psychological aspects as the life history of the patient, the relations between his experiences, emotions and behavior, the changes in his (social) situation. It is clear that the study of the psychopathology of religion could not flourish in such an atmosphere.

5. The Twentieth Century: Contrary Notions Searching for the Soul: Psychoanalysis

The reaction could not fail to appear, however. By demythologizing the demonological interpretation of mental illness scientific psychiatry also lost the human empathy for the patient. One of the most important figures from the countermovement, which focused again on the things the patient experienced subjectively and which tried to take the patient's story and his symptoms seriously, was Sigmund Freud (1856-1939). It was a stroke of a genius, when he stated that the patient really is in the grasp of dark powers, unknown to himself. However, these powers are not of a supernatural nature, they are very human, and they are intrapsychic. By translating the former religious language into psychological language, one could detect how in demonology psychic reality is expressed symbolically, a psychic reality that exists in hidden desires, anxieties and attempts to deceive the censorship mechanisms (Vergote, 1987). When the patient claims to be possessed by the devil, this is not an incidental nonsense uttered by an inflicted brain, using the accidental idiom of its surroundings. The statement does contain sense, but it is a sense that has to be discovered. Since the rise of psychoanalysis the older demonology could suddenly be reevaluated as a earlier form of the same seeking and feeling for insight and understanding of the mentally diseased. For the psychopathology of religion this was a great step forward. It showed it was possible to understand all kinds of pathological religious emotions and behavior as conditioned and structured by a mutilated, ill psyche.

As so often, however, the scale tipped in the other direction: Freud and many of his followers couldn't avoid the temptation of making the new insight as embracing as the older demonological one. Now that mental illness has shown to be a matter of psychological, not of supernatural order — could this not be as well the case with religion as a whole? Continually reasoning along the principle of analogy, Freud made bold statements. He compared religious practices to the obsessive actions of the neurotic patient. As the compulsive neurosis comes into being because of feelings of guilt about insufficient control of sexual and/or selfish desires — could it not be then that religion is derived from some feeling of guilt too? Freud answered this question affirmatively: human religion came into being because of feelings of guilt about the murder of the father, somewhere in the beginning of history. And individual religion originates from the life-long existing need for a (strong) father. God is the exalted father of man's childhood.

Freud's essays on culture and religion are beautiful and compelling, however, he transgressed flagrantly the frontiers of his professional competence. A cultural phenomenon such as religion cannot be derived from the (psyche of the) individual; it ought to be the other way round: the individual has to be understood from an analysis of his culture. Fruitful as the new psychological insights introduced by psychoanalysis were, the discussion was obscured a great deal by the fact that the evaluation of religion, even within the psychopathological work, was determined by pre-scientific biases. It was not because of psychological, but because of ontological and anthropological arguments that Freud's analyses were so critical towards religion. Unnecessary storms of protest have been the consequence, psychoanalysis for a long time, and sometimes even today, was repressed in religious circles. As is well known, other psychoanalists have tried to safeguard religion from Freud's critique and they defended a position that implied that religion belongs to human nature, so that the criteria for mental health should include some remarks on religion (for example Jung, Maeder, Fromm). However, they were just working with another anthropological model, they were in fact as biased as Freud was. For the methodology of psychopathological research this was no step forward.

6. Phenomenology

The methodological frontiers were better guarded by another psychological school that tried to correct the one-sidedness of the bio-medical psychiatry by psychological viewpoints. Part of the (early) work of the well known philosopher Karl Jaspers (1883-1969) belongs to this school. He started as a psychiatrist and was at the beginning of the so-called phenomenological movement in psychiatry (Spiegelberg 1972, 1982), which also tried to focus again on what the patient himself said, on the subjective experiences and that tried to develop alternatives for the psychological research methods that came from the tradition of the natural sciences. The phenomenologists, following Dilthey (1894), searched for appropriate methods to explore the nature of the psyche. With regard to the psychopathology of religion, Jaspers spoke of a 'methodological consciousness', meaning the epistemological insight that all knowledge (also scientific knowledge) is determined by the conditions and the capacities of the means by which it was obtained. So knowledge always has its boundaries, is always just partial. For the psychopathology of religion this means that the religious phenomena (and also the 'symptoms') have a double aspect: insofar as they are behaviour and experiences they are submitted to psychophysical conditions, and accessible for psychological and psychopathological research. The religious quality, however, is inaccessible to this kind of research, and has to be judged upon by theology or by philosophy (Heimann, 1961).

The phenomenological school had more attention for religion than the (former) somatically oriented school. Phenomenology could be and usually is combined with the former somatic orientation. One of the best known publications in this field has been Einführung in die Religionspsychopathologie (Introduction to the psychopathology of religion) by Kurt Schneider (1928). He started from a organic understanding of mental disease and described the abnormal religious phenomena that occur with the different clinical pictures. His book was meant for pastors, to teach them to recognize pathologically determined forms of religion in order to be able to collaborate with psychiatrists. Schneider makes no statements about the value or the genesis of the religious symptoms, and in this way gives less insight than the (critical) psychoanalytic school. On the other hand, he had the advantage of leaving aside the quarrel as to whether religion or the patient's religiosity has to be evaluated positively or negatively, as belonging to human nature or not.

7. The Historical-Cultural Psychological Perspective

Our small tour through history is drawing towards its end: we are approaching the present already. In the last decades a historical-cultural perspective has been elaborated upon in psychology. This perspective tries to give due to human historicity: man is a cultural and historical being, who is born into a culture and a religion. These exist prior to the individual, they are objective, and the individual —normally— is taken into the culture and bears its characteristics. It might be, that by personal vicissitudes, someone is psychically mutilated and disturbed. The consequences can be, then, that this person is not or no longer adequately integrated in the objective culture (eventually inclusive of religion). This perspective has the advantage of being modest and empirically oriented. It does not assume that man is by nature either religious or irreligious. Rather, it supposes that man can become religious or irreligious, and that it is this process that has to be investigated. To learn whether a particular behavior, language or sentiment is psychopathological in nature, this perspective takes a double approach. It turns to the culture concerned for a verdict, also in the case of religion. The representatives of the individual's (religious) culture should tell whether a particular religious manifestation is normal or not. Thus this perspective avoids the fallacy of labeling as 'pathological' behavior that the researcher is not acquainted with, but that might be appropriate within a religious (sub)culture. This is the cultural aspect of the perspective, it derives its inspiration from descriptive phenomenology (that is also employed in the sciences of

religion). The second approach is a psychopathological one and makes reference to psychological standards, not to the content of the behavior or experience. It investigates whether the psychological roots of the particular behavior or experience are pathological in nature. This second (historical) is inspired by psychoanalysis: where and how things went wrong in the individual's (early) psychohistory.
Hence, to do research in the psychopathology of religion, one has to discern two levels:
1. the common religious convictions and behaviour of all participants of the culture concerned.
2. the individual organization of life within the collective system.

A psychopathologist of religion can only make statements with regard to an individual in a specific, historical culture. To be able to make such statements he must be acquainted with the human psychic structure as well as with the culture his patient is a participant of. This position is defended, among others, very eloquently in the work of the psychologist-theologian-philosopher Antoine Vergote (*1921), emeritus professor from the university of Louvain, Belgium. He attained a (preliminary) synthesis by combining phenomenological and psychoanalytic insights with historical and anthropological data. Provided with the outlined methodological insight and equipped with the knowledge required, Vergote offers fine historical-psychological analyses, for example of Theresia d'Avila's mystical experiences, of the voices of Jeanne d' Arc and of the visions and stigmata of Thérèse Neumann.

8. Conclusion

From the perspective of the last position, it is clear —a proposition that takes us back to our point of departure— that it is hardly possible to give general, a priori formulations concerning the relation between religion and mental illness. The relation can be structured in many ways and one always has to consider how the relation is structured in any specific case. Hopefully our short exploration has shown something of the long, and often very difficult way which was needed to arrive at this formulation, which may even sound evasive. All kinds of viewpoints have been defended in history: a prioris such as religion is beneficial for health or, the other way around, religion hinders personal growth and autonomy. All kinds of reasoning and practices have existed: demons have been regarded as the cause of illness and religious rituals (e.g., exorcism) as the appropriate remedy, there has been (and still is) non-specific religious care of the insane, there has been the view that neglected religious symptoms al together because it considered psychic disturbances to be just a matter of the mixture of bodily fluids or of brain damage. It seems that scientists have actually taken every possible stand.

Nevertheless, some progress has been made. Grosso modo, the blunt a prioris have been left behind: it is generally recognized that for a specific individual (he might be a psychiatric patient) specific religious practices can be harmful, whereas for another the same practices might be helpful. Some kind of religious devotion with one person can be a sign of a condition of genuine mental health with another whereas, it can be the manifestation of an infantile restraint or of a mental disease. Empirical research shows that with regard to mental health, religion can be a haven, a hazard, a therapy, an expression or a suppression of mental pathology (Spilka et al., 1985). The old question whether religion is right or wrong, whether it is the cause of or the remedy for mental disease or not, has shown to be unfruitful as the starting point for the psychopathology of religion. (Too much apology for the own religious position was mixed up with the answers.) Psychoanalysts, working with the same research methods, have reached opposing positions on religion, according to their different anthropologies. Phenomenologists tried to avoid a judgment and described religion with clinical pictures (as we had with Schneider), without asking questions concerning the value or the impact of these religious forms. More satisfying, however, seems to be the historical-psychological position where there is a verdict whether the observed religious phenomena are pathological or not, but where this verdict is left to the appropriate experts: to the religious culture or community concerned, and where the psychopathologist tries to understand how these (deviant) religious phenomena came into being. On the other hand, however, we have to realize, as spiritual health does not necessarily correlate with psychological understanding of health, that, from a psychological point of view, behaviour which is acceptable to or even stimulated by a religious culture can be structured in a pathological way. Perhaps one should better consider research into these matters as belonging to the regular psychology of religion, not to the psychopathology of religion.

REFERENCES

Albertus Magnus. *Opera Omnia*. Paris: Vivès, 1890-1898.

Beek, H.H. (1974). *Waanzin in de Middeleeuwen. Beeld van de gestoorde en bemoeienis met de zieke*. Hoofddorp: Septuaginta.

Bromberg, W. (1975). *From shaman to psychotherapist: a history of the treatment of mental illness*. Chicago: Henry Regnery Company.

Dilthey, W. (1894). Ideen über eine beschreibende und zergliedernde Psychologie. In: W. Dilthey. (1964). *Gesammelte Schriften*. Band V (p. 139-241). Stuttgart: Teubner.

Drinka, G.F. (1984). *The birth of neurosis. Myth, malady and the victorians*. New York: Simon and Schuster.

Freud, S. (1907). *Zwangshandlungen und Religionsübungen*. [Transl.: Obsessive actions and religious practices. In: The Standard Edition of the complete psychological works, vol. IX (p. 116-127). London: Hogarth Press, 1959.]

Freud, S. (1913). *Totem und Tabu. Einige Übereinstimmungen im Seelenleben der Wilden und der Neurotiker*. [Transl.: Totem und Taboo. Some points of agreement between the mental lives of savages and neurotics. In: The Standard Edition of the complete psychological works, vol. XIII (p. 1-162). London: Hogarth Press, 1955.]

Freud, S. (1927). *Die Zukunft einer Illusion*. [Transl.: The future of an illusion. In: The Standard Edition of the complete psychological works, vol. XXI (p. 2-58). London: Hogarth Press, 1961.]

Griesinger, W. (1844). Recension über: M. Jacobi (1844), 'Die Hauptformen der Seelenstörungen in ihren Beziehungen zur Heilkunde nach der Beobachtung geschildert. Band I: Die Tobsucht'. In: W. Griesinger (1872). *Gesammelte Abhandlungen*. Band I: Psychiatrische und nervenpathologische Abhandlungen (p.80-106). Berlin: Hirschwald.

Heimann, H. (1961). Religion und Psychiatrie. In H.W. Gruhle et al. (Eds.), *Psychiatrie der Gegenwart. Forschung und Praxis*. Band III. Soziale und angewandte Psychiatrie (pp. 471-493). Berlin: Springer.

Heinroth, J.C.A. (1818). *Lehrbuch der Störungen des Seelenlebens oder der Seelenstörungen und ihrer Behandlung. Vom rationalen Standpunkt aus entworfen, zwey Theile. Erster oder theoretischer Theil*. Leipzig: Vogel.

Heinroth, J.C.A. (1822). *Lehrbuch der Anthropologie. Zum Behuf academischer Vorträge, und zum Privatstudium. Nebst einem Anhang erläuternder und beweisführender Aufsätze*. Leipzig: Vogel.

Hippokrates. *Oeuvres complètes d'Hippocrate*. (P. Littré, Ed.). Amsterdam/Parijs: Hakkert, 1839-1861 en 1973-1978.

Hole, G. (1977). *Der Glaube bei Depressiven. Religionspsychopathologische und klinisch-statistische Untersuchung*. Stuttgart: Enke.

Howells, J.G. (Ed.) (1975). *World history of psychiatry*. London: Baillière Tindall.

Ideler, K.W. (1847). *Der religiöse Wahnsinn erläutert durch Krankengeschichten*. Halle: Schwetschke.

Ideler, K.W. (1850). *Versuch einer Theorie des religiösen Wahnsinns*. Halle: Schwetschke.

Jaspers, K. (1913). *Allgemeine Psychopathologie*. Berlin: Springer.

Kaplan, D., & Manners, R.A. (1972). *Culture theory*. London: Prentice-Hall.

Kopp, P. (1933). Psychiatrisches bei Albertus Magnus. *Zeitschrift für die gesamte Neurologie und Psychiatrie*, 147, 50-60.

Krafft-Ebing, R. von (1883[3], 1890[4]) *Lehrbuch der Psychiatrie*. Stuttgart: Enke.

Schneider, K. (1928). *Zur Einführung in die Religionspsychopathologie*. Tübingen: Mohr.

Siegler, M., & Osmond, H. (1974). *Models of madness, models of medicine*. New York: MacMillan.

Spiegelberg, H. (1972). *Phenomenology in psychology and psychiatry*. Evanston: North-Western University Press.

Spiegelberg, H. (1982[3]). *The phenomenological movement. A historical introduction*. Den Haag: Mouton.

Spilka, B, Hood, R.W., & Gorsuch, R.L. (1985). *The psychology of religion: an empirical approach*. New Jersey: Prentice-Hall.

Vergote, A. (1987). *Debt and desire. Two axes of human existence, of religion and of psychopathology*. New Haven: Yale University Press.

Verwey, G. (1985). *Psychiatry in an anthropological and biomedical context. Philosophical presuppositions and implications of German psychiatry, 1820-1870*. Dordrecht/Boston: Reidel.

Zilboorg, G. (1941). *A history of medical psychology*. New York: Norton.

CHAPTER 2
MENTAL HEALTH AND RELIGION: A THEORETICAL SURVEY

M.H.F. van Uden & J.Z.T. Pieper

1. Mental health

In the last section of his principal work *Als ziende de Onzienlijke* ('As seeing the invisible') (1974), the Dutch psychologist of religion and culture Han Fortmann elaborately dealt with the relationship between religion and mental health. He starts off by enunciating that, scientifically speaking, mental health is not easily definable. When we find a definition of mental health, we have to realize its cultural relativity. What is strange and out of line in one culture may be an altogether normal way of behaviour in another. Therefore Fortmann points out that we have to consider the function the behaviour has for the person, rather than the outward appearance. 'The hallucinations and the visions that Indians in California summon to themselves through psychedelica and fasting, differ from the visions of psychotic patients by the difference in the function they have for the individual' (Fortmann 1974, p. 306). The same behaviour is an expression of a cultural habit in one case and an expression of a splintered personality in another. Moreover, in a certain culture ideological (political, philosophical and theological) presuppositions influence the determination of what is mentally sane and what is not. Therefore the many definitions of mental health only have relative or limited value. However, there are a number of definitions that try to get round these limitations as much as possible by using a wide, open and/or relatively abstract formulation.

In this manner Paloutzian (1983) defines mental health in terms of:

— the absence of excessive feelings of guilt;
— realistic estimation and acceptance of one's shortcomings;
— the experience of not too much, but not too little tension in one's life;
— the ability to deal with problems;
— reading a satisfactory social life;
— having a sufficient amount of feelings of happiness.

Fortmann himself gives the following formulation:

'the ability (freedom!) to realize oneself (e.g. in work) ánd to lose oneself..... The term "freedom" is not sufficient in itself. One should add that it is a freedom that functions in two ways: self-actualization and surrender' (Fortmann, 1974, 361).

If we take a look at the literature that relates mental health to religion, it appeares that rather diverse subjects are brought together under the common denominator of mental health. Mental health can refer to a) personal charateristics, b) (deviant) social behaviour and to c) psychiatric or psychopathological issues. Personal characteristics can refer to dogmatism, authoritarianism, suggestibility and overscrupulousness, that we all suffer from to some extent. The aspect of mental health only comes up when a person is excessively determined by such a characteristic. In the category of deviant social behaviour, we find themes like alcoholism and drug addiction, criminality, sexual deviations, etc. In these cases mental health is mainly related to their social stigma. In psychiatric or psychopathological cases (mental health in the narrower sense), the instability of the individual is the highest. The milder neurotic disorders must be distinguished from the more serious, psychotic, ones that need professional (clinical) help in most of the cases. In the following paragraph, we will see a number of concrete examples of each category.

2. The complex interrelation of religion and mental health

Before we deal with the interrelations of religion and mental health, we want to state briefly how we use the term 'religion' in this article. In defining religion a distinction is often made between substantial and functional definitions. Substantial definitions refer to a specific quality of religious phenomena. They usually derive their content from the judeo-christian tradition. At least there is a reference to a transcendent reality. Functional definitions are directed towards the result that is brought about by religion. A result that is mentioned frequently is 'an answer to the ultimate questions of life'. This answer can be derived from God, humanism, but it can also be found in interpersonal relationships, self-actualization and enjoyment of life. We will not limit ourselves to a specific definition. However, since research in the psychology of religion is mainly situated in Judeo-Christian culture, references to a relationship with a transcendent, more or less personal God will be prevalent in the material to be dealt with.

In current literature equivocal relations between religion and mental health, such as Freud's (1927) statement that religion keeps man immature and consequently mentally unhealthy, will not be found. Most authors start from the principle that there are various relations between religion and mental health. Argyle and Beit-Hallahmi (1975) mention three possible relations. First, religion can benefit the individual's wellbeing and happiness. Second, religion can be seen as a form of psychopathology or at least as a factor that leads to unadjusted behaviour of the individual. Third, emotionally unstable people can turn to religion in an attempt to rise above their problems.

Paloutzian (1983) sums up four possible relations: 1. people with mental disorders become religious, hoping to be able to control their problems; 2. religion makes originally healthy people unhealthy; 3. some forms of religion are pathogenous, other forms are beneficial to mental health; 4. there is no connection between religion and mental health.

According to Spilka, Hood and Gorsuch (1985) the relationship can be differentiated further. Religion can:

1. cure the pathological by working as a therapeuticum;
2. repress the pathological by subpressing potential deviant behaviour by religious socialisation;
3. hide the pathological when religion becomes a haven;
4. express the pathological in religious form;
5. cause the pathological when it is the cause of mental insanity.

As this division maps out the field of research most differentiatedly, we will now use it.

2.1. Religion as therapy

Concerning religion we find a large scale of activities and experiences having an implicitely therapeutic function. Especially participation in *religious rituals* (confession, exorcism, celebrations, pilgrimage etc.) can have a considerable curative effect. Also *intense religious experiences* such as the mystical experience, speaking in tongues and conversion are well-known for their therapeutic aura.

Even though 'primitive' societies were more liable to have rituals than our modern industrialized one, a number of important rituals are still intact in the twentieth century. One of the most important social functions of the church in our western society is to offer rituals concerning radical transitions in life such as birth, marriage, illness and death.

The weekly visit to church may not be frequent anymore but on occasions such as baptisms, weddings and funerals the major part of the community stays in contact with the church. Since the church obviously provides for a need in this respect, the question emerges what function and effect these kinds of rituals have. Elsewhere (Pieper 1988) it was pointed out that the individual can prosper from a ritual in two ways. First, the ritual channels emotions, thus benefiting the individual's stability. It can allow for the expression of emotions that are not verbalized easily. The ritual uses well-tested channels providing that the individual is not overwhelmed. In the case of a wedding it may concern feelings of festivity and joy, in the case of a baptism feelings of wonder, in the case of a funeral feelings of meaninglessness regarding the meaning of existence. In these cases, symbols within the ritual provide means to come into contact with anxieties or the archetypes (Jung) in the collective unconscious, in a way that is not too threatening.

Second, the ritual provides a frame of interpretation on the cognitive level, thus guiding the concrete life situation by attributing a specific sense and meaning to it. In the case of a funeral this may be the Christian belief in an afterlife, implying a possible reunion with the deceased in the future. Rituals also facilitate the transition to a new role by providing a frame of explanation: an ideology legitimizing the new role and explaining how to act within it. In the context of rituals of initiation Van der Hart (1984) points out that the tribe's myths and central symbols (the cosmology) are passed over to newcomers in this manner. He pointed out elsewhere (1981) that similar rituals may also be relevant outside the religious domain, namely in the current practise of psychotherapy when initiating a transition to a new attitude to life. Associating closely with this concept Derks, Pieper and Van Uden (1991) have described pilgrimage as a transforming ritual. Apart from religious changes a pilgrimage can cause positive effects on a person's mental well-being. Research (Morris 1982; Van Uden and Pieper 1990; Pieper and Van Uden 1991) has proved the actual therapeutic effect of pilgrimages to Lourdes concerning the mental well-being of the pilgrims. Pilgrimages such as these evidently decrease feelings of anxiety and (partly also) depressive feelings.

Let us now consider a number of intense religious experiences that may have a positive effect on the individual's psychosocial economy, starting with the mystical experience. Boisen, who himself endured a number of psychotic periodes in his life, sees a close connection between certain forms of mental disorder and certain forms of mystical experience (Stroeken 1983). Boisen feels that such a mixture of psychotic/mystical experience is an attempt to endure an imminent desintegration of the personality. In most cases the result is a constructive reorganization, a restoration of the unity of the self. A quotation from an interview taken in another context gives insight about the depth of experiences such as this.

'I also think that in those days, that I was doing very badly, that I spent in isolation-cells, that I was so scared, that I was also a danger to myself,

that I wanted to be dead... That I heard songs again just then... That was the only thing that gave me the feeling, that didn't abandon me, or something like that.
Well, parts of psalms that came to mind suddenly. When things were really black, when I didn't know how to carry on, then it always got to me very joyfully: "Count your blessings one by one'. Well, at a moment like this I didn't feel blessed at all, but they were very cheerful songs and darned, then I had a blessing all of a sudden that I could count. And then 'Praise the Lord'. And that I found, in itself it was great of course, because that was quite something in itself! Something to live for alone, because it comes to your mind. Yes, yes, it was just enough to go on" (Pieper 1988, p. 74).

In this case we find an experience of a religious/mystical character that calls desintegration of the personality to a halt.

Another example we derive from the psychiatrist Gyselen's contribution to the study *Hoe menselijk is mystiek?* (How Human Is Mysticism) (Gyselen et al. 1979). Gyselen deals with the life of a 52-year-old patient and the positive effect a certain mystical experience had in the course of the psychiatric process.

"This turning point occurs during a walk on a road in the countryside. 'Suddenly a weight fell off of me. I felt light. The air trembled and had a heart that was beating. The trees were my allies. The bricks lived and trembled and were intensely coloured. Your heart beats on the rhythm of the vibrations all around, then. You feel one with all that is, and that all that is, is good. The colour of the clouds gave me a feeling of peace, the nature knew me exactly... This occurence, I am inclined to say: this Divine occurence, I would almost label it best as a Divine intervention in the earthly existence of the man who I was at that time. I can describe it in the best way as a radical movement away from my me as I had always experienced it, while the other me was a spectator of my person. This new me felt absorbed, no, felt part of Something who is cosmic, who is now and always. Something real beyond description. I remember now that I saw myself and that I was filled with abhorrence. And I also thought that in fact anyone who was interested, could see me like this: full of sin, arrogance and vanity. And I understood that in my intellectual zeal to understand everything rationally, in fact I wanted to be my own God. And then it seemed to me that I made a jump: a surrender to the faith. The realization that one doesn't necessarily have to understand everything with one's mind but that he can live in peace and inner tranquility, knowing this with each and every fibre of your body that since God is, everything is good. And that God supports the Life in me, me and everything and everything. And that I know another word synonymous to Life: Love — fiery. I think that this experience didn't last very long, maybe it was only a flash. But I think that it was still enough to relish a sort of tranquility for months that I hadn't known before. A tranquility that started by seeing everything new....'" (Gyselen, 1979, pp. 17-18).

Gyselen concludes that the experience can be interpreted as 'an attack on the illness' and that, from a psychological point of view this mystic experience doesn't make the patient sicker in any case, but, quite to the contrary, brings him closer to his true self.

An experience that clearly concerns the reintegration and transformation of the personality is conversion. People speak of a new self, a second birth etc. A state of doubt and discomfort passes into tranquility and joy. This can be made clear easily by saint Augustin's story of his conversion. In the eighth book of his *Confessiones* he describes his state of mind as follows:

"And then, after a deep contemplation from hidden depths had surfaced all my misery and had placed it before the eyes of my heart, a violent storm broke, carrying an enormous rain of tears with it". Augustin isolates himself "and suddenly, there I hear a voice from a neighbouring house, a voice that said singingly and repeatedly, the voice of a boy or of a girl, I know not: 'Take and read, take and read'"! Augustin takes the next best passage from the Bible and starts to read (Romans 13,13): "'Not in carousing and drunkeness, not in bedrooms and indecencies, not in quarrel and envy, but wear the Lord Jesus Christ and do not spoil the flesh in eagerness'. I did not want to read any further and it was not necessary. For at once, at the end of the sentence, a light of security flew into my heart and all the darkness of my wavering and doubting fled away'" (Augustin 1963, 245-246).

The last subject we want to deal with is prayer. Clark (1958, p. 325) sees prayer as an 'inexpensive substitute for the psychiatrist's couch'. In the direct contact with God, one can ask for help, guidance and remission of sins. In extreme situations of crisis (such as during war) even the most hardened atheist often resorts to prayer in one form or another. Irrespective of a real intervention of God, from a psychological viewpoint prayer can radiate a reassuring and liberating influence. In this case prayer works as a coping-mechanism: one tries to get a grip on a situation by attributing sense and meaning to it. Recently Janssen, De

Hart en Den Draak (1989) derived similar conclusions from an empirical survey among 192 dutch highschool pupils:

'So, praying primarily seems to be a way of coping with inevitable, uncurable unhappiness'....'So prayer can be seen as a way of constructing reality, as a way of making sense in a multi-interpretable world'....'We defined praying as a verb, as an activity: praying is a mechanism to construct and interpret one's experience' (Janssen et al. 1989, p. 37).

2.2. Suppression of deviant behaviour by religious socialization

Because of a strict religious upbringing or socialization, potentially deviant behaviour can be channeled into socially acceptable behaviour. It is well known for example that education in religious families often is aimed towards controlling undesirable emotions such as anger and agression. This second function of religion will be most effective in countries like the U.S.A. where socially acceptable standards coincide with religious standards. The suppression of deviant behaviour can take place in three ways:

First, the religious community can exercise a radical influence on the individual by censuring and sentencing undesirable and encouraging and rewarding desirable behaviour.

The closer the relationships between the members of the community, the more radical the individual can be 'shaped'. A well-known example of this influence is alcohol and drug abuse. In the U.S. many young people from traditional protestant or Jewish families use alcohol and drugs much less than secularized youngsters in the same age-group. We find strong group-pressures within new religious movements (some based on Western, some based on eastern religious and philosophical traditions). The press often points at the dangers connected to this. An survey of psychological and psychiatric studies in this field (Richardson 1985) shows however, that joining a community like this mainly has a benificial effect on the health of the people that are concerned. Richardson deals with research on groups like the 'Jesus-people', 'Ananda Marga', 'Unification Church', etc. His study shows that the social ties within the group decrease neurotic phenomena effectively and lead to the resocialization of young people that were alienated from social life before.

We find an example of this in Van der Lans (1981) study *Volgelingen van de Guru* (Followers of the Guru). A 26-year-old man, who has been a member of the 'Divine Light Mission' for five years relates as follows:

"I was totally obsessed with LSD and high all day. I was dealing with astrology, Gurdjieff, Uyldert, Hesse, Kerouac, buddhism. I was searching terribly, I had no work, no study, very few friends". He had very little contact with his parents, even though they supported him financially. Because of the LSD he got into an identity crisis: "My ego, all of my personality collapsed. It was as if I had to start all over again...I had clearly recognized the question in myself: What am I doing here? Why can't I function in this world like everyone else? I had worked up a real desire to get up in the morning and to go to work...". Then he got into contact with the 'Divine Light Mission' through a friend. The premies, "with their short hair and their silly suits", were peculiar company to him. "But then I got 'satsang'. Somebody was trying to get his experience across. That was enough for me. I recognized it totally and felt that this was what I wanted". Since his initiation he hasn't used any drugs nor smoked cigarettes. The relationship with his parents is good now. "They think it's great that I look as neatly as this all of a sudden, with short hair. Apart from that they are not interested" (Van der Lans 1981, 56-57).

Eaton and Weil (1955) did important research on the Hutterites, a Christian sect with communities in North America and their results can be interpreted in the light of the effect of strict religious socialization. The Hutterites' Bible-centred faith emphasizes brotherly love and communal ownership of property. Their way of life, from birth until death is defined strictly. The presupposition was that a supportive and controlling system such as this one, into which the members are born, would result in a lower number of neurotics and psychotics, because even if someone would deviate from normal behaviour, the community would react with a love-filled and therapeutic attitude. Well, this appeared to be the case indeed with neurotic problems, but with respect to the more serious, psychotic ones, the effect appeared to be the reverse. Second, not only the social pressure of the community of believers, but also the content of belief (dogmas and doctrines) can have a controling effect. A good Christian has to live by the Ten Commandments and many other doctrines of faith. With ideas of a punishing God added, this can have an extreme influence on social behaviour. The French sociologist Durkheim found a connection between religion and suicide. Roman Catholic countries such as Spain and Italy, in which suicide is a mortal sin, would show considerably lower percentages of suicide than protestant countries such as England and Iceland. It should be mentioned however that Argyle & Beit-Hallahmi (1975) compared the numbers of suicides in 18

European countries in the year 1960 and concluded that Durkheim's thesis didn't hold (anymore).

Thirdly the acquisition of desired behaviour, can occur through the imitation of religious models. Social learning theory teaches that imitation of models and examples is one of the most important ways in which children acquire new styles of behaviour. Models may be found in the existing religious community (religious leaders, well-known pastors, preachers etc.) or in the religious tradition (biblical heroes, Jesus and his apostles, martyrs, saints etc.). As a psychological phenomenon, this is closely related to social role theory of the Swedish psychologist of religion Sundén (1966). With respect to religious experience, he refers to 'Rollen-übernahme' as the taking over of roles of persons in biblical and other traditionally religious stories.

2.3. Religion as a haven

A religious system can function as a haven, as a secure sanctuary that gives shelter against the tensions and troubles of daily life, in a number of ways. The monastic life offers a regulated, controlled existence that provides protection against the precariousnesses of the life outside the monastery's walls. Acceptance by a religious group can alleviate the fear of social isolation and rejection. The belief in divine protection increases the feeling of security. Let us take a look at a number of examples.

A study on Jehovah's Witnesses (Spencer 1975) concluded that, compared to the general population, their rate of schizophrenia was three to four times higher. According to Spilka et al. (1985) Jehovah's Witnesses appear to attract people who are looking for an ultra-traditional spiritual community with a strict moral code, in order to find protection against the temptations of life.

Members of new religious movements in many cases appear to have a past characterized by severe psychological problems, drug addiction, and sometimes criminality. Joining a religious movement can be seen as an attempt to get away from that past. A quote from the earlier-mentioned booklet *Followers of the Guru* (Van der Lans 1981) shows this clearly:

"What was the central point? How shall I put this? That I wanted to find God, that I wanted to become happy, that I wanted to know the meaning of my life; what is it all about? Actually everything was subordinated to this. I had disengaged myself from everything, all my attention was fixed on this. I abandoned my school, left theatre-school, went from Amsterdam to South Limburg, because someone lived there that I felt could teach me something. I gave away everything I possessed, my furniture, records, books. I simply did away with it all. I burnt my boats behind me" (Van der Lans 1981, p. 79).

Apart from this religious sects with strong, authoritarian leaders can attract immature, dependable personalities. Galanter, Rabkin, Rabkin and Deutsch (1979) established that about 4 in 10 'Moonies' (members of the Unification Church of leader Moon) had serious psychological problems prior to joining this community.
The search for a secure religious haven is not easy. Especially with sects and new religious movements we see a number of mentally unstable individuals switching from one group to another. Their ties to a specific group are weak. The number of switches from one group to another seem to increase in accordence with the degree of mental insecurity of the people involved. Apart from that it should be mentioned that most of the members of such groups function normally. Also, social circumstances, such as contact with friends and acquintances have a strong influence on the chances of participation in movements of this kind (Lofland and Stark 1965).

The monastic life also appears to have a considerable attraction on neurotic and pre-psychotic persons (Kurth 1961). Once the entrance is made, it can prevent admission into a mental clinic. Often however, the protective shield does not work for too long. Also Kurth found more cases of mental disturbance in cloistered orders (such as the Carmelites), than in the more socially active ones (such as orders that are involved in education like the Ursulines). Judging by the following quote from the book Nonnen ('Nuns'), (Bernstein 1978) concerning a woman who entered a convent right after her mother's death, the monastic life can also provide protection when dealing with far-reaching life-events:

"A woman who would have been rejected almost certainly with the hard tests of today came out of grief when her mother died, thirty years ago: 'I was eighteen and very sad and upset. And as soon as the doors closed behind me, I felt at ease, I knew I was in the right place'" (Bernstein 1978, 70).

2.4. Religion as an expression of mental disorder

Religion can enable the individual to express mental aberation, as it were in a 'masked' way. Bizarre behaviour can be permitted within the context of a religious system. It is true that the individual will be regarded as different and peculiar, but the label 'mentally disturbed' will not be attached to him or her openly.

Some descriptions of mystical experiences seem very similar to descriptions of the behaviour of patients with severe mental disturbances. An example, quoted from Antoon Vergote's study *Bekentenis en begeerte in de religie* ('Confessions and Desire in Religion') (1978), may clarify this:

"The honourable Agnes Blannbekin, born in Vienna towards the end of the thirteenth century, is fully occupied with the question of what actually happened with the 'Holy Foreskin' of Jesus, a question that was touched upon by some theologians in those days, seemingly aggravating by chance the question whether the resurrected body was violated or not. God ended Agnes' agonizing worries by revealing to her that our Lord brought the foreskin back to life with him, on the day of the resurrection. Fortunately, God didn't add that he was going to reveal to saint Birgitta that the holy forskin was still hidden in ...Rome.
For Agnes this revelation is the start of a sequence of remarkable ecstacies that are told by her 'unworthy father confessor', as the Franciscan Ermenic introduces himself.
So we see how Agnes, in a certain year when on the day of the circumcission —as per usual— she is crying bitterly, starts to contemplate about where the foreskin of the Lord may be, even though she was already told in the revelation. Hark now. 'Soon she felt a tiny skin on her tongue, like the skin of an egg but softer, and that tiny little skin she swallowed. When she had swallowed it, she felt this extremely tiny skin on her tongue again, just like before, and so she swallowed it once more. And this occured to her a hundred times indeed... The sweetness accompanying the digestion was so strong that she sensed a delightful transformation in all her limbs and joints. During this revelation she was filled with light within in such a way, that she could observe herself totally'. The Lord favoured her still more with innumerable tender and pure touches with his hand or with a lamb coming from the altar. Agnes herself was filled with an excitement in her chest every time that God visited her that was so intense that it went through her body and that it burned as a result, not in a painful but in a most pleasurable manner'. No wonder the blooddrainer was astonished with her blood-letting, because the girl's blood was so hot that it was boiling" (Vergote 1978, pp. 261-262).

This is an illustration of the fact that a religious experience can raise suspicions of mental insanity. For that matter, well-known mystics like St. Teresa are depicted as hysterics, Jeanne d'Arc was diagnosed as paranoid and schizophrenic among other things and Dostoevski and the apostle Paul were classified as epileptics.

Glossolalia (speaking in tongues) can in some cases also refer to an underlying pathology. During meetings of the Pentecostal movement, speaking in tongues functions as an emotional confession. The sounds that are produced by the 'tongue-speakers' are usually meaningless. It is a string of vowels and consonants that is expressed in an emotional manner coupled with rhythmic movements of the body. The sounds cannot be identified as an existing language, apart from fragments from the bible that are often mixed into it. Goodman (1972) argues on the basis of the extreme emotional excitement (e.g. when a charismatic religious leader urges the participants to let themselves go during mass-meetings) that the normal cortical control of language production stops and that lower sub-cortical centers of the brain take over the production of language. In this case unconscious personal problems can play a part. Vroon (1978) relates speaking in tongues to the Tourette-syndrome, which is characterized by the uncontrolled expression of curses and coarseness in a distorted voice.

In 1 Cor. 14, 5-15 the New Testament states speaking in tongues as a phenomenon that is warned against by Paul:

"Now, I want you all to speak in tongues, but especially for you to prophesy. The one who prophesies is greater than the one who speaks in tongues unless he interprets in order that the church may be built up. Now, brothers, if I come to you speaking in tongues, how will I benefit you unless I speak to you either by revelation or by knowledge or by prophecy or by teaching?
... So also if you produce unintelligible speech by the tongue, how will anyone understand what is being said? for you will be speaking to the air. ... if I do not understand the meaning of the voice, I will be a barbarian to the one who is speaking; and the one who is speaking will be a barbarian so far as I am concerned. So you also, since you are zealous for ecstacy of the spirit, keep striving for the upbuilding of the church so that you may excel. Therefore, let the one who speaks in a tongue keep praying that he may interpret. For if I pray in a tongue, my spirit is praying, but my mind is unproductive".

Paul points out the danger of what he refers to as "the enchantment of the spirit". An interpretation is necessary.
This goes to show again that there is a possibility for the religious to become an expression of psychopathological phenomena.

The third theme that can clarify how the pathological may be expressed in the religious is scrupulosity. This is the case when a person experiences a continuous doubt and insecurity about sin and guilt and when a person is absorbed by the question if he is tresspassing one rule or another. This obsession causes compulsive and ritualized actions that intend to control doubt and insecurity. The religious ritual can satisfy the need for such compulsive actions. For, until recently, within the Catholic church especially, believers were supposed to observe ritual rules strictly. For example, many conditions had to be fullfilled before the Holy Communion could be received. As early as 1907 Freud pointed at the relationship between individual compulsive actions and collective religious rituals. He mentions the following similarities between the compulsive actions and the religious ritual: 1. the moral dilemma that arises when the action is neglected; 2. the conscientious way in which they are performed; 3. the fact that these actions are isolated from other daily activities; 4. the fact that interruptions are forbidden. Freud ends his argument with the following final conclusion that antagonized generations of theologians and believers.

'According to these similarities and analogies it could be ventured to understand obsessive-compulsive neurosis as the pathological counterpart to religious development, to define neurosis as an individual religiosity; to define religion as a universal compulsion neurosis' (Freud 1907, 21).

Religion is a collective obsessive-compulsive neurosis, that can save an individual neurosis; again we see how the psychological problem (the neurosis) is expressed through the religious domain.

The final possible expression of mental disturbance through religion we are going to mention concerns priesthood. Disturbances in the personality can cause people to think that they are destined for priesthood. Mental troubles can motivate people to turn to the clerical life as an outlet for emotional problems. This can be the case, for instance, when celibacy becomes a cover-up for problems concerning sexuality and intimacy. The number of mental disturbances among the clergy is higher than the number among the average population.

Kennedy et al. (1977) identified 65% of a sample of Roman Catholic priests as either maldeveloped or underdeveloped socio-psychologically speaking. The question is of course of cause and effect. The research performed by Hoenkamp-Bisschops (1991) shows clearly how much the obligation of celibacy can lead to all kinds of problem behaviour.

Nowadays it seems that very few people can deal with a celibate life-style in a healthy way.

2.5. Religion as a hazard to mental health

Finally it is also possible that religion and faith in God present a hazard to mental health, causing mental disfunctioning or worsening mental problems. The latter is the case when the function of a haven and the function of expression go together with a loss of sense of reality to such a degree that possible non-religious therapeutic interventions are refused. God is then played off against the therapist who, on the basis of his inferior position, has to come off second best compared to an omniscient and omnipotent entity. The religious tradition provides a lot of possibilities regarding content, such as miracles, prophetic predictions, original sin, punishment by God like the destruction of Sodom and Gomorra, that patients embrace gladly to legitimize or continue their mental disorder or deviant behaviour. In his study *The three Christs of Ypsilanti*, Rokeach (1964) reports the confrontation between three psychiatric patients who are all convinced to be the true incarnation of Christ. For two years they are exposed to each other's convictions, thus revealing their rigid thinking and inability to change positively. Generally speaking, so also in cases of not strictly pathological problems, there is a danger that religion may prevent the necessary confrontation with reality when functioning as 'opium of the people'. A sedation from time to time is possible, but a permanent anaesthesia causes destructive stagnation. However, the following case of Mr. Cox proves that there is a thin line between sedation and stagnation. Mr. Cox was interviewed in the context of a research on the function of faith in the process of mourning:

'In his current religiosity his wife has taken up an important place: "The devotion of Mary comes back to me, but my wife, she stands above her. Because she is next to God, I wouldn't dare to use God's name in the second place, so my wife comes second and on my heavenly mother Mary third, let me say it like this then, and I beg her every day to help me". According to Mr. Cox, contact with the Supreme Being is possible, but only through a mediator: "For me, that is my wife, she is my mediator. I still have contact with her often, so I let it all run through her. And then I receive facts, I have them right here on paper, about 380 pages already. I keep a record of this regularly, the things that she predicts me or that she dictates. Because I have spiritual contact with her, this is possible. I used to be able to summon her myself. Then I went to her grave and spoke with her. Then I heard her voice and she gave me

advice". Every year Mr. Cox commemorates the passing away of his wife:
"These weeks, well, they are horrible moments for me. I experience everything again. This year I ran out of the house. My table in the living room was covered with candles and flowers and her picture was in the middle. The candles burned with it all day". In this "remembrance-week" he doesn't want to be disturbed. In his wall-unit Mr. Cox has installed an altar: "It has a niche, and in it stand 6 candles and her big photograph. On my desk I have a picture, on my drawer too. For as long as I shall live, I promised her, I will put flowers with them. Until today I have done so. On my desk a small candle burns all through the day. I'd rather not talk about it very much, because I will never forget it" (Van Uden 1985, pp. 53-54)'.

Here the adoration of his wife as a saint, a form of neurotic regulation of fear, helps Mr. Cox him to survive, but at the cost of a considerable amount of his freedom.

Moreover religion can cause mental problems by itself. Freud argues that, in the battle between 'Id' and 'Superego', religion takes the side of the Superego. Religious commandments and prohibitions are intended to curb sexual and agressive impulses. Then also, since religion is aiming towards moral perfection, the tresspassing of these laws causes feelings of guilt and sin. In extreme cases this can cause compulsive feelings of guilt that can dominate and paralyze a person's life. Also this can lead to, often extreme penitance varying from the thrashing out of sin by flagellants in the Middle Ages to public confessions of guilt in our current TV-era.

In the Netherlands the issue of guilt and sin was researched by Aleid Schilder (1987). Her study *Hopeloos maar schuldig* ('Helpless, But Guilty') on a strict Dutch-Reformed part of the population, gave some insight into the paralyzing effect guilt feelings can have on people's work, thinking and doing. She showed how messages like 'you are shouldered with original sin, that you can't do anything against' can cause or intensify depression as an expression of "learned helplessness" (Seligman). A part of a diary of one of her clients looking back at her depression, shows how these two factors are interrelated:
"In our church sin is constantly preached about, that you can't do anything by yourself, that you are a miserable human being, that you can't do anything good out of yourself. And that was emphasized so much, and at home (i.e. in the past A.S.) idem dito. When you have heard that you are a miserable person, you become programmed like

that. I think that love and mercy of God are not talked about enough; feelings are never allowed to be added. But I do have feelings, a whole lot as for me. As I had to learn with my mind that I was a miserable person, my feeling couldn't do anything else but feel miserable!" (Schilder 1987, pp. 76-77).

On a cognitive level religion can also be a hazard to mental health. The emphasis on obedience and blind belief benefit immaturity and unrealistic thinking. When religion provides simple, uncomplicated solutions for complicated questions of existence, it encourages more unrealistic attitudes. Both aspects (obedience and the intolerance of ambiguity) are found in so-called authoritarian personalities. These authoritarian personalities can cause considerable damage to society when they are organized in a broader context such as the Klu Klux Klan.
In extreme cases such an absolute obedience can lead to calamities such as the mass-suicide in Jonestown (Guyana) in 1978. Jim Jones led 912 of the members of his cult (the People's Temple Movement) into death. We derive a dramatic description of this event from Conway and Siegelman (1979).

"Then Jones addressed the population of Jonestown and told them that the member of congres and the journalists were dead and that the military forces of Guyana were on their way to Jonestown to torture and kill the inhabitants of the commune. "It is time to die in dignity", Jones said, thus for the last time repeating a vow that he had taken often before: to lead his followers in a 'mass-suicide for the glory of socialism'. Then, on Jones' orders, the temple doctor and his medical team brought to the front a battered washing-tub filled with strawberry lemonade that had been mixed with large quantities of cyanide, tranquilizers and sedatives. Jones told the gathering: "The time has come to meet each other in a new place. Bring the babies first", he ordered; and his nurses injected the poison into their throats. Then the rest of them came to the front, complete families at once, every one drank a cup of poison and was guided away by the temple-guards and forced to lie down in rows, facing down. Within a few minutes the people started to gasp for air, as blood was flowing out of their mouth and nose, until the last convulsive movements started. According to witnesses the ritual lasted for almost five hours. All through this time Jim Jones was seated on his high chair in the pavilion and repeated: "I have tried, I have tried, I have tried". And then: "Mother, Mother, Mother, Mother". When it was all over, Jones was lying on the platform face-forward, with a bullet through his head. And 912 people were dead' (Conway and Siegelman 1979, p. 245).

3. Explanations for the differences in effect

The five possible relationships between religion and mental health that we dealt with in the second paragraph can be divided into two global parts. In the first four cases religion has a positive effect: healing and repressing the pathological and softening when it provides a haven or when it expresses the pathological. It is questionabele, however, if the softening is beneficial in the end. In the fifth case the relation is negative. This division into two categories is quite common in the empirical research that was performed over the last decades. On the basis of a meta-analysis of 24 studies on psychopathology, Bergin (1983) concludes that religion can sometimes be related to psychopathology and sometimes to mental health.

In order to explain the differences in the results in the various studies we have to point at a number of methodological questions. First, most of the empirical studies are interested in the correlation between religion and mental health. This type of research can establish a connection, a correlation, but it cannot establish the direction of the connection: if we assume that the relationship is negative, it cannot be established what is the cause and what is the effect (the old question: what came first the chicken or the egg?). If we assume that pathology came first, then religion can be seen as the expression of the pathological. If, however, we assume that religion came first, then religion can be seen as the cause of the disturbance.

Second, it is very difficult to compare the various studies, because the ways in which 'religion' and 'mental health' are measured differ in different studies. Concerning religion, questions can be asked about religious beliefs (which have a range of varieties), but also about religious experiences or about religious behaviour such as church attendance. When measuring mental health huge handbooks, full of numerous tests and instruments, can be consulted that focus on aspects of mental health such as anxiety, depression, self-esteem, authoritarianism, self-ideal/self-discrepancy, etc.

Third, intervening variables can have a veiling influence. This is the case when an established relation between religion and mental health is actually caused by a third variable (the intervening one), which is related to both religion and mental health, forging them together. An example of such a variable is social-economic class: when people from a low social-economic class can be characterized by having both an authoritarian style of raising their children ánd by being very religious, chances are big that the children from this class will be both very authoritarian and very religious. Research on children in this class may

lead to the wrong conclusion that highly religious people are authoritarian.
This conclusion is wrong because the established relation is really caused by the fact that an authoritarian style of upbringing and religiosity go together in this class. Other variables of this kind are sex, age and ethnical origin. Serious research projects, therefore, will have to deal with the possible influence of such intervening variables and will have to control their effects in the analysis of data.

Apart from these answers, that refer to influences of the methodology used, another answer can be given to explain the differences in the various studies concerning the relations between religion and mental health. Even if all methodological obstacles could be avoided, the relation would still be twofold, as essentially there are two forms of religion: healthy and unhealthy religion. The first form is related to healthy, the latter to unhealthy personal and social characteristics. This shows a lot of similarity with the well-known distinction between intrinsic and extrinsic religion. In the case of the intrinsic form religion is valuable in itself and goes together with personal adjustment. In the case of the extrinsic form, religion is a means for other purposes, such as security and social status and it goes together with a non-balanced personality. Baker and Gorsuch (1982) actually established differences between intrinsic and extrinsic believers: the first ones scored lower on a number of anxiety-indicators such as ego-weakness and paranoid feelings. Spilka et al. (1985, p. 315) draw the following conclusion in this respect:

'A faith which provides an open-minded, competent guide for everyday living is found in conjunction with good adjustment and effective coping behavior. A shallow, externalized religion that is needed when things aren't what one desires is more likely to be a correlate of shortcoming in personality and social interaction'.

Again the question comes to mind as to what is the cause and what is the effect. Does a mentally healthy person develop an intrinsic religiosity or does intrinsic religion cause mental health? It is feasible that the relation is twofold, in other words that the variables of religion and person can be both effect and cause. An example, centred around the imagery of God, may illustrate the former. It appears that disordered people develop 'disordered' imagery of God. The God in question is either threatening or punishing or avenging, or the image of God is unclear or confused. Both of these images of God have negative effects on mental health. In the first case feelings of guilt and sin increase, causing the feeling of self-esteem to sink to a new low. In the latter case life is deprived of sense and meaning. This downward spiral can be stopped, however, by deep radical religious experiences, such as mystical experiences, conversion, but also by experiences around birth, love, illness and death. Then, instead of the negative image of God, a loving and forgiving God appears, causing a positive effect on mental health through an increasing feeling of self-confidence and self-esteem.

To summarize, the relation between religion and mental health is complex. This complexity is related to the fact that every individual can deal with forms of religion that are provided by the culture differently. Whether religion is healing or not, from a psychological viewpoint, will depend on its functioning in the person's total mental economy (Van Uden 1985). As James (1902) put it: ultimately healthy religion can only be recognized by the fruits it yields.

REFERENCES

Argyle, M. and Beit-Hallahmi, B. (1975). *The social psychology of religion*. London: Routledge and Kegan Paul.

Augustinus, A. (1963) *De belijdenissen (vertaling Gerard Wijdeveld)*. Utrecht: Fontein.

Baker, M. and Gorsuch, R. (1982) Trait Anxiety and Intrinsic-Extrinsic Religiousness. *Journal for the Scientific Study of Religion*, 21, 119-122.

Bergin, A.E. (1983) Religiosity and Mental Health: A critical Reevaluation and Meta-Analysis. *Professional Psychology: Research and Practice*, 14, 170-184.

Bernstein, M. (1978) *Nonnen. Van een mysterieus bestaan achter kloostermuren naar de emancipatie van een oude levensstijl*. Baarn: In den Toren.

Boisen, A.T. (1952) The General Significance of Mystical Identification in Cases of Mental Disorder. *Psychiatry*, 15, 287-296.

Clark, W.H. (1958). *The Psychology of Religion*. New York: Macmillan.

Conway, F. and Siegelman J. (1979) *Knappen*. Amsterdam/Brussel: Elsevier.

Derks, F., Pieper, J. and Uden, van M. (1991) Transformatie en confirmatie. Interviews met bedevaartgangers naar Wittem en Lourdes. In: Uden, van M., Pieper, J. and Henau, E. (eds.) *Bij Geloof. Over bedevaarten en andere uitingen van volksreligiositeit*. Hilversum: Gooi en Sticht, 105-123.

Eaton, J.W. and Weil, R.J. (1955). *Culture and mental disorders*. Glencoe Ill.: Free Press.

Fortmann, H.M.M. (1974). *Als ziende de onzienlijke* (deel 1 en 2), Hilversum: Gooi en Sticht.

Freud, S. (1907). *Zwangshandlungen und Religionsübungen*. Freud Studienausgabe, 1975, Band 7, 11-21. Frankfurt: S. Fischer Verlag.

Freud, S. (1927). *Die Zukunft einer Illusion*. Gesammelte Werke, Vol. 14, London, 1961.

Galanter, M., Rabkin, R., Rabkin, J. and Deutsch, A. (1979) The Moonies: A Psychological Study of Conversion and Membership in a Contemporary Religious Sect. *American Journal of Psychiatry*, 136, 165-169.

Goodman, F.D. (1972). *Speaking in Tongues: A Cross Cultural Study of Glossolalia*. Chicago: University of Chicago Press.

Gyselen, M. (1979) Mijn patiënt was meer dan ziek. In: Gyselen, M. et al. *Hoe menselijk is mystiek?* Baarn: Ambo.

Hart, van der O. et al. (1981), *Afscheidsrituelen in psychotherapie*. Baarn: Ambo.

Hart, van der O. (1984). *Rituelen in psychotherapie: Overgang en bestendiging*. Deventer: Van Loghum Slaterus.

Hoenkamp, A. (1991). *Varianten van celibaatsbeleving. Een verkennend onderzoek rond ambtscelibaat en geestelijke gezondheid*. Baarn: Ambo.

James, W. (1902.) *The Varieties of Religious Experience*. New York, Longmans, Green.

Janssen, J., Hart, de J. and Draak, den C. (1989) Praying Practices. *Journal of Empirical Theology*, 2, 28-39.

Kennedy, E.C. et al. (1977) Clinical Assesment of a Profession: Roman Catholic Clergyman. *Journal of Clinical Psychology*, 33, 120-128.

Kurth, C.J. (1961) Psychiatric and Psychological Selection of Candidates for the Sisterhood. *Guild of Catholic Psychiatrists Bulletin*, 8, 19-25.

Lans, van der J. (1981). *Volgelingen van de goeroe. Hedendaagse religieuze bewegingen in Nederland*. Baarn: Ambo.

Lofland, J. and Stark, R. (1965) Becoming a World Saver: A Theory of Conversion to a Deviant Perspective. *American Sociological Review*, 30, 862-874.

Morris, P.A. (1982) The effect of pilgrimage on anxiety, depression and religious attitude. *Psychological Medicine*, 12, 291-294.

Paloutzian, R.F. (1983). *Invitation to the psychology of religion*. Glenview, IL : Scott/Foresman.

Pieper, J.Z.Th. (1988). *God gezocht en gevonden? Een godsdienstpsychologisch onderzoek rond het kerkelijk huwelijk met pastoraaltheologische consequenties*. Nijmegen: Dekker en van de Vegt.

Pieper, J. and Uden, van M. (1991) De huidige Lourdesbedevaart. Motieven en effecten. In: Uden, van M. en Pieper, J., *Bedevaart als volksreligieus ritueel*. Heerlen: UTP-teksten 16.

Richardson, J.T. (1985) Psychological and psychiatric studies of new religions. In: Brown, L.B., *Advances in the Psychology of Religion*. Oxford, Pergamon, 209-223.

Rokeach, M. (1964). *The Three Christs of Ypsilanti*. New York: Knopf.

Schilder, A. (1987). *Hulpeloos maar schuldig. Het verband tussen een gereformeerde paradox en depressie*. Kampen: Kok.

Spencer, J. (1975) The Mental Health of Jehovah's Witnesses. *British Journal of Psychiatry*, 126, 556-559.

Spilka, B., Hood, R.W. and Gorsuch, R.L. (1985). *The psychology of religion. An empirical approach*. Englewood Cliffs, NJ: Prentice Hall.

Sundén, H. (1966). *Die Religion und die Rollen. Eine psychologische Untersuchung der Frömmigkeit*. Berlin: Töpelmann.

Stroeken, H. (1983). *Psychoanalyse, Godsdienst en Boisen*. Kampen: Kok.

Uden, van M.H.F. (1985). *Religie in de crisis van de rouw. Een exploratief onderzoek d.m.v. diepte-interviews*. Nijmegen: Dekker en van de Vegt.

Uden, van M. (1988). *Rouw, religie en ritueel*. Baarn: Ambo.

Uden, van M.H.F. and Pieper, J.Z.T. (1990), Christian Pilgrimage. Motivational structures and ritual functions. In: Heimbrock, H.G. and Boudewijnse, H.B. (eds.). *Current studies on rituals. Perspectives for the psychology of religion*. Amsterdam/Atlanta: Rodopi, 165-176.

Vergote, A. (1978). *Bekentenis en begeerte in de religie. Psychoanalytische verkenning*. Antwerpen: De Nederlandsche Boekhandel.

Vroon, P. (1978). *Stemmen van vroeger. Ontstaan en ontwikkeling van het zelfbewustzijn*. Baarn, Ambo.

CHAPTER 3
THE PSYCHOLOGICAL EXPLANATION OF RELIGION AS WISH-FULFILMENT: A TEST-CASE: THE BELIEF IN IMMORTALITY

Jozef Corveleyn

1. The paradox

A remarkable paradox characterizes the psychology of religion. On the one hand, psychologists of religion are modest about their competence to speak about the 'object' that is involved in the religious behavior they observe and try to understand. They intentionally limit themselves to the observable aspects of religious behavior (Vergote, 1984). About the reality, the existence of the object of religious belief, they feel compelled to keep silence: this question falls outside the realm of their scientific competence. This restriction is generally observed in the psychological study of belief in a life after death. Psychologists can study the presence, the intensity, and the motivational context of this expression of the human desire for immortality, but they are always aware of their incompetence to prove the existence of an 'afterlife'.

On the other hand and at the same time, the psychology of religion falls from time to time into a seductive trap, the trap of integral explanation. Some scientists of religion try to achieve a total explanatory theory about religion as such. They take the interesting but necessarily partial insights they obtain in the course of their particular psychological, sociological, or historical scientific research as the foundation of a total theory. This is what William James (1902) did. He 'explains' religion as the product of a basically natural religious experience. A similar jumping to conclusive explanation can be found in Freud. In his pamphlet The Future of an Illusion (1927), he explains the religious phenomenon as the result of the psychologically understandable but logically superfluous attachment of man to an illusion. Man wishes to believe in a father-god to avoid the painfulness of, and to diminish the anxiety provoked by, his confrontation with negativity in life: the dangers of nature and the absurdity of death.

2. Epistemological transgression

These explanations are epistemological transgressions: they start from an empirically well-founded psychological insight into one aspect of religious behavior - for Freud: religious attitude is mainly motivated by the need to avoid anxiety - and leap into the non-psychological domain of metaphysics: the question of the existence or non-existence of the object of belief. This jump is implicit in Freuds presumption. The proposition 'the belief in God as such is an illusion' implies the metaphysical proposition 'God does not exist'. This is an epistemological reduction.

3. Academic psychologists: Freud's followers?

Although the link Freud made between death anxiety and religious belief (e.g., in life after death) is very questionable from an epistemological point of view, this thesis has had a remarkably strong influence on academic psychology. Freud's thesis (1927) consists of a psychological hypothesis and a philosophical presumption. The hypothesis is about the interaction between an affective component - death anxiety and a particular coping strategy: religious attitude and belief. Generalizing and inflating this interaction onto a global theory explaining religion as such is driven by rationalistic ideological concerns. The main component of this theory is motivational: man becomes religious when he tries to avoid anxiety and to compensate for insecurity and helplessness.

The great seductive power of Freud's thesis for psychologists and other scientists may well be largely due to this motivational aspect. As will be shown below, psychological research on psychological attitudes towards, and styles of coping with, death has in any case been strongly influenced by Freud's position. And this applies not only to psychological hypothesis construction but also, at least implicitly, to the way many psychologists draw general explanatory conclusions from their empirical data concerning the whole phenomenon of religious belief.

The narrowing influence of Freud's motivational explanation on attitudinal and coping research in academic psychology is reflected in two characteristics of this research.

First of all, many authors restricted their research to the question of the existence of a causal (functional) relationship between death anxiety and religious belief. Often (Lester, 1967a; Templer, 1970; Feifel and Branscomb, 1973) only two very simple questionnaires were used, one concerning anxiety about some representations of death, the other containing more or less sophisticated questions about whether the subject is a religious believer. Correlations were found in two directions. Martin and Wrightsman (1965) for example, found that 'religious participation is significantly and negatively correlated with two of [their] death-concern measures' and they concluded 'that the general tenor of the findings may be interpreted to indicate that religion serves as a means of confronting and reducing one's fear of death' (pp. 321 and 322, my italics). Swenson (1961) and also Feifel and Branscomb (1973) found similar correlations and drew the same general conclusion: the stronger the belief, the less the fear of death. This observation is intended to serve as a confirmation of Freud's thesis. Other authors, however, have reported positive correla-tions as a proof for the same thesis. In his 1959 study, Feifel observed more intense fear of death in more religiously involved persons and used the same explanation for this finding as he used later on (Feifel and Branscomb, 1973) to explain the observation of a negative correlation. The overall importance of Freud's thesis in the conception of classical psychological research on coping with death, is also reflected in an even more curious use of this thesis as a starting point for empirical research. Williams and Cole (1968) translated the functio-nal Freudian thesis as follows: 'Reasoning from Freud's postulations, one would expect both prevailing insecurity and preoccupation with death to be characteristic of the highly religious' (p. 111). In fact, they observed that 'a group of low religiosity subjects manifested the greatest degree of conscious, prevailing insecurity' (my italics) and they nearly explicitly concluded that Freud's affirmation that 'religion is the product of insecurity' (p. 116) is thereby rejected. In all the studies we mentioned, the same hidden agenda is present: the ambition to explain religion via the functional-motivational pathway.

The second characteristic of the empirical psychological research on the attitude towards death is the striking restriction of the scope of attention to only one affective attitudinal category, that of anxiety or stress or concern. This one-sidedness manifests itself most notably in large-scale research projects such as those reported by Lester (1967a, 1967b, 1970, 1971) and Templer (1970, 1971, 1972), Templer and Dotson (1970); Templer, Lester, and Ruff (1974), Templer and Ruff (1971), and Templer, Ruff, and Franks (1971). This is the elevation of spontaneous psychological insight to the level of scientific evidence: who is not afraid of death? Supported by the most popular Freudian hypothesis about religion and human psychology, researchers have focused their attention on a commonsense idea. In doing so, they fail to make use of the findings of psychodynamic research.

4. Psychodynamic research

4.1. Freud about death

In many of his writings, Freud (1909, 1915a, 1915b, 1916, 1917, 1923, 1927, 1930, 1933a, and 1933b) tried to elucidate the complex psychological attitude of man towards death and towards the representation of an after-life. Fear or anxiety are not the only or even the dominant affective attitudes. First of all, there is a clear psychological distinction between the attitude towards one's own death and towards the loss by death of others, be they strangers or loved ones.

In everyday life the theme of death is concealed, the reality of death of others being avoided or denied. Freud's evaluation of the spontaneous attitude is in the same line as Heidegger's (Heidegger, 1927): by denial, man tries to avoid the possibility of a connection between the reality of the death of others and his own death by reducing death in his mental conception from something necessary to something accidental (Freud, 1915a, p. 342). This avoidance by "redefinition" is, in the first place, not due to anxiety in the face of one's own death but, as Freud argues, serves above all to circumvent confrontation with an intolerable secret affective reaction towards the death of the other: lack of concern or more overt hostile thoughts (for example, 'it's his turn!', or; 'it's a pitty he is dead, but in any case he wasn't doing very well anyway'). This unconscious, agressive component also seems to play an important role in the mourning process after the loss of a loved person (Freud, 1915a; 1915b, and 1917). In his pessimistic-realistic view of love relationships, Freud stresses this aspect: even our most tender and warmest relationship is not totally free of hostility that stimulates the unconscious death wish (Freud, 1915a, p. 353). Another affective component in coping with the death of a loved person is rebellion. The most intolerable aspect in the death of a loved one is not primarily the absence but the brutal fact of the end of life, which contradicts our spontaneous, albeit unconscious, narcissim: the vital power man feels does not suffice to prevent the destruction of life.

Towards one's own death, man's psychological attitude is very complex. When it is consciously meditated upon, the dominant emotion is fear. Thus, it is understandable that spontaneous psychology takes it for granted that this emotion characterizes man's most fundamental attitude towards death. Clinical observation contradicts this conclusion. Freud showed that anxiety is a secondary reaction. The primary attitude is non-acceptance of death-as-end that confronts man with the limits of his narcissism or feeling of vital power. Freud's clinical observa-tions can be summarized as follows (Freud, 1915a, p. 341 and p. 347). First

of all, he stressed, as did Heidegger (1927), that man does not have a direct representation of his own death. However, an important characteristic of the phenomenon of daydreaming that is mentioned by Freud in this context shows the power of an implicit, most of all operating unconsciously, narcissitic fantasy of immortality. The central theme in most daydreaming activities is one's own life in progress. In this activity, conscious censorship is very weak (Varendonck, 1922). By daydreaming, man rephrases and reconstructs his life not hindered by the limitations he encounters in everyday life. Nothing is impossible in this active dreaming acitivity. Normally, there is no place in daydreaming for self-limitation or for taking into account the finitude of vital power. When he is absorbed in his deepest wishfulfilling dreams, man feels, or better is, immortal. The above mentioned rebellion is one side of man's narcissism; the fantasy of immortality that shows its primary importance in spontaneous ideations is the other. This observation does not contradict the commonsense observation that, when man consciously reflects about life and death, he feels anxiety. The existence of this basic fantasy of immortality makes it psychologicaly understandable that man does not, in fact, show much concern about death and finitude in his everyday life, in spite of his rational awareness of it. The fantasy of immortality in itself is not pathological (Lifton, 1973). On the contrary, it contributes to a healthy mental life that is characterized by creativity in the broadest sense of the word. 'Life is impoverished, it loses interest, when the highest stake in the game of living, life itself, may not be risked', argued Freud (1915a, p. 343). A sufficient degree of disregard for the possibility of death enables man to take the risks that are inevitable in life. This kind of narcissism gives him vitality. Zilboorg's (1943, also 1938) observations in war point in the same direction. For him, the fear of death is a primary fact in
our mental functioning that requires a constant coping effort. The major coping mechanism is negation or denial that contributes to the 'self-inflationary propensities of man
which keep his sense of insecurity on a more or less subliminal level' (Zilboorg, 1943, p. 470). This coping strategy is not pathological, it makes life livable, even in the worst of circumstances (war).

Freud's ideas about the 'psychology of death' are much more balanced than one would expect on the basis of his popularized functional thesis about the link between fear of death and the wish fulfilling beliefs in God and in life after death. Fear of death is not the only basic affective reaction towards the end of life, it is not even the primary one in the normal course of life. A strong sense of immortality, operating most of all unconsciously, is an essential part of a healthy mental life.

4.2. Clinical psychology research

Besides the classical survey research about the attitude towards death, there is a clinical tradition of empirical research about the psychological meaning of death. In this tradition, which is often neglected in scientific reviews, one finds a confirmation of the greater comple-xity of the psychological meaning of death than is suggested by the questionaire research in the academic psychology tradition. The actual body of such clinical literature is rather small. I give some interesting examples.

Bromberg and Schilder (1933 and 1936) detected a great variety of influential psychological meanings of death in normal subjects as well as in subjects of different psychopathological groups. The most important difference between normal and pathological groups is that psychologically disturbed subjects emphasize one or another particular meaning of death by separating it from the plurality of possible meanings. The authors found a number of meanings. Death is sometimes experienced as the final way out of an unbearable life situation. This meaning is almost always implicitly present in the longing to die (see also Friedlander, 1940), which is in itself not confined to suicidal patients but, as their data showed, is a thought or fantasy that is also common in normal subjects. In this context, death is paradoxically considered to be a new life, a life that is free of the tensions of the present life. Another meaning dimension of death is death as a means to put pressure on important others to obtain more affection. This death representation can become very elaborate on the fantasy level. The subject secretly enjoys the supposed emotional reactions of his loved ones whom he considers to be failing in their duties of attention and affection. Finally, some subjects cherish the representation of their own death —in fact the longed for life after death— as a state of absolute perfection: a state of being without weaknesses or faults (see also Hoffman and Brody, 1957). Other meanings of death that have been observed (see also Greenberger, 1965) in psychodynamic studies, are death as non-existent, death as punishment for untolerable aggressivity and/or sexual desires (see also Alexander, 1929), death as the possibility of reunion with the mother or another love object, and finally death as a lover. Of course, several of these themes are creatively developed in poetry and other literary forms. Bromberg and Schilder (1933 and 1936) located the origin of this great variety of death representations in the early infantile relational experiences (reliable, threatening, troubled by continuous threat of separation, etc.).

In the research about the meaning of death in children and in adolescents, a great variety of meaning dimensions has also been observed, in addition to the genetic psychological fact of the phased development of the death representation (cognitive and affective) in childred (e.g. Chadwick, 1929; Schilder and Wechsler, 1934; Nagy, 1948; Safier, 1964; Hug-Hellmuth, 1965; Melear, 1973; Spinetta, 1974).

What is striking in the clinical and psychodynamic research literature on the psychological meaning of death is the great thematic variety of death representations, not only in children but also in adult subjects and not only in psychologically disturbed subjects but also in the so-called normal groups. One has to conclude that, in normal adult life, death is psychologically present probably in more than in one way in the same individual. An adult assumes the rational idea (knowledge) of death as the irrevocable end of physical existence. This idea, when made conscious, is loaded most of all with anxiety or fear. And it can be called normal for one to try to cope with this anxiety by means of the mechanism of repression or denial. Clinical studies, however, have proven that the death representation is not one-dimensionally negative and that it is not always loaded with anxiety. Finally, it is curious that none of the reviewed clinical studies report the subjects making a spontaneous appeal to religion as part of their coping strategy towards death.

5. Realistic psychology? Fear of death and religion in extreme situations

An additional encouragement to leave the narrow scope of the research tradition in academic psychology comes from a source of evidence that is not much in use in that psychology: the testimonies of persons who have been cruelly and irrevocably confronted with death in extreme situations. If religious belief and, more specifically, religious belief in an after-life, can be explained motivationally as caused by death anxiety, as Freud argued in one of his approaches and as the classical survey research in psychology would contend, then one would expect to find the evidence for this link in situations where the reality of death is dominantly present and inexorable. I will leave aside here the psychomedical research on assistance and counseling for the dying patient (e.g. Kübler-Ross, 1969 and 1985) as well as the few studies that have been conducted about persons who like living dangerously (dangerous sports and/or professions) (e.g. Lester, 1971) but rather consider the experience of concentration camp survivors. It is impossible to review here the huge amount of rich scientific studies on this topic and the growing stream of personal testimony literature. I will select some paradigmatic references.

Bruno Bettelheim's (1943) famous article entitled "Individual and Mass Behavior in Extreme Situations" is based on his personal experience in Dachau and Buchenwald. It is not a subjective report nor an impressionistic discourse. In collaboration with fellow prisoners, he systematically registered the main types of psychological reactions of men to the concentration camp situation. Althought death was continuously present as part of the camp terror, the theme of coping with that monstrous threat is almost totally absent as an explicit topic. It could be said that all of the reactions Bettelheim describes can be considered variations of the coping strategy in that situation. It is remarkable that the representation of personal death is not reported as a conscious preoccupation among the respondents. Neither is there a reference to explicit, religious ideation concerning death and the eventuality of an after-life. Probably because our topic was not in the focus of Bettelheim's attention, he does not give an explicit psychological elucidation of this phenomenon. Nevertheless, he implicitly indicates some lines of explanation (see also Bettelheim, 1960, 1968, 1986).

First of all, he underlines the generally observed reticence of camp survivors to talk about the most terrible experiences they endured during camp life after their liberation. He observed the same reticence in senior camp inhabitants, and he understands this attitude as a kind of amnesia. When they do speak about their most threatening and humiliating experiences, they do it in a rationalizing defensive way. During camp life, the most terrible aspects of that life and the most terrifying situations are often experienced as unreal (derealization) and as not personally involving the prisoner himself (depersonalization) (Bettelheim, 1943, p. 75). In his general psychological study, Chodoff (1966) reports the same coping patterns. To the extreme situations in the camp life, formerly normal persons react with what would be, in normal circumstances, pathological mechanisms of denial, with episodes of derealization and depersonalization, and even with inappropriate feelings of happiness. It is striking also in this study, that no explicit ideational or affective preoccupation with death is reported. The only explicit concern of the surviving camp prisoner is his life here and now and the protection of his personal integrity and of his privacy.

Another, more precise observation of Bettelheim (1943) points in the same direction: persons who were worried too much about the atrocity and the insecurity of their condition, who were continuously overwhelmed by their anxiety and by fear of death, had the least chance of survival. The text is not formal and explicit about this point but is very suggestive in this direction. Bettelheim's (1943) text and also Chodoff's (1966) make clear that anxiety is not the only or consciously the most important affective attitude towards death. In any case, they make it clear that the anxiety reaction is not the soundest or most adequate coping strategy when a person is really in direct confrontation with death. A good amount of negation can be called a sound coping and selfdefense strategy.

And what can we find in those studies about the 'link' between death (anxiety) and religious belief and, more specifically, religious belief in an afterlife? Neither Bettelheim nor Chodoff report the presence of explicit religious ideation about life after death. Nor do they report an increase of religiosity or religious activity in extreme situations. Bettelheim (1943, p. 87-88) observed enhanced day dreaming activity in older prisoners with eschatological and messianic themes, but these thoughts were not embedded in a religious atmosphere. Other research (e.g. Cohen, 1979) and testimonial literature (e.g., Micheels, 1989; Levi, 1987, 1988; Appleman-Jurman, 1988) seem to confirm these observations. Levi, who was a fine observer of himself as well as of others, never mentions that religious thoughts and attitudes were called upon by his fellow prisoners to alleviate their misery. He does not deny the possible incidence of increased belief as being helpful for some particular person, but he did not observe an explicit appeal to it. The observations of Cohen (1979) point in the same direction. Levi (1987) even offers a contrary consideration: to strenghten the will to survive in such an inhumane situation as Auschwitz, it was, in a certain sense, necessary to give up all frames of reference, not only religious ones, but also all other accustomed modes of thinking and of affective life (Levi, 1987, p. 31).

In none of the testimony literature is religion signaled as motivationally based on even the most extreme need situation of man. Death anxiety as such is not 'naturally' appealing for religious involvement as a means to alleviate that terror.

6. Further research is needed...

The 'psychology of death' and more specifically the religious psychological concern about the potential link between the experience of death and religious attitudes need further, more detailed, and more clinical investigation. Two conclusions can be drawn from our preliminary study.

First of all, further research must widen its scope when studying the psychologically relevant representational - cognitive and affective - working through of the reality of death: attention must be paid to a large and very differentiated field of psychological meanings that are attributed to death, and a broader variety of affective attitudes must be taken into account. Technically speaking, there is a need for larger and more refined instruments to approach this field than were the small questionnaires that have hitherto been used in academic psychological research on the topic. Indeed, I would argue for the systematic use of the indepth interview technique in this kind of research. Such a research project is in the development phase at the Centre for Psychology of Religion of the University of Leuven.

Psychology of religion has to leave the all too narrow motivational hypothesis stemming from Freud on the link between need and death anxiety and the religious attitude. More recent classical survey research (Magni, 1971 and 1973; Spilka et al., 1977) has already added many nuances to the question, but this research needs, in our view, further development in conjunction with the clinical approach.

REFERENCES

Allport, G. (1958). *The Nature of Prejudice*. New York: Doubleday.

Allport, G., & Ross, J.M. (1967). Personal religious orientation and prejudice. *Journal of Personality and Social Psychology*, 5, 432-444.

Alexander, F. (1929). The need for punishment and the death-instinct. *International Journal of Psychoanalysis*, 10, 256-269

Appleman-Jurman, A. (1988). *Vergeten kan ik niet*. Baarn: Anthos.

Bettelheim, B. (1943). Individual and mass behavior in extreme situations. *Journal of Abnormal and Social Psychology*, 38, 417-452. Reprinted in B. Bettelheim, Surviving the holocaust (pp. 60-96). London: Collins.

Bettelheim, B. (1960). *The Informed Heart. A Study of the Psychological Consequences of Living under Extreme Fear and Terror*. Harmondsworth: Penguin Books. (Ed. Peregrine Books, 1987).

Bettelheim, B. (1968). The ultimate limit. *Midway*, 9, 3-25. Reprinted in Bettelheim, B. (1986). Surviving the Holocaust (pp. 16-30). London: Collins.

Bettelheim, B. (1986). *Surviving the Holocaust* (Fontana Paperback). London: Collins.

Bolt, M. (1977). Religious orientation and death fears. *Revue of Religious Research*, 19, 73-76.

Bromberg, W., & Schilder, P. (1933). *Death and dying. A comparative study of the attitudes and mental reactions toward death and dying*. Psychoanalytic Review, 20, 133-185.

Bromberg, W., & Schilder, P. (1936). The attitude of psychoneurotics toward death. *Psychoanalytic Review*, 23, 1-25.

Chadwick, M. (1929). Notes upon the fear of death. *International Journal of Psychoanalysis*, 10, 321-334.

Chodoff, P. (1966). Effects of extreme coercive and oppressive forces: Brainwashing and concentration camps. In S. Arieti (Ed.), *American Handbook of Psychiatry* (Vol. 3, pp. 384-405). New York: Basic Books.

Cohen, E.A. (1979). *De negentien treinen naar Sobibor*. Amsterdam: Elsevier.

Corveleyn, J. (1990). Geloven in het hiernamaals, een wensdroom? Psychologische reflecties. In J. Lambrecht and L. Kenis (Eds.), *Leven over de dood heen: Verslagboek van een interdisciplinair Leuvens colloquium* (pp. 145-191). Leuven/Amersfoort: Acco.

Delooz, R. (1971). Qui croit à l'au-delà? In A. Godin (Ed.), *Mort et présence. Etudes de psychologie* (pp. 17-38). Bruxelles: Lumen Vitae.

Diggory, J.C., & Rothman, D.Z. (1961). Values destroyed by death. *Journal of Abnormal and Social Psychology*, 63, 205-210.

Feifel, H. (1959). Attitudes toward death in some normal and mentally ill populations. In H. Feifel (Ed.), *The Meaning of Death* (pp. 114-130). New York: McGraw Hill.

Feifel, H. (Ed.). (1959). *The Meaning of Death*. New York: McGraw Hill.

Feifel, H. (1974). Religious conviction and fear of death among the healthy and terminally ill. *Journal for the Scientific Study of Religion*, 13, 353-360.

Feifel, H., & Branscomb, A.B. (1973). Who's afraid of death? *Journal of Abnormal Psychology*, 81, 282-288.

Freud, S. (1909). *Bemerkungen über einen Fall von Zwangsneurose*. Gesammelte Werke VII, 379-463.

Freud, S. (1915a). *Zeitgemässes über Krieg und Tod*. Gesammelte Werke X, 324-355.

Freud, S. (1915b-1991). Wir und der Tod. *Psyche. Zeitschrift für Psychoanalyse und ihre Anwendungen*, 45, 132-142, and Die Zeit of 20 VII 1990, Nr. 30. First published in: ZweimonatsBericht für die Mitglieder der österr. israel. Humanitätsvereine B'nai B'rith, Bd. 18/Nr.1, 41-51. Editorial article: Nitzschke, B. (1991).

Freud, S. (1916). *Vergänglichkeit*. Gesammelte Werke X, 358-361.

Freud, S. (1917). *Trauer und Melancholie*. Gesammelte Werke X, 427-446.

Freud, S. (1923). *Das Ich und das Es*. Gesammelte Werke XIII, 235-289.

Freud, S. (1927). *Die Zukunft einer Illusion*. Gesammelte Werke XIV, 323-380.

Freud, S. (1930). *Das Unbehagen in der Kultur*. Gesammelte Werke XIV, 421-506.

Freud, S. (1933a). *Warum Krieg?* Gesammelte Werke XVI, 13-27.

Freud, S. (1933b). Ueber eine Weltanschauung. In S. Freud, *Neue Folge der Vorlesungen zur Einführung in die Psychoanalyse* (Gesammelte Werke XV, pp. 170-197p.)

Friedlander, K. (1940). On the "Longing to die". *International Journal of Psychoanalysis*, 21, 416-426.

Gebsattel, V. von. (1938). Die Welt des Zwangskranken. *Monatschrift für Psychiatrie und Neurologie*, 99, 10-74.

Godin, A. (Ed.). (1971). *Mort et présence. Etudes de psychologie* (Cahiers de Lumen Vitae. Psychologie de la Religion, 5). Bruxelles: Ed. Lumen Vitae.

Godin, A. (1971). La mort a-t-elle changé? In A. Godin (Ed.), *Mort et présence. Etudes de psychologie* (pp. 233-256). Bruxelles: Ed. Lumen Vitae.

Godin, A. (1988). Espérer en faisant mémoire. Réflexions psychologiques sur la crise des "fins dernières" dans les croyances chrétiennes. In L.V. Thomas (Ed.), *Réincarnation, immortalité, résurrection* (Publications des Facultés Universitaires Saint-Louis, n° 45) (pp. 91-132). Bruxelles: Facultés Universitaires Saint-Louis.

Greenberger, E. (1965). Fantasies of women confronting death. *Journal of Consulting Psychology*, 29, 252-260.

Hampe, J.C. (1988). *Sterven is heel anders: Ervaringen met de eigen dood* (2e uitg.). Baarn: Ten Have.

Heidegger, M. (1927). *Sein und Zeit*. Tübingen: Niemeyer.

Hoelter, J.W., & Epley, R. (1979). Religious correlates of fear of death. *Journal for the Scientific Study of Religion*, 18, 404-411.

Hoffman, F.H., & Brody, M.W. (1957). The symptom, fear of death. *Psychoanalytic Review*, 44, 433-438.

Hug-Hellmuth, H. von. (1965). The child's concept of death (1912). *Psychoanalytic Quarterly*, 34, 499-516.

James, W. (1902). *The Varieties of Religious Experience. A Study in Human Nature*. Glasgow: Collins (Ed. 1977, Fountain Books).

Jeffers, F.C., Nichols, C.R., & Eisdorfer, C. (1961). Attitudes of older persons toward death: A preliminary study. *Journal of Gerontology*, 16, 53-56.

Kahoe, R.D., & Dunn, R.F. (1975). The fear of death and religious attitudes and behaviour. *Journal for the Scientific Study of Religion*, 14, 379-383.

Kalish, R.A. (1963). Some variables in death attitudes. *Journal of Social Psychology*, 59, 137-145.

Kübler-Ross, E. (1969). *Lessen voor levenden. Gesprekken met stervenden*. Baarn: Ambo.

Kübler-Ross, E. (1985). *Over de dood en het leven daarna*. Baarn: Ambo.

Leclaire, S. (1956). Jérôme ou la mort dans la vie de l'obsédé. *Psychoanalyse*, 2, 111-140.

Lester, D. (1967a). Fear of death of suicidal persons. *Psychological Reports*, 20, 1077-1078.

Lester, D. (1967b). Experimental and correlational studies of the fear of death. *Psychological Bulletin*, 67, 27-36.

Lester, B. (1970). Re-examination of Middleton's data. *Psychological Reports*, 27, 136.

Lester, D. (1971). Sex differences in attitude toward death: A replication. *Psychological Reports*, 28, 754.

Levi, P. (1987). *Is dit een mens* (2e uitg.). Amsterdam: Meulenhoff.

Levi, P. (1988). *Het respijt* (2e uitg.). Amsterdam: Meulenhoff.

Lifton, R.J. (1973). The sense of immortality: On death and the continuity of life. *American Journal of Psychoanalysis*, 33, 3-19.

Magni, K.G. (1971). La peur de la mort. In A. Godin (Ed.), *Mort et présence. Etudes de psychologie* (pp. 129-142). Bruxelles: Ed. Lumen Vitae.

Magni, K.G. (1973). The fear of death: Studies of its character and concomitants. In L.B. Brown (Ed.), *Psychology and Religion* (pp. 329-342. Baltimore: Penguin.

Martin, D., & Wrightsman, L.S., Jr. (1965). The relationship between religious behavior and concern about death. *Journal of Social Psychology, 65, 317-323.*

Meissner, W.W. (1958). Affective response to psychoanalytic death symbols. *Journal of Abnormal and Social Psychology*. 56, 295-299.

Melear, J.D. (1973). Children's conception of death. *Journal of Genetic Psychology*, 123, 359-360.

Micheels, L.J. (1989). *Doctor # 117641: A Holocaust Memoir*. With a foreword by Albert J. Solnit. New Haven/London: Yale University Press.
Middleton, W.C. (1936). Some reactions toward death among college students. *Journal of Abnormal and Social Psychology*, 31, 165-173.
Nagy, M. (1948). The child's theories concerning death. *Journal of Genetic Psychology*, 73, 3-27.
Nitzschke, B. (1991). Freuds Vortrag vor dem Israelitischen Humanitätsverein "Wien" des Ordens B'nai B'rith: Wir und der Tod (1915). Ein wiedergefundenes Dokument. *Psyche: Zeitschrift für Psychoanalyse und ihre Anwendungen*, 45, 97-131.
Ochsman, R. (1984). Belief in afterlife as a moderator of fear of death? *European Journal of Social Psychology*, 14, 53-67.
Patrick, J.W. (1979). Personal faith and the fear of death among divergent religious populations. *Journal for the Scientific Study of Religion*, 18, 298-305.
Pfister, O. (1928). Die Illusion einer Zukunft. *Imago*, 14, 149-184.
Rhudick, P.J., & Dibner, A.S. (1961). Age, personality, and health correlates of death concerns in normal aged individuals (Attitudes toward death in older persons: A symposium). *Journal of Gerontology*, 16, 44-49.
Safier, G. (1964). A study in relationships between the life and death concepts in children. *Journal of Genetic psychology*, 105, 283-294.
Schilder, P., & Wechsler, D. (1934). The attitudes of children toward death. *Journal of Genetic Psychology*, 45, 406-451.
Siegel, R.K. (1980). The psychology of life after death. *American Psychologist*, 35, 911-931.
Spilka, B., Stout, L., Minton, B., & Sizemore, D. (1977). Death and personal faith: A psychometric investigation. *Journal for the Scientific Study of Religion*, 16, 169-178.
Spinetta, J.J. (1974). The dying child's awareness of death: A review. *Psychological Bulletin*, 81, 256-260.
Swenson, W.M. (1961). Attitudes toward death in an aged population. *Journal of Gerontology*, 16, 49-52.
Templer, D.I. (1970). The construction and validation of a Death Anxiety Scale. *Journal of General Psychology*, 82, 165-177.
Templer, D.I. (1971). The relationship between verbalized and nonverbalized death anxiety. *Journal of Genetic Psychology*, 119, 211-214.
Templer, D.I. (1972). Death anxiety in religiously very involved persons. *Psychological Reports*, 31, 361-362.
Templer, D.I., & Dotson, E. (1970). Religious correlates of death anxiety. *Psychological Reports*, 26, 895-897.
Templer, D.I., Lester, D., & Ruff, C.F. (1974). Fear of death and femininity. *Psychological Reports*, 35, 530.
Templer, D.I., & Ruff, C.F. (1971). Death Anxiety Scale means, standard deviations, and embedding. *Psychological Reports*, 29, 173-174.
Templer, D.I., Ruff, C.F., & Franks, C.M. (1971). Death anxiety: Age, sex and parental resemblance in diverse populations. *Developmental Psychology*, 4, 108.
Thomas, L.-V. (1988). L'eschatologie: permanence et mutation. In L.-V. Thomas (Ed.), *Réincarnation, immortalité, résurrection* (Publications des Facultés

Universitaires Saint- Louis, n° 45) (pp. 1-42). Bruxelles: Facultés Universitaires Saint-Louis.

Thomas, L.-V. (Ed.). (1988). *Réincarnation, immortalité, résurrection* (Publications des Facultés Universitaires Saint- Louis, n° 45). Bruxelles: Facultés Universitaires Saint- Louis.

Varendonck, J. (1922). *Über das vorbewusste phantasierende Denken* (Internationale psychoanalytische Bibliothek, Vol. 12). Mit einem Geleitwort von Prof. Dr. Sigm. Freud. Leipzig/Wien/Zürich: Intern. Psychoan. Verlag.

Vergote, A. (1984). *Religie, geloof en ongeloof. Psychologische studie.* Antwerpen/Amsterdam: De Nederlandsche Boekhandel.

Williams, R.L., & Cole, S. (1968). Religiosity, generalized anxiety, and apprehension concerning death. *Journal of Social Psychology*, 75, 111-117.

Zaleski, C. (1987). *Other World Journeys. Accounts of Near-Death Experience in Medieval and Modern Times*. Oxford: Oxford University Press.

Zilboorg, G. (1938). The sense of immortality. *Psychoanalytic Quarterly*, 7, 171-199.

Zilboorg, G. (1943). Fear of death. *Psychoanalytic Quarterly*, 12, 465-475.

CHAPTER 4
RELIGION AS PSYCHOPATHOLOGY: EXPLORING A METAPHOR

Benjamin Beit-Hallahmi

The phenomenon of religion challenges us to deal with two related questions. The first is that of its psychological origins and essence; the second is that of its functions and consequences for groups and individuals. These questions lead us to examine the nature of religious ideas and the interaction between such ideas and individual personalities.

My aim in this chapter is to explore the implications, the potential, and the limitations of using the observations and concepts of psychopathology as a way of understanding religious phenomena. Religion, in all its manifestations, may be *sui generis*, but to explain it we need metaphors taken from other realms of human experience. Attempting to develop a psychological theory of religion, we are all in search of the right metaphors and analogies. Religion has been looked at through the metaphors of philosophy, science, art, neurosis, psychosis, and realistic coping (see Pargament, this volume). My own favorite analogues, when trying to decipher the psychological processes involved in religion, have been art and psychopathology (Beit-Hallahmi, 1989).

Using neurosis as a metaphor for religion (and religion as a metaphor for neurosis) has been common since Freud first pointed out the similarity between compulsive symptoms and religious rituals and called religion a "universal obsessional neurosis" (Freud, 1907, p. 127). But when we look at religious ideas and claims, the correct diagnostic label seems to be found not in the field of adult neurotic behavior, but in observations of infantile, and maybe paranoid psychotic ideations. We are led in this direction by another well-quoted comment by Freud: "The whole thing is so patently infantile, so foreign to reality, that to anyone with a friendly attitude to humanity it is painful to think that the great majority of mortals will never be able to rise above this view of life" (Freud, 1927, p. 74). Childishness is indeed the hallmark of religious beliefs, and psychotic thinking may be the normal experience of every young child. The fairy tale flavor of all scripture stories is unmistakable, except that adults are willing to accept them not only literally, but as important, central truths.

This kind of ideation in an adult may be rightly judged to be bizarre, or at least defective in terms of the ego's reality testing. The obvious similarity between paranoid ideation and religious belief systems has often been noted (La Barre, 1972 ; Meissner, 1978, 1988) and its implications should be examined. Edward B. Tylor's classical theory of animism (1871) suggested that direct experiences with dreams, visions, hallucinations as well as with death created the theory of the soul and the beginnings of religion.

All religions promise their followers everlasting life through the immortality of the soul, but some religious leaders promise their followers literal, physical, immortality, and some followers claim to accept that promise. In the 1930s in the United States, a man known as Father Divine was supposed to have given his followers everlasting life: "...many of us who are in this place will never lose the bodies we now have. God is here in the flesh, and he is never going away from us, and we will remain here forevermore. This is heaven on earth" (Fauset, 1944, p. 105). What are we to make of this obvious delusion? Immortality delusions operate to shore up the depresssed individual ego, leading to a "mania" which may be functional, at least in the short run.

One may ask whether a conscious commitment to religious ideation would not undermine reality testing in general. When we listen to the stories about disembodied voices coming from heaven, and infantile fantasies about miracles and promised triumphs, we have to ask to what extent accepting such ideas affects one's negotiations with social and physical reality, and whether it does not betray a fatal character flaw in the believer.

Religious belief systems are made up of ideas of reference - connections between the human microcosm and the macrocosm of the universe - and ideas of influence - influences directed from an imagined macrocosm to the human microcosm - two classical criteria of psychotic ideation in the individual. This led La Barre (1972) to conclude that religions were indeed paranoid defenses, while Meissner (1988) admitted that separating the paranoid elements out of Christian beliefs would be impossible.

The question of explaining religion within the psychopathology framework has been clearly posed by Arieti (1976): "There is no doubt that hallucinations and delusions of any sort, religious or not, are abnormal phenomena... Must we accept the idea that in some of its beliefs religion is a form of collective schizophrenia, and in some of its practices a form of obsessive-compulsive psychoneurosis, different from the psychiatric syndromes because it is socially acceptable?" (p. 252).

Arieti's dilemma is that "...mystical experiences seem to correspond to what are called hallucinations and delusions in psychiatric terms. Must we then conclude that people who have such experiences are suffering from schizophrenia, paranoia, or other psychoses? Not necessarily" (1976, p. 251). One reason is that "...whereas hallucinations are rare in paranoia and well-systematized paranoid conditions, they are common in mystical experience" (p. 252).

The production of mystical experiences requires a special psychological process, combining normal and pathological mechanisms: "But what are the phenomena that bring about hallucinations and delusions, in the absence of intoxication and psychosis? They seem to me to be related to hysterical and hypnotic mechanisms... In mystical experiences we have a condition of autohypnosis: the subject puts himself into a state of trance and projects power to the divinity... In religious experiences as in the aesthetic process, the various levels of mentation are concordant. This concordance leads to religious value... The subject does not believe his will is involved. He feels that he is the recipient of an experience, a passive agent... This strong religious force is the result, first, of religious preparation, then of a state of over belief, and finally of a state of authohypnosis" (p. 253).

What Arieti calls religious value, and regards positively, is what we may call the prophecy commitment (or delusion). "The individual who experiences them has a marked rise in self-esteem and a sense of his being or becoming a worthwhile and very active person. He has been given a mission or a special insight, and from now on he must be on the move doing something important - more important than his own life... he has been chosen to perform something of stupendous proportions" (p. 251).

To sum up Arieti's theory of the religious, it is based on the assumption of a special process, relying on projection and hystetrical mechanisms, but with positive, creative outcomes in terms of faith, optimism, and meaning.

While the description of the religious process itself (atheistic, reductionist) is quite in keeping with other psychoanalytic conceptions, it is the valuation of the outcome which is likely to be challenged. La Barre (1972) has described a similar process, but would not accept Arieti's judgment of the outcome. He would easily point to crazy messiahs all over the world who have had this sense of mission, with tragic results for themselves and others.

A Theory of Normal Pathology

Having stated my initial assumption, let me now present two paradoxes which challenge the psychopathology analogue:

1. Religious ideas are crazy, that is they represent conscious expressions of immature, pathological processes, but religious people are clearly not insane, and they (as a group) manage to deal quite well with everyday reality.
2. For some seriously disturbed individuals, religious ideas can sometimes be therapeutic.

These two paradoxes may seem to undermine the value of my suggested analogue, and I will try to offer adequate answers to this implied challenge.

I want to solve the first paradox by suggesting that pathology is more prevalent, and at the same time well under control, in most human beings. What I would like to propose here is that pre-logical, infantile, crazy ideas are common, experienced by all of us, and we should approach religious ideation in light of this basic datum. By normal pathology I mean the psychotic within all of us, primary process thinking, the infantile, the weird, hypnagogic experiences which we all share.

We all respond to psychotic ideas and psychotic images, as those reflect inner processes that are common to all. There is a great deal of similarity and continuity between "insane" ideas and productions in art, mythology, religion, and literature (MacGregor, 1989). Freud (1915-1916) stated we all become psychotic every night, when we dream, and so we understand, and produce, psychotic ideation naturally.

Psychoanalysis has given us an important notion, relevant to our discussion here, which is that psychopathology is a matter of quantity, not quality. There is only one human psychology, animated by one set of structures and dynamics, with pathology being an intensification of normal processes. There is a continuum starting with "normality", through "neurosis" and ending with psychosis. An individual judged to be normal is so judged because of an imaginary "average" of behaviors, some of which may be abnormal. And likewise, an individual judged to be psychotic is so judged because of an imaginary "average" of behaviors, some of which may be quite normal. Instances of both normal and abnormal human events can serve us equally well in developing our understanding of the human psyche and its operating rules.

It is easy to see that religious believers hold bizarre beliefs, but mostly use them only in a religious context. They allow themselves this escape from reality only under very specific circumstances. The miraculous events which run counter to everything we know about nature and humanity are usually believed to have happened long ago and far away. They have no real implications for the management of immediate reality. They may be a source of enjoyment and moral inspiration, and thus can enhance functioning, not interfere with it. This is one instance of a more general phenomenon: "In the work of art, as in the dream, unconscious contents are alive; here too, evidences of the primary process are conspicuous, but the ego maintains its control over them, elaborates them in its own right, and sees to it that the distortion does not go too far" (Kris, 1952, p. 103).

This specific and controlled movement away from reality is known in psychoanalytic theory as regression in the service of the ego.

This term is another metaphor, of course, for one of the most amazing and, indeed, miraculous phenomena in normal human behavior. "It can be considered a sign of the ego's strength if occasionally and for a specific purpose, it is capable of tolerating the mechanisms of the 'ID'" (Kris, 1952, p. 116).

Music and artistic productions, as well as religion, may induce in us hypnotic-like processes (Arieti, 1976), but the regression involved is still, in most cases, specific and controlled, still in the service of ego.

In this context, the derivatives of Winnicott's concept of the transitional state are worth looking at closely:

"I am therefore studying the substance of *illusion*, that which is allowed to the infant, and which in adult life is inherent in art and religion... We can share a respect for *illusory experience*, and if we wish we may collect together and form a group on the basis of the similarity of our illusory experiences" (Winnicott, 1971, p. 3 - italics in the original).

A close reading of Winnicott shows that his idea of transitional phenomena does not stray far from the more traditional, and better known, concept of regression in the service of the ego: "It is assumed here that the task of reality-acceptance is never completed, that no human being is free from the strain of relating inner and outer reality, and that relief from this strain is provided by an intermediate area of experience which is not challenged (arts, religion, etc.) This intermediate area is in direct continuity with the play area of the small child who is 'lost' in play" (Winnicott, 1971, p. 13). Collective fantasies, like fairy tales or movies, are to be used and enjoyed, and religious fantasies are utilized in the same way. Harry Stack Sullivan called myths "Dreams that satisfy the needs of many" (Sullivan, 1953, p. 339). This means that myths belong to the parataxic mode, a pre-logical way of thinking, but serve a useful function for groups and individuals. Faur (1990), following Freud, shows major Christian mythological ideas to be oedipal fantasies, accepted and used by believers without any evidence of detrimental effects, like other works of art.

Hansson (1986) showed that very old people invest more in their religion than in social relations, because for them the main problem is coming to terms with death and separation from loved ones. They have lost many sources of social support through death and so finding new contacts does not make much sense. What may look from the outside like growing isolation and a withdrawal from the world actually signifies better coping, but coping alone, with the help of religious ideas and religious objects.
Here religion offers what no other source can provide, and the regression from reality is highly beneficial.

Going further in our explorations of normal pathology, we note the universality of magical thinking and compulsive rituals. Individuals engage in developing minor delusional systems of magical accounting, paying attention to numbers which are lucky or unlucky, and ascribing causality and moral value to events in the world around them. I ran across a vivid example just a short while ago. A woman journalist, who came to interview me about occult ideas, confessed to me that she herself believed that anything bad that ever happens to her is punishment and retribution for her own misdeeds, and that she has her own system of moral bookkeeping, unrelated to any official religious belief systems.

Hallucinations, considered a psychotic symptom, are probably much more prevalent in the general population than we tend to assume, and here again the issue is one of quantity in any given individual. Romme and Escher (1989) described a conference for people who hear voices, held in Holland. This conference was publicized on Dutch radio, and hundreds of individuals showed up. Some of them described their experiences with their private voices as extremely beneficial. The voices they heard came from guides who made their lives better. Others reported real agonies caused by voices.

The similarity in occult visions of all ages and places, pointed to by all students of religion may be tied to the similarity in psychotic ideation. It is matched by the universality of artistic creations and myths. Paranoid delusions, hallucinations, and other severe symptoms, reflecting universal human concerns, are found in all human cultures, and the overall prevalence of schizophrenia seems to be uniform in all ages and societies. The sociologist Edward Shils suggested that "the propensity to seek contact with transcedent powers and to impute charisma is rooted in the neural constitution of the human organism" (Shils, 1975, p. 97). Jaynes (1977) also speculated that both schizophrenic hallucinations and religion reflect our basic neurological wiring. As psychologists we are interested in the conscious and unconscious manifestations of this neural propensity, reflected in the universal readiness for regression, faith, and psychosis.

Object relations theory provides a theoretical basis for understanding the projected world of the spirits in relation to the internal world of objects. Its starting point is the existence of an inner world of mental representations, reflecting the self and objects to which it is attached. The world of imaginary objects is created at an early stage of object relations, when substitute objects are projected to stand for real objects which are missed and presumed lost (Cf. Freud, 1923). We develop imaginary compensation for object loss, and replace the bad object with an ideal one.

Religious belief systems describe a struggle between good and evil in the imaginary world far from us (and sometimes very close to us) in the form of the devil, demons, and spirit possession. And where does this struggle come from? "Who are the gods who panic? Who are the monsters and werewolves, ogres and witches? Or the bogeys, vampires, and vultures who appear in dreams and mysteries and threaten one's life? Whence those fears and figments; the notion of fantastic beings and domains no human is able to fathom? We encounter them everywhere. They are an integral part of the vast repertoire of human imagination, nay, the human condition. Their supernatural craft stems from that inspiration which in one way or the other belongs inevitably to everyone's childlike sense of impending doom or disaster and only magic, ritual, or prayer can tame or dispel" (Muensterberger, 1972, p. ix).

The art metaphor for religion is limited by the social convention about the truth of religion and the artifice in art. What separates art from religion is the latter's claim for truth and superiority over reality. The power of religious claims and the idea of the holy, shadows of individual psychosis, seem to be beyond reality testing. The experience of the holy and the uncanny (Levy, 1984) is what separates religion from secular belief systems. Lutzky (1991) suggested that this "numinous" experience stems from early object relations. She has proposed a solution to the mystery of the origins of the sacred. There is a connection between the sacred and the internal object, between early experience and the numinous. Hutch (1991) offers a related theoretical notion of the *residuum*, which "is the psychological origin of all religious myths, rituals, doctrines, communities and ethics" (p. 85). "The *residuum* is the sum total of prototypical affect laden traces or images... which, arising from infancy, remains the person's more or less fixed projection on the world and others." (p. 84).

Religious Ideas and Diagnosed Psychotics

Conventional social beliefs inspire or produce the specific contents of schizophrenic hallucinations, which in an individual raised in a religious environment are likely to be religious (West, 1962). Practicing mental health professionals may be faced with an issue of differential diagnosis (cf. Numbers & Numbers, 1985), which is not our concern here, but does have implications for our analysis: "A problem then for practicing doctors seems to be to distinguish these two areas of religion and mental illness... A solution to the problems of separating insanity from religious experience is to look at them, not as mutually exclusive natural states located in the physical world, but rather as being in particular domains of culture. The same biological events set up resonances in each system of reference" (Littlcwood & Lipsedge, 1989, p. 192).

Is it possible that personal pathology may lead us to choose certain ideas? That crazy people are more likely to choose certain crazy ideas to believe in? That disturbed individuals are more likely to develop strong commitments to religious ideas and religious groups? It is clear that psychotic or near psychotic individuals treat religious ideas in a special way, and embrace them, failing in "religious" reality testing as they fail in no other area of behavior.

Let us look at the case of Oric Bovar (1918-1977), a former opera coach, who led a small group in New York City in the early 1970s claiming he was Jesus Christ, and that he could raise the dead back to life. When one of his disciples died, he kept the body and was found by police praying over it. He was charged with a misdemeanor for keeping the body. On April 11, 1977, the day he was supposed to stand trial, Oric Bovar jumped out of a 10th floor window.

Individuals who are diagnosed as psychotic are the only ones who seem to take religious ideas literally, which we then use as proof of their insanity. They don't get the "normal" meaning of religious claims in the same way in which they don't get jokes, and fail in interpreting common proverbs. What they lack is the ability to regress in the service of the ego; what they possess in abundance is the ability to experience the sacred as close to them. This has led several researchers to speculate about the structural-neurological connection between schizophrenia and religious ideas (Jaynes, 1977).

But let us turn to the second paradox in the relationship between religion and psychopathology, mentioned above. We have to consider how religion offers solace to some individuals who are psychotic or borderline psychotic. What we find is that in some cases, whether in major religions or in "deviant" new religious movements, such people find a community, social support, a real acceptance, and a greater tolerance for "crazy" ideas. "Nor is it hard to discern that all the ties that bind people to mystico-religious or philosophico-religious sects and communities are expressions of crooked cures of all kinds of neuroses" (Freud, 1921, p. 132).

Highly disturbed individuals seek relief, support, and acceptance in formal or informal interactions, and this search leads them to a variety of settings available in their communities. Beyond the intended social service and treatment organizations, they may join "underground structures", which are often ignored by official social agencies and caregivers. In these unofficial settings they might be frustrated and exploited, but they may also be helped, through the unique fit between their own psychological makeup and the organization's particular culture.

Salvation groups are social networks organized around a message of esoteric knowledge, available to members only, which sometimes enables them to experience dramatic personality transformations ("conversions"). The message is usually religious, but may also be totally secular. In all cases these groups are belief minorities, regarded by society at large as deviant. A marginal worldview will attract marginal individuals, and the alienated, the lonely, and the seriously disturbed, are, not surprisingly, overrepresented among members of these groups.

While the groups are inherently deviant in terms of their basic beliefs, which we may regard as delusional, they provide some highly disturbed individuals with a supporting environment, thus unintentionally offering what would be viewed as therapeutic intervention when given in formal, professional settings.

Salvation testimonials presented in these groups include claims of physical and psychological change, telepathy, and miraculous cures of minor and major ailments, including addictions. While we may doubt the reliability of such claims, there is some evidence that membership in these deviant salvation groups may lead to improved functioning in the broader community. In a few cases, dramatic improvement is achieved. In some cases, hospitalization or re-hospitalization are prevented. In other cases, the burden on mental health and welfare agencies is lessened. In many cases, much is gained in subjective, human terms.

The "psychotherapeutic" effects of both conventional and deviant religious beliefs and, especially, religious communities, can be viewed again as evidence for a special affinity between what is religious and what is psychotic. Beyond the undeniable value of these groups as social support systems, and the unconditional love they sometimes offer the rejected psychotic, the special attraction of a collective paranoia for a deranged individual must be powerful (and comforting). However, we should keep in mind that the relief offered may be temporary and limited (Witztum, Greenberg, & Dasberg, 1990).

Limitations and Criticisms of the Psychopathology Analogue

We may now turn to the conceptual deficiencies of our analogy, which must have already occurred to the attentive reader.

One source of criticism is our heavily psychological and individualistic bias. Two extreme positions may be taken regarding the genesis of religious faith: "psychology and nothing else" versus "society and nothing else". So far we have looked at psychological factors exclusively. We always have to consider "symptoms", and beliefs, in their psychological, social, and historical context.

Our colleagues in anthropology and sociology may go a bit further, and remind us that religion exists only in a social way and religious groups develop for social causes. There are strong historical reasons for why certain private ideas become social and inspire social movements. The real causes are historical, political, economic. The rise of religious ideas is predicated on necessary historial conditions, because such ideas are the medium for expressing social issues. Individual dreams are social dreams in more than one way, not only reflecting universal human experiences, but the deprivations and struggles of social groups (Argyle & Beit-Hallahmi, 1975). We may invoke the famous Durkheimian dictum about how only social facts should be used to explain other social facts. In this context, our analogy is indeed false.

An interpretation of religion within the framework of individual psychopathology is deficient because it ignores its interpersonal context (first at the level of dyadic communication), its social context (the level of group formation and group dynamics), and its historical context. Indeed, religion is always social, and a religious belief system held by only one individual might as well be a psychosis. The sole criterion for differentiating individual psychosis from religion is interpersonal and social.

Collective ideas of religion would be considered psychotic if an individual held them. The criterion for judging them should be social, and they are always held in an interpersonal context.

Our concern here is exactly with the question of how a psychosis acquires a social nature, and how paranoid ideas are collectivized and become mere social conventions.

Social Learning and Conventional Beliefs

The interpretation of religion as a purely social fact seems uniquely suited to majority, conventional, religious beliefs.
Religious people, and even deeply religious ones, have not invented their religion. Conventional religious beliefs are usually acquired through social learning (Argyle & Beit-Hallahmi, 1975). These ideas are not private creations. The social learning of religion presents religious ideas, which may be crazy, as part of social reality. The received social consensus may have little to do with individual dynamics. "...the most significant difference between a religion, as held by a person, and a state of systematized delusion resides in the element of social participation. Some people necessary to the particular person have incorporated in their several personalities approximately the same structure of transcendental beliefs and rituals... there is a community of assumptions... It is not necessary to set up a special teaching situation in order to inculcate in the young the most consistent and constantly manifested traits of the family culture-complex. Very special educative situations indeed are needed if one is to eradicate the effects of this most facile sort of acculturation. It is safe to assume that the nucleus of one's personal religion has been acquired in this automatic way..." (Sullivan, 1964, p. 81).

Social learning may imbue certain pre-logical or paleological ideas with apparent immunity to critical thinking. Arieti (1956, 1976) has referred to paleologic thinking as "the foundation of many societal or collective manifestations - rituals, magic, customs, and beliefs- that are transmitted from generation to generation and accepted without questions being raised as to their validity".

Can We Combine Psychodynamics and Sociodynamics?

"Two different psychological theories might be developed to explain two different kinds of religious involvement. One is the low-involvement religion, the religion of identity, learned within the family of origin and having little emotional significance; and the other is the high-involvement religion, often the religion of converts, who learned it outside their family of origin and invest much emotional energy in it" (Beit-Hallahmi, 1989, p. 100). Identity religion, i.e. low involvement religion, does not present a need for a discussion of individual dynamics. We should not find much psychological investment among most conventional believers because there is only little ego-involvement in their faith, which is indeed only identity religion. When social learning is involved, we are dealing with a low level of ego involvement, and the consumption of a social product. When looking for high involvement, we should examine new religious groups, likely to be considered deviant.

The Creation of New Ideas and New Movements

The real question we are faced with is the formation and acceptance of original, or at least new, religious ideas. On a social level, the production of such ideas means forming new social groupings and challenging existing authority structures.
This is only partially related to the social learning of conventional beliefs, and may be compared to the phenomenon of conversion, another form of innovation.

Going back to the concept of regression in the service of the ego, we might suppose that mild regression involved an acceptance of social beliefs, while a major regression leads to the invention of original ones. We do not have to assume that only psychotic people are responsible for new religious ideas, but we can assume that individual psychodynamics are involved in those exceptional cases where religious innovation occurs. Psychotic people may be original and creative when it comes to religion, but they have to achieve social acceptance and group formation. Any private delusion may become commonly held (Littlewood & Lipsedge, 1989). "Deviant" religious views are simply minority views, which may one day become socialized.

Students of religious movements often encounter lone prohpets, individuals who proclaim new discoveries of truth and salvation, but remain unheeded by the world. They are likely to be judged deviant and deranged, but how different are they from leaders of new movements? What is the difference between the founder of a religious movement, such as Rudolf Steiner (Beit-Hallahmi, 1993) and somebody like D.P.Schreber (Freud, 1911; Schreber, 1955)? While Steiner's ideas may strike us as bizarre, they contain no ideas of reference. Personal references within a system of deviant beliefs about the spiritual world are evidence of pathology, recognized as such by believers and non-believers alike. Thus, Schreber was much more unlikely to attract followers.

Moving from the individual to the social "normalizes" religious ideas. A truly psychotic production is totally uncommunicative, private, and provokes anxiety in the observer. Psychotic ideation which wins converts and followers must undergo processing and elaboration to make it develop beyond private experience.

Then it becomes "art", an artistic production, in the sense of providing some relief to at least a few individuals, who may become real followers. This is tha making of a religious leader.

The move from madness to vision, from individual dynamics and pathology to socially held beliefs, and from group dynamics to history, must involve more than the limited pathological dynamics of a folie a deux (or a trois). The appearance of shared beliefs, especially if considered deviant by the larger society, demands a serious investment of psychic energy and social capital. Group formation involves a psychological investment on the part of members in group beliefs, in the group leader and in other members (Freud, 1921). What is commonly known as charisma may be the followers' fantasy created in response to the leader's pathology, and then projected on him, provided that an overall social need for such a process exists.

Psychopathology and History

The apperance of new religious belief systems, heretofore unknown in a culture and the formation of new religious groups breaking new cultural ground must be tied to major historical changes.

We have witnessed an example of this process recently, and indeed only an analysis combining psychological and historical concepts can begin to do justice to its complexity. This is the appearance of both religious and secular salvation movements in Israel within a short time in the 1970s, which is clearly connected to historical developments during that poriod, namely a continuing political crisis and the resultant experience of stress and distress by members of the society (Beit-Hallahmi, 1992; Sobel & Beit-Hallahmi, 1991). The crisis experienced by the whole society is felt on the individual level as greater vulnerability. Those with paranoid or schizotypic predispositions will respond with new religious ideas, or to religious ideas, whether new or old. A high degree of personal involvement in old and new religions has been found to be connected to a personal history and present evidence of serious psychopathology (Witztum, Greenberg, & Dasberg, 1990). When we deal with high invovlement religion, we may need to resort to theories of personality dynamics and psychopathology.

While the appearance and acceptance of religious movements should be interpreted with due regard to historical and social factors, psychology and psychopathology are still needed to explain individual differences in personal commitment to religious ideas. Under the same set of historical conditions, not everybody joins even the most successful movement, nor are followers committed in the same way. Durkheim was right, but all social facts are built on a psychological foundation. The psychopathology we all share is naturally social, but we still share it as individuals.

REFERENCES

Argyle, M & Beit-Hallahmi, B. (1975) *The Social Psychology of Religion*. London: Routledge & Kegan Paul.

Arieti, S. (1956) Some basic problems common to anthropology and modern psychiatry. *American Anthropologist, 58*, 26-30.

Arieti, S. (1976) *Creativity: The Magic Synthesis*. New York: Basic Books.

Beit-Hallahmi, B. (1989) *Prolegomena To The Psychological Study of Religion*. Lewisburg, PA: Bucknell University Press.

Beit-Hallahmi, B. (1992) *Despair and Deliverance: Private Salvation In Contemporary Israel*. Albany, NY: SUNY Press.

Beit-Hallahmi, B. (1993) *Dictionary of Modern Religious Movements*. New York: Richards Rosen.

Faur, J. (1990) De-authorization of the Law: Paul and the oedipal model. In J.H. Smith & S.A. Handelman (Eds) *Psychoanalysis And Religion*. Baltimore: Johns Hopkins University Press.

Fauset, A.F. (1944) *Black Gods of the Metropolis*. Philadelphia: University of Pennsylvania Press.

Freud, S. (1967) Obsessive actions and religious practices (1907). In *The Standard Edition of the Complete Psychological Works of Sigmund Freud*, Vol. IX, 115-127. London: Hogarth Press.

Freud, S. (1958) Psychoanalytic notes on an autobiographical account of a case of paranoia (Dementia paranoides) (1911). In *The Standard Edition of the Complete Psychological Works of Sigmund Freud*, Vol. XII, 9-82. London: Hogarth Press.

Freud, S. (1967) *Introductory Lectures* (1915-1916). In *The Standard Edition of the Complete Psychological Works of Sigmund Freud*, Vol. 15. London: Hogarth Press.

Freud, S. (1921) Group psychology and the analysis of the ego. In *The Standard Edition of the Complete Psychological Works of Sigmund Freud*, Vol. 18, 65-143. London: Hogarth Press, 1955.

Freud, S. (1923) A seventeenth-century demonological neurosis. In *The Standard Edition of the Complete Psychological Works of Sigmund Freud*, Vol. 19, 72-102. London: Hogarth Press, 1967.

Freud, S. (1927) *The Future of An Illusion*. In *The Standard Edition Of The Complete Psychological Works*. Vol. XXI, 1-56. London: Hogarth Press, 1971.

Hansson, R.O. (1986) Relational competence, relationships, and adjustment in old age. *Journal of Personality and Social Psychology, 50*, 1050-1058.

Hutch, R. A. (1991) *Religious Leadership: Personality, History and Sacred Authority*. New York: Peter Lang.

Jaynes, J. (1976) *The Origin of Consciousness in the Breakdown of the Bicameral Mind*. Boston: Houghton Mifflin.

Kris, E. (1952) *Psychoanalytic Explorations in Art*. New York: International Universities Press.

La Barre, W. (1972) *The Ghost Dance*. London: Allen & Unwin.

Levy, R. (1984) The emotions in comparative perspective. In K.R. Scherer & P. Ekman (Eds.) *Approaches to Emotion*. Hillsdale NJ: Erlbaum.

Littlewood, R. & Lipsedge, M. (1989) *Aliens and Alienists*. London: Unwin Hyman.

Lutzky, H. (1991) The sacred and the maternal object: An application of Fairbairn's theory to religion. In H. Siegel, J. Lasky, & S. Warshaw (eds.) *Psychoanalytic Reflections*. New York: New York University Press.
MacGregor, J.M. (1989) *The Discovery of the Art of the Insane*. Princeton: Princeton University Press.
Meissner, W.W. (1978) *The Paranoid Process*. New York: Jason Aronson.
Meissner, W.W. (1988) The origins of Christianity. In Boyer, L.B. & Gronick, S. (Eds) *The Psychoanalytic Study of Society*, *13*,71-92.
Muensterberger, W.(1972) Introduction to G. Roheim, *The Panic of the Gods*. New York: Harper.
Numbers, R.Z. & Numbers, J.S.(1985) Millerism and madness. *Bulletin of the Menninger Clinic*, *40*, 289-320.
Romme, M.A. & Escher, A. (1989) Hearing voices. *Schizophrenia Bulletin*, *15*, 209-216.
Schreber, D.P.(1955) *Memoirs of My Nervous Illness*. London: Dawson.
Shils, E.(1975) *Center and Periphery*. Chicago; University of Chicago Press.
Sobel, B. & Beit-Hallahmi, B. (Eds) (1991) *Tradition, Continuity, Conflict: Jewishness and Judaism In Contemporary Israel*. Albany, NY: SUNY Press.
Sullivan, H.S.(1953) *The Interpersonal Theory of Psychiatry*. New York: Norton.
Sullivan, H.S.(1964) *The Fusion of Psychiatry and Social Science*. New York: Norton.
Tylor, E.B. (1871) *Primitive Culture*. London: Murray.
West, L.J. (Ed) (1962) *Hallucinations*. New York: Grune & Stratton.
Winnicott, D.W.(1971) *Playing and Reality*. New York: Basic Books.
Witztum, E., Greenberg, D. & Dasberg, H.(1990) Mental Illness and religious change. *British Journal of Medical Psychology*, *63*, 33-41.

Acknowledgements.

I would like to thank Emanuel Berman, Michal Eilat, Antoon Geels, Henry Rosenfeld, and Eliezer Witztum for ideas, suggestions, and criticisms.

CHAPTER 5
RELIGION AS TRANSGRESSION: PSYCHOLOGICAL MECHANISMS INVOLVED IN RELIGION AND MENTAL ILLNESS

Halina Grzymala-Moszczyńska

The issue of religion and mental health will be addressed within the framework of "transgression theory" as elaborated by Jozef Kozielecki (1986, 1987). The concept of transgression as he uses it means "going beyond established borders" in a physical as well as in an intellectual or behavioral sense. There are also other scientific disciplines where the concept appears but it does not occupy a central position within them. Kozielecki's concept of transgression displays certain similarities with concepts in other areas of psychology, for example in Bruner's (1978) work on going beyond available information, in McClelland's (1961) on enlarging personal knowledge, and in Maslow's (1968) on the need for self-actualization.

Different kinds of transgression activities are also of interest in sociology and history, as activities undertaken by groups of individuals and societies (i.e., rebelling against authorities of the country in order to reshape existing social structures, conquering new lands in order to enlarge an empire, etc.). Psychiatrists may describe the strivings of their patients to "transgress" - that is to trancend - the broken life space and limitations in functioning by means of building personal philosophies that are more or less cohesive (Kepinski, 1972). Within the psychiatric context the problem of transgression concerns socially accepted and agreed upon norms as to what is "normal" in a given society under given circumstances. According to Bastide (1972), the label "pathological" could be attached to any behavior that stimulates defence mechanisms in a social structure. It does not mean, however, that under all circumstances the behavior is pathological. But even clear pathology could be understood in the way that it transgresses social norms for the sake of preserving individual identity. We will return to this problem later on, while discussing the question of motivation involved in religion and mental illness.

Religious myths and religious practices represent efforts to transgress the "conditio humana" and because of that, they are of interest not only to theology but also to other disciplines, for example, psychology, psychiatry, philosophy, anthropology and sociology. In psychology, transgression represents human activity directed towards exceeding the boundaries of the individual's past achivements. It originates in the hope of transcending the limits of the individual's previous external and internal states, and a sense of pride about expected results.

A contrasting activity is represented by protective behavior. Its aim is to avoid the loss of important values (food, safety, etc.) or to challenge an experienced deficit. Protective activity aims at preserving a vital balance in one's relation with the environment and minimizing unwanted states of mind and body. Transgression activities could be divided into different kinds, depending on their subject:

— activities directed towards things (building new tools, for example, computers, which allow for the expansion of human capacities)
— activities directed towards other people (altruistic actions as well as the construction of instruments for stronger social control)
— activities directed towards the self (self-creation, exercizing strong will),
— activities directed towards symbols (building up new, unconventional thought structures, enlarging personal knowledge throught art, science, philosophy and religion).

The kinds of transgressions specified above could also be divided according to their relative novelty. We can differentiate between creativity and innovation on the one hand and expansion on the other.

The two main kinds of behavior specified above differ also in terms of the motivation involved. The typical motivation for protective behavior would be mainly of an homeostatic character, i.e., it aims at keeping or regaining a balance with the environment. Transgression behavior could also be stimulated by homeostatic motivation. If the usual means do not provide a person with a sufficient amount of food, there is a search for new sources and new technologies in order to obtain a necessary supply and, as a result, to restore a balance in the relation with the environment. However, the specific motivation for transgressive behavior is mainly "hubristic" and cognitive in nature. Hubristic motivation is a term coined by Kozielecki and comes from the Greek word hubris or hybris. It meant for the ancient Greeks wanton insolence or arrogant pride that roused a god's anger. Our use of the term disregards its pejorative connotation. Kozielecki describes the first kind of motivation in the following terms: "hubristic motivation is understood as an entire striving to assert and enhance one's self importance... its scale ranges from 'I am a non entity' to 'I am a person of prime importance...'

Manifestations of hubristic motivation are of particular importance.

1. Striving for superiority is of the vertical type. The scale of importance to which this striving is related resembles a social ranking scale: the position of the self on the scale is brought into relation to the position of the other person; in other words, it is an attempt to improve one's position. Because of that, the person may undertake very ambitious expansive or creative transgressions.
2. Striving towards perfection is of a horizontal type. The person strives for ever-greater achievements, seeking to excel and to reach perfection. A fundamental aspect of this striving is that both the aspiration level and the success assessment are in reference to the self rather than to others. The striving towards perfection is a one-person game.

The other kind of motivation that is an important factor in transgression is cognitive motivation, known also as competence motivation. The idea is that humans engage in novel behavior in order to satisfy their exploratory drive, to enjoy themselves intellectually, or to have an aesthetic experience when getting to know new things.

Cognitive motivation has a number of characteristic features. It is nonhedonistic in that it is not geared towards pleasures as such. As a rule, it is heterostatic and hence not accountable to the simple laws of need satisfaction" (Kozielecki 1987, pp. 431-432).

Cognitive motivation becomes stimulated by the novelty of the subject, its complexity, cognitive conflict between old and new information and, finally, by uncertainty and the lack of accurate information.

Two main kinds of behavior (protective and transgressive) differ also in terms of the quality of their intellectual representation. Protective tasks are mostly based on information directly available in the environment. Transgression tasks require information coded in long-term memory and not easily available for checking. This very feature stimulates creation of both myth and illusion.

Both religion and mental illness belong to the group of activities called symbolic transgressions. Religious myth contains allegoric, unrealistic elements and it is dominated by non-linear structures of time. Because of that it acquires universalistic meaning not bound to a particular place or historical moment. Religious myths operate on a cultural level and belong to the accepted heritage of the society.

In mental illness we have to deal with content chiefly built up from illusion. In everyday language as well as in some scientific works, the terms myth and illusion are often confused with each other. Illusion consist of an inadequate interpretation of the facts or the taking of false appearances for reality. Illusion remains private and egocentric.

Illusion as present in mental illness is an attempt to solve basic epistemological, ontological and eschatological questions. The problems triggering these efforts belong, however, to the real surroundings of the ill person. The content of the illusion concerns the ill person, his or her perceived mission for the future of humankind, and the world's attitude towards him or her.

An illusion has meaning only for the individual in question, but in a specific situation it can have a meaning for a group of people. One of the models of the founding of new religious movements refers to the mental illness of leaders who during psychotic states are able to build systems of compensation that solve their own problems as well as the problems of those who become their followers. As an example we could take the case of L. Ron Hubbard, the inventor of Dianetics, which later evolved into Scientology.

Religious myth cannot be falsified or verified. The evaluation of myth is limited to the dichotomy of belief-unbelief, eventually belief-doubt. Acceptance of religious myth stems from the elaboration of internal information, attitudes, emotions, and desires. The content of mental illness can only be partially falsified as far as it concerns real persons and the real world. It mirrors, however, the reality of the internal world of the ill person, which is based upon information derived from long-term memory rather than from an outside reality. Illusion present in mental illness displays high rigidity and resistance to cognitive conflict, especially when it concerns contradictory information coming from the outside. Religious myth represents new, universalistic values. Polarization of characters and states is structured according to a sharply toned, "black and white" schema. The contents of the psychotic states of mind move between extremes: ecstasy and elation versus damnation and evil.

Because of the psychological structure of religious myth it could bring both positive and negative consequences for its follower, being powerful stimulant for mental cohesion as well as a clearly destructive power.

Different forms of religiosity seem to be stimulated by different kinds of motivation. Extrinsic religiosity, in which the believer uses his religion for self-serving ends, seems to be stimulated by homeostatic and superiority motivation. This motivation produces close-minded commitment to a single point of view and discourages open-mindedness and flexibility. It could faster deformed and hostile attitudes towards outsiders, based on a conviction of one's own superiority. It causes aggression towards people who do not share the same religious beliefs.

In contrast, the intrinsic religious orientation, according to which religion provides the master motive in life, seems to be mainly motivated by striving towards perfection. This motivation helps to assimilate and accept moral values and to overcome one's suffering. But as a side effect, it could produce a quite fanatical and rigid true believer (at least as far as Allport's Intrinsic scale operationalizes the dimension). Homeostatic motivation can also contribute to this orientation and produce a positive sense of personal competence and control based on a reliance on God. The combination of both motivational aspects helps to build an image of the world operating according to a predictable structure.

The quest orientation "reflects a self-directedness and reliance on one's own ability to think through complex, ultimate questions" (Batson, Schoenrade & Ventis, 1993, p. 260). The orientation seems to be motivated by cognitive motivation, which stimulates ambitious undertakings. This motivation is based upon self-reliance and stimulates open-mindedness. Different kinds of motivation which stimulate one's religiosity determine the different roles it plays within the individual psyche.

Construction of the content of illusion in the psychotic state seems to be ruled by homeostatic motivation. For example, Cameron (1959) analyses the example of the ill person who lost his confidence in and understanding of the surrounding world. Coleman (1972) stresses that illusions might also play the role of confirming one's own importance. They help to win acceptance. They stimulate the building of reformist, messianic and grandiose thoughts. This kind of illusion seems to be stimulated mainly by hubristic motivation, particularly by striving for superiority, but also to some extent by cognitive motivation.

In stressing the presence of altruistic motivational structures in at least some cases of mental illness we approach the problem of pathology in a positive way, i.e., the mentally disturbed patient is seen as someone different but in no way inferior in comparison to the rest of the population. This theoretical stance has existed in Europe only since the beginning of the 19th century. Mental disturbances began to be perceived as crossing the borders in order to explore a new vision of the world. It was mirrored in Romantic art, poetry, drama and painting. The earlier approach,the so-called deficit approach, saw psychiatric patients as persons who had lost the possibilities of normal emotional, intellectual, and social functioning due to some physiological imbalance, faulty education or simply possession, and towards whom all means should be used in order to restore them to normal ways of functioning. From the beginning of the 19th century questions concerning mentally disturbed persons were reshaped into another form: what did he or she gain through mental illness, what extra values were thereby introduced into his or her internal life? Some attributes of mental illness even appeared in the image of the Romantic hero, as a symbol of his or her unusual capacities.

The source of the illness was no longer attributed to the individual but to his or her historical situation which exercised strong pressure on the individual. To be different no longer meant being someone of less worth but represented instead a kind of splendid isolation from the world of common people.

Within a context of Polish Romantic art transgressions of the norms of normal life were often connected to transgressing the norms of the self-preservation instinct in order to sacrifice one's own life for the sake of the freedom of the country. This very goal also supplied the transgression of the borders of normality with an extra positive value.

Thus, the comparison of religion and mental illness in terms of motivation and content leads us to the conclusion that those processes, though quite different in terms of content, can be identical in terms of the dynamics involved. In this respect my conclusion is in agreement with Beit-Hallahmi's analysis concerning the similarities between art and religion (Beit-Hallahmi 1989).

REFERENCES

Bastide, R. (1972). *Sociologia chorób psychicznych*. Warszawa: Państwowe Wydawnictwo Naukowe.

Batson, C.D. Schoenrade, P., & Ventis, W.L. (1993). *Religion and the Individual: A Social Psychological Perspective*. New York: Oxford University Press.

Beit-Hallahmi, B. (1989). *Prolegomena to the Psychological Study of Religion*. Lewisburg: Bucknell University Press.

Bruner, J. (1978). *Poza dostarczone informacje*. Warszawa: Państwowe Wydawnictwo Naukowe.

Cameron, N.(1959). The Paranoic Pseudo-Community Revisited. *American Journal of Sociology, 65*, 52-58.

Coleman, J.C. (1972). *Abnormal Psychology and Modern Life*. Glenville: Scott & Foresman.

Kæpiński, A. (1972). *Schizofrenia*. Warszawa: Państwowy Zakład Wydawnictw Lekarskich.

Kozielecki, J. (1986). A Transgressive Model of Man. *New Ideas in Psychology, 4*.

Kozielecki, J. (1987). *Koncepcja transgresyjna człowieka*. Warszawa: Państwowe Wydawnictwo Naukowe.

Maslow, A.H. (1968). *Toward a Psychology of Being*. New York: Van Nostrand Reinhold.
McClelland, D.C. (1961). *The Achieving Society*. Princeton, New Jersey: Van Nostrand Reinhold.

CHAPTER 6
RELIGION AS A MEANING SYSTEM: A CONCEPTUAL MODEL FOR RESEARCH AND COUNSELING

Jan van der Lans

When the subject of religion and mental health is under discussion, it is inevitable that we are confronted with the fact that both concepts are not unequivocal. It is hardly possible to compare the results of empirical research, because of the dissimilarity of measures used for measuring mental health as well as for religiosity. This situation impedes the development of theories.

One of the ways in which the global concept 'mental health' has been narrowed is to conceive of it as 'psychological well-being'. It is generally assumed that religiosity contributes to psychological well being and there are numerous empirical studies about the relation between these two variables.

Witter et al. (1985) published a quantitative meta-analysis of the results of 28 empirical studies on this relationship, published over a period of 50 years, and came to some interesting conclusions. Religion appears to account for between 2 and 6% of the variance in adult subjective well-being. Generally (and not surprisingly), religion is a less potent predictor of subjective well-being than income, occupational status, health, adjustment, family and work satisfaction, and neuroticism. Religion is a better predictor of well-being, however, than age, gender and race. The relation between religiosity and well-being varies with how religion is operationalized: religious activity (frequency of church attendance) is more strongly related to subjective well-being than the inportance or interest someone attaches to his religion. The same has been found by later researchers (Steinitz, 1980; St. George & McNamara, 1981; Markides, 1983).

Of course, the measures for subjective well-being were dissimilar in the various studies, but yet comparable. Most scales measured life-satisfaction, happiness, morale or quality of life. Petersen & Roy (1985) investigated in a large sample of the city of Memphis to see whether two other dimensions of psychological well- being (anxiety and worthwhileness of life) were affected by four different aspects of religiosity. Contrary to Witter et al. (1985), they did not expect a general positive effect of religiosity on psychological well-being, but predicted that the relationship between religiosity and well being would depend on which aspect of religiosity and of well-being is considered. In this sample a correlation was found between frequency of church attendance and well being. It is however conspicuous that this religiosity measure is only related to one of the dimensions of well being. Ss, who frequently attended church, report fewer anxiety or psychological stress feelings than low attenders. Obviously, this is an effect of the social integration function of religion, as the investigators conclude, because other aspects of religion (belief, salience) did not correlate with this dimension. The strongest correlation between religion and well being was found with respect to the dimension 'worthwhileness of life'. Here, religion appeared to be a stronger predictor than other factors, like age, education, race, marital status, and equivalent with the influence of perceived health. A regression analysis demonstrated, however, that this relationship was related to the salience-aspect of religiosity. It seems to me that this fact makes the relationship less impressive than it was at first glance, because of the contamination between the two variables. A high score on this second dimension of well being (worthwhileness of life) means that the individual perceives that he leads a goal-oriented existence. And religious salience "refers to the extent to which one's religious faith is a central or ultimate component of his life" (p. 51).

It is important to note that Petersen & Roy hoped to find empirical support for the hypothesis that religiosity contributes to well being because religion contrbutes to meaning-giving. "Religion provides an overarching interpretive scheme, which allows the individual to make sense of his existence" (p. 51) and to find an explanation for the contingencies of life. Unfortunately, none of the religion measures which Petersen & Roy used was suited to measure to what extent religion functions as a meaning-giving system.

The results of an investigation recently published by Chamberlain & Zika (1988), demonstrate the necessity of taking into consideration the concept of meaning-giving, when the relation between religion and psychological well-being is discussed. In their sample of women, they found a correlation between religiosity, operationalized as a personal meaning-system (assessed by two King & Hunt subscales: Orientation to Growth and Cognitive Salience) and life-satisfaction. According to Ed Diener in his outstanding review article (1984), life-satisfaction is one of the three basic components of subjective well-being. Religiosity also correlated with most of the measures, they had used to assess meaning in life. Meaningfullness appeared to be a much stronger predictor of psychological well-being, however, than religiosity. The correlations between the measures for meaningfullness and well-being hardly changed when the effect of religion was taken into account. Thus, that religiosity, at least as it was assessed in this study, does not contribute something specific to psychological well-being. Or, that a sense of meaning and purpose, the sense that the world is comprehensible and one's life is manageable are more essential conditions for psychological well-being than being religious.

One of the limitations of a questionnaire survey is that it is like an instantaneous snapshot, not giving insight into changes that take place when conditions are fluctuating. There are no indications that in Chamberlain & Zika sample there were also Ss who suffered from a psychological crisis. Theoretically, it is to be expected, that the meaning-giving function of religion or its substitute plays a primary role not in everyday life but during crisis. Maton (1989) remarked that, when investigating the influence of religiosity on well-being, it is importatn to control for the level of life stress.

New interest in the meaning-giving function of religion

Several writers in the past have considered the meaning-giving function of religion as its most essential characteristic with regard to mental health. Through its system of symbolic ideas and rites it should protect people against feelings of meaninglessness and help them to understand the world (James, 1902; Tillich 1952; Allport 1950, 1961; Fromm 1950; Yinger, 1966; Frankl, 1962). The meaning-giving function of religion is again emphasized in modern society, by writers who attribute the increase in alienation, demoralization and meaninglessness to the cultural processes of secularization, unchurching and privatization of religion. In the Netherlands, an increasing number of practitioners in the mental health field are now waking up to the fact that to be able to help clients, who ask for therapeutic guidance because of an emotional or behaviour problem, the clients' world-view or life-philosophy cannot be left out of consideration (Dijkhuis, 1988). When someone asks for help, it is because life has become traumatic to him in one way or another. In order to restore psychological balance, the client must be able to change things or to redefine the situation so that life becomes meaningful again in the light of some central value.

Therefore, the counselor should always pay attention to the client's life-philosophy. One's life-philosophy is adequate when it function as a source for meaning.

According to some clinicians, improving the client's "meaning giving" competence should be one of the aims of every psychotherapeutical intervention (Bertens, 1985; Frank, 1982). In the Netherlands, some training institutes for mental health workers have appointed a staff member who is an expert on this border area between religion, weltanschauung, meaning-giving and psychotherapy. The growing awareness of the interrelation of these issues leads to more and more frequent appeals to the psychologist of religion for theoretical clarification and supporting research. In my university, graduate courses in clinical psychology of religion have now been developed for psychology students who prepare themselves for a professional career as a clinical psychologist and psychotherapist. The curriculum aims at introducing the students into theories concerning the role of meaning-giving, both preventive and curative, with respect to psychological problems.

A conceptual model of meaning-giving (see Appendix)

The central position of the concept of meaning-giving in the curriculum makes it necessary to develop a theoretical rationale about the interaction between religion, meaning giving and mental health. A prerequisite for theorizing about these variables is a more accurate definition of the concepts involved. Besides, the fact that in our society, the number of those affiliated with religious denomination has diminished to 40% of the population, makes it necessary for the psychologist of religion to gain insight into other resources of existential meaning than religion in the substantial sense of the word.

In this paper I will present a theoretical scheme that has been developed for three purposes. First, to help the students think about meaning-giving as a phased psychological process. Second, to discuss the irreplaceable role religion or a secular life-philosophy plays within this process, not at any moment but in critical periods. Thirdly, this conceptual scheme has proved to be a useful theoretical frame for the construction of interview schedules.

In order to display that meaning-giving is a multi-level process, the model is constructed as a kind of flow chart with options and subroutines.

The construction of models, in which complex behavioral processes are analyzed into elements, can be very useful. A formal model is especially useful for making precise descriptions and for tracing psychological control mechanisms. In psychophysiological and psychonomic research, the use of such models has proven to be advantageous in the building of psychological theories. As psychologists of religion, we should accept the challenge to represent the behavior we are studying in models. (Religious behavior may be less mechanistic than handwriting or learning, but hardly more complicated!) It could improve the general theoretical weakness of our discipline.

Now I will explain the model briefly and offer a theoretical justification for it.

1. The scheme differentiates tasks, sources of meaning, moments at which decisions of more than routine character have to be made, and two levels of meaning-giving.
2. In this model, meaning-giving is conceived as grounded in two kind of needs: the need for an orderly, recognizable and explainable world, and the need to experience life as worthwhile and manageable. Consequently, meaning-giving involves two tasks: orientation and evaluation. Meaning-giving is not something special, but a mental activity of common occurrence. In interacting with his environment, a subject is often confronted with novel and unexpected events or with the necessity to take decisions. Meaningfullness is conceived as the outcome of a succesful orientation and a positive evaluation with respect to an event or a situation. Both an intrinsically motivated commitment to a situation and subjective well-being are possible only if these two tasks of meaning-giving succeed. Mostly, these tasks proceed as background-tasks, but at crucial moments they need our focal attention.
3. Several theories have been formulated and verified empirically about cognitive mechanisms people use in making their environment accountable. According to Lerner, 'belief in a just world' is such an assumption, that people use to gain cognitive control over a situation. Religious and other cultural belief systems provide their followers with ideas and images, that can be used to explain situations and events and to make sense out of it. Lerner (1980) has pointed to the example of the Protestant ethic, which makes people believe that fortunate events are a reward for efforts and misfortune means punishment.
4. The process of meaning-giving is more than just recognizing and accounting. It also implicates an evaluation. A new or ongoing activity, a social relationship, or an occurrence can only be experienced as meaningful when it suits at least one of the central goals which give direction and positive thrust to one's life.
   In recent research on decision making it has become evident that also our self-image plays a large role when we have to judge whether it is meaningful or not to start with or to continue an activity or a relationship. Self-images and goal-images form the evaluative

standards that determine our judment about the meaningfulness of something.
5. Commitment to a situation is only possible when it has meaning for us. That is, when something is apprehended as understandable, manageable and estimated as worthwhile. In its turn, intrinsically motivated commitment has often been considered as a condition for and as the most obvious indicator of mental health. Vergote (1978), summarizing statements by Freud, points out that there are four basic human commitments, which differentiate between psychological health and illness: the ability to work, to communicate, to love and to enjoy. It seems evident, that these basic commitments are only possible in regard to a situation that has meaning for a subject. As soon as a person is faced with a situation which he does not understand or cannot manage, these basic commitments will be inhibited.
6. The capability of a person to cope with such a meaning-giving problem depends on the appropriateness of the resources of meaning that are available.

In everyday life, in accounting for events and situations, we lean on a collective world-view, that has been defined by Luckmann as "an encompassing system of meaning, containing typifications, interpretive schemes and recipes for conduct on different levels of generality" (1967, p. 55). Besides this collective world-view, we use our self-image and all kinds of intermediate personal goals to assess a situation, a relationship or an activity as wortwhile or not. However, when a meaning-giving problem causes symptoms of serious psychological stress, these ordinary sources of meaning are apparently insufficient. More fundamental resources must be activated then. This is often the case when someone is labouring under a serious loss (be it a loss of a loved one, or of physical health, of motoric or sensoric abilities, a job, a belief-system, etc.). Such occurrences may be catastrophic, as we know. They break down an orderly subjective world and may arouse a serious identity problem: "who am I?", "Is it still worthwhile to live on?", "Why me?"

During the last 15 years, social psychologists have investigated how victims of severe accidents and cancer patients react to their illness and try to regain control (Bulman & Wortman, 1977; Wong & Weiner, 1981; Taylor, Lichtman & Wood, 1984; Taylor, 1985; Feather, 1985; Gotay, 1985; Schulz & Decker, 1985; Maton, 1989). The findings suggest that the connection between attribution and succesful coping with stress is different for the various kinds of trauma. A general finding has been that many patients in such circumstances are not only involved in questions of causal attribution (blaming), but also in searching for a new purpose. Gotay (1985) found that patients in an early state of illness use other kinds of attributions than patients in an advanced state. Especially in the latter group, religious attributions ('God's will') were more frequently mentioned. Taylor et al. (1984) found that cognitive control, i.e. control by meaning-giving, appeared to be more strongly associated with adjustment than behavior control or other types of control.

Especially when it is not possible to withdraw from a stress-arousing situation, conscious reflection upon and a search for ultimate meaning and values may be necessary to prevent the outbreak of an enduring crisis of meaning. Traumatic circumstances and events as mentioned above cause a rupture of one's life story and therefore seriously weaken the idea of personal identity. The tasks of re-orientation and re-evaluation that are required now, apply to the whole of one's personal existence. At this level, a religious or philosophical symbolic system may help to solve this kind of meaning-problem. The importance of such a system of symbolic ideas is of course not that it takes away the pain, but can make it bearable by giving it a meaning. In cultural-anthropological studies, we find a lot of examples of the use of religious symbols and myths as successful therapeutic strategies for people who undergo a transitional crisis.

Summary and conclusions

The model that has been presented in this paper has been elaborated to remove the fog surrounding the concept of meaning-giving and to clarify this complicated psychic process and its relation to subjective well being. In scientific work, the general purpose of using models is to discover the presumed order in a confusing multitude of variables. In operational research, models are used for tracing weak points in a (commercial or industrial) system and to test alternative solutions for improving the workings of the system. During the last decade, highly elaborated models have been introduced in medical and psychiatric clinics for computer-assisted diagnostical work (expert systems). The claim of the meaning-giving model is very modest. First, it serves an educational purpose. It reminds students that meaning has to be viewed as a central element in everyday behavior, comprising two subsystems, one cognitive-attributional and one motivational-attitudinal, in either of which a meaning-giving problem may arise. This approach helps students to theorize about meaning-giving in terms of psychological concepts instead of in philosophical categories. By differentiating two levels of meaning-giving, the level of routine orientation and evaluation of objects and events in the world of every day life, and the level of meaning-giving with respect to the whole of existence, the model provides a theoretical explanation for the empirical fact that religiosity is not a general predictor of psychological well being. In this respect, the model also stimulates discussion on the goals of psychotherapy and especially about whether and when religious issues should be introduced into a psychotherapy process, and how the roles of the psychotherapist and of the pastor should be distinguished then.

Obviously, the model is still very defective. The different elements are too globally formulated and need further specification.
Some may critize the presumed centrality of meaning-giving in the psychic economy of striving for well-being. However, according to Frank (1982), all methods of psychotherapy start from the assumption that humans react to their own way of interpreting facts and events and that the inadequacy of these interpretations has caused the psychological problem to be treated. A psychotherapist will therefore always start with making a recapitulation of the way the client is interpreting and evaluating life. The goal of every psychotherapy, of whatever theoretical approach, is to change the way in which the client perceives himself and other people. In this view, improvement of the client's meaning-giving competence is one of the aims of every psychotherapeutical intervention. For this reason, the counselor or therapist have to find out what are the client's sources of meaning. For the same reason, he should inspect the client's life-philosophy. Is the religious system in which the client has been socialized, still functioning adequately or does the client have another system of beliefs and images at his disposal from which he can borrow life-goals and cognitive orientation with respect to existential problems?

It is exactly to this part of the curative task of mental health professionals, that the psychology of religion can contribute with new theoretical insights and research instruments.

REFERENCES

Allport, G. (1950). *The individual and his religion: a psychological interpretation.* New York: Macmillan.

Allport, G. (1961). *Pattern and Growth in Personality.* New York: Holt, Rinehart & Winston.

Antonovsky, A. (1987). *Unraveling the mystery of health: how people manage stress and stay well.* San Francisco: Jossey-Bass Publications.

Battista, J. & Almond, R. (1973). The Development of meaning in life. Psychiatry, *36*, 409-427.

Beach, L. R. & Mitchell, T. R. (1987). Image Theory: Principles, Goals, and Plans in Decision Making. *Acta Psychologica*, *66*, 201-220.

Bertens, P. (1985). De psychotherapie en haar verloren dimensie. *Tijdschrift voor psychiatrie*, *27*(1), 5-14.

Bulman, R. J. & Wortman, C. B. (1977). Attributions of Blame and Coping in the "Real World": Severe accident vistims react to their lot. *Journal of Personality and Social Psychology*, *35*(5), 352-363.

Chamberlain, K. & Zika, S. (1988). Religiosity, life meaning and well being: some relationships in a sample of women. *Journal for the Scientific Study of Religion*, *27*(3), 411-420.

Crumbaugh, J.C. & Maholick, L.T.(1964). An experimental study in existentialism: The psychometric approach to Frankl's concept of noogenic neurosis. *Journal of Clinical Psychology*, *20*, 200-207.

Diener, E. (1984). Subjective Well-Being. *Psychological Bulletin*, *95*(3), 542-575.

Dijkhuis, J. H. (1988). Levensbeschouwing: een miskende dimensie van psychotherapie. in J. H. Dijkhuis, & J. H. M. Mooren, *Psychotherapie en levensbeschouwing*. (pp. 9-25). Baarn: Ambo.

Feather, N. T. (1985). Attitudes, Values, and Attributions: Explanations of Unemployment. *Journal of Personality and Social Psychology*, *48*(4), 876-889.

Frank, J. D. (1982). Therapeutic components shared by all therapies. in J. H. Harvey, & M. Parks (eds.), *Psychotherapy research and behaviour change*. (The masters' lecture series 1). (pp. 9-38). Washington D.C.: American Psychological Association.

Frankl, V. (1962). *Man's Search for Meaning: An Introduction in Logotherapy*. Boston: Beacon Press.

Fromm, E. (1950). *Psychoanalysis and Religion*. New Haven, Conn.: Yale University Press.

Gotay, C. (1985). Why me? Attributions and adjustment by cancer patients and their mates at two stages in the disease process. *Social Sciences and Medicine*, *20*(8), 825-831.

James, W. (1902). *The Varieties of Religious Experience*. New York.

Lerner, M. (1970). The desire for justice and reaction to victims. In J. Macauly, & L. Berkowitz (eds.), *Altruism and Helping Behavior*. (pp. 205-229). New York: Academic Press.

Lerner, M. J. (1980). *The Belief in a Just World. A Fundamental Delusion*. New York: Plenum Press.

Lichtman, R. R., Taylor, S. E. & Wood, J. V. (1985). Research on the chronically ill: Conceptual and Methodological Perspectives. in A. Baum, & J. Singer, *Advances in environmental psychology*. Hillsdale: Erlbaum.

Luckmann, T. (1967). *The Invisible Religion. The Transformation of symbols in industrial society*. New York: The Macmillan Company.

MacIntyre, A. (1981). *After Virtue*. London.

Markides, K. S. (1983). Aging, Religiosity, and Adjustment: A longitudinal analysis. *Journal of Gerontoloy*, *38*, 621-625.

McNamara, P. H. & St.George, A. (1979). Measures of religiosity and the quality of life: a critical analysis. in D. Moberg (Ed.), *Spiritual well-being: Sociological perspectives*. Washington, DC: University Press of America.

Petersen, L. R. & Roy, A. (1985). Religiosity, Anxiety, and Meaning and Purpose: Religion's consequences for psychological well-being. *Review of Religious Research*, *27*(1), 48-62.

Schulz, R., & Decker, S. (1985). Long-Term Adjustment to Physical Disability: The role of social support, perceived control and self-blame. *Journal of Personality and Social Psychology*, *48*(5), 1162-1172.

Steinitz, L. Y. (1980). Religiosity, Well-being, and Weltanschauung among the Elderly. *Journal for the Scientific Study of Religion*, *19*(1), 60-67.

Taylor, S. (1983 Nov). Adjustment to threatening events. *American Psychologist*, *38*, 1161-1173.

Taylor, S. E., Lichtman, R. R., & Wood, J. V. (1984 Mar). Attributions, beliefs about control, and adjustment to breast cancer. *Journal of Personality and Social Psychology*, *46*(3), 489-502.

Tillich, P. (1952). *The courage to be*. New Haven, Conn.: Yale University Press.

Vergote, A. (1978). *Bekentenis en begeerte in de religie. Psychoanalytische verkenning*. Antwerpen/Amsterdam: De Nederlandsche Boekhandel.

Witter, R. A., Stock, W. A., Okun, M. A., & Haring, M. J. (1985). Religion and subjective wellbeing in adulthood: A quantitative synthesis. *Review of Religious Research*, *26*(4), 332-342.

Wong, P. T., & Weiner, B. (1981). When people ask"why?" questions, and the heuristics of attributional search. *Journal of Personality and Social Psychology*, *40*(4), 650-663.

Yinger, J. M. (1969). A structural examination of religion. *Journal for the Scientific Study of Religion*, *8*(2), 88-109.

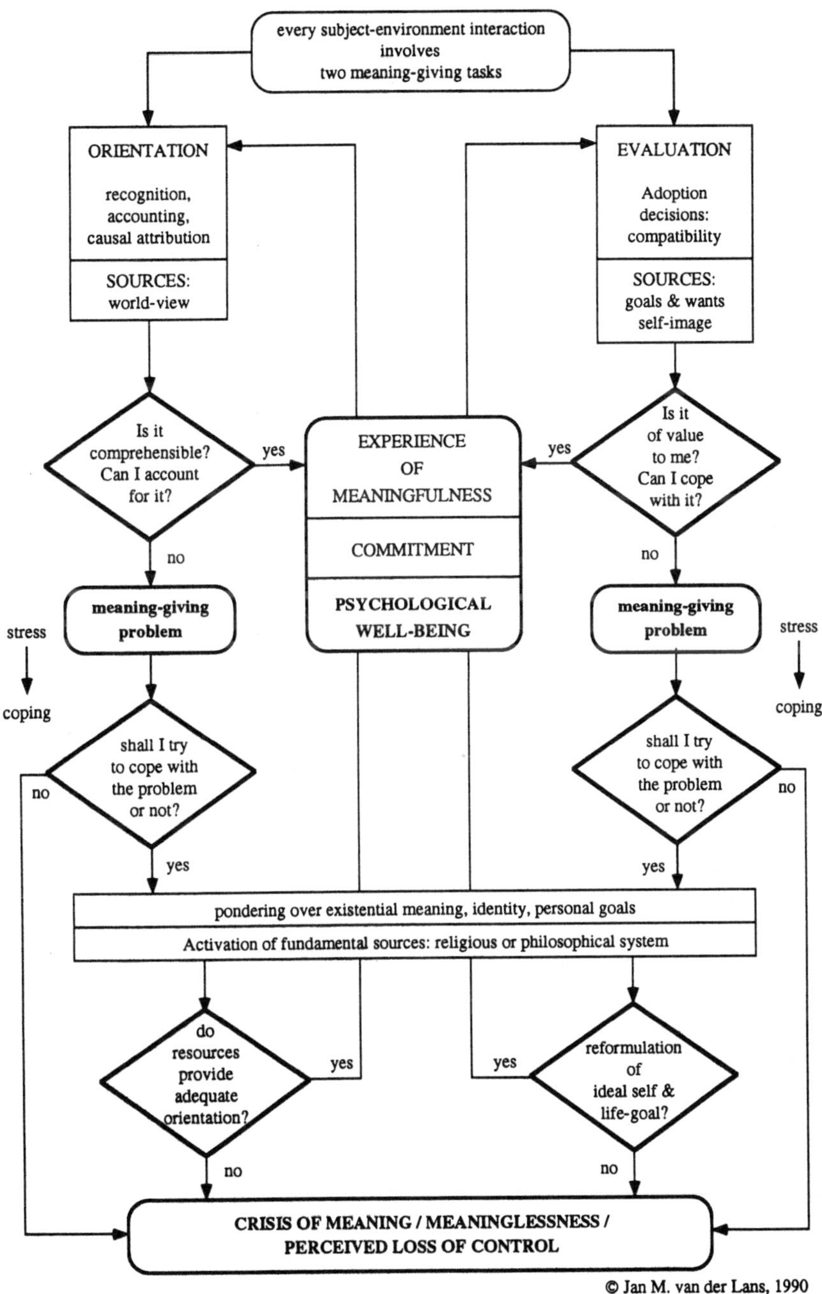

© Jan M. van der Lans, 1990

CHAPTER 7
RELIGION, MENTAL HEALTH, AND THE LAW: ASSESSING THE "CULT CONTROVERSY"

James T. Richardson

In 1982 I reviewed the literature on psychiatric and personality assessment of members of new religions, popularly referred to as "cults", at a conference on new developments in psychology of religion, held at Wolfson College, Oxford, the proceedings of which were subsequently published (Brown, 1985). Because of the continuing controversy about the new religions, particularly in America, I have decided to update that earlier review, offer some interpretation of the newer data, and discuss some important legal developments related to data on the mental health of participants in new religions.

First, I will review major findings and conclusions of that earlier paper (Richardson, 1985), which examined a number of studies focusing on some of the more controversial groups and movements. Included were psychological assessment studies of (1) a nation-wide, communal, Jesus Movement organization which I and others had studied in considerable depth (Richardson, Stewart, and Simmonds, 1979; Simmonds, Richardson, and Harder, 1976; Simmonds, 1978); (2) an Eastern-oriented, California, "new age" group, Ananda Cooperative Village (Nordquist, 1978, and Rosen and Nordquist, 1980); (3) the Unification Church (Galanter, 1980; Galanter, et al., 1979; Kuner, 1983); (4) the Children of God and Ananda Marga groups in Europe (Kuner, 1983); (5) a fundamentalist campus group at an elite American college (Nicholi, 1974); (6) the Divine Light Mission (Galanter, 1978; Galanter and Buckley, 1978); and other assessment research (Ungerleider and Wellisch, 1979). I also critiqued one report of a major "anti-cult" psychologist, Maragret Singer, who has served as a legitimator for groups opposed to new religions (Singer, 1979), and briefly discussed a number of other relevant works done by sociologists and social psychologists (Barker, 1981; Wuthnow, 1976; Beckford, 1978; Derks and van der Lans, 1982; Wright, 1983; Skonovd, 1983; Anthony, Robbins and McCarthy, 1980; Bromley and Richardson, 1983; Richardson, 1980 and 1982; and Shupe and Bromley, 1980).

This earlier body of work was impressive in coverage and consistency of findings. Noteworthy was the finding from studies of communally oriented groups that a new personality type was being fostered in or attracted to such groups. Nordquist's work on Ananda Cooperative Village showed a typical member to be comparatively high in social compassion and more concerned about environment and living a more simple, noncompetitive life. I summarized Nordquist and Rosen's findings by saying (Richardson, 1985: 213-214): "Taken as a whole, these results do not suggest personality disorders or major psychopathologies. They reflect a different setting and lifestyle centered around values of self-realization and even altruism."

Our work on the Jesus Movement group revealed what we first called a "dependency prone" personality, but which more participant observation demonstrated to be quite functional within the communal context of the group. Dramatic behavioral changes associated with participation (stopping use of drugs, alcohol, tobacco, and pre-marital sex) and the loving atmosphere within the group made us aware that the apparently maladaptive pattern we found "fit" that particular context well, and had positive value for participants.

Kuner's (1983) application of the MMPI to European members of the Unification Church, Ananda Marga, the Children of God, and a control group revealed overall group profiles within the normal ranges, with few member's scores indicating poor mental health. He added that members had better scores than control group members and seemed to live with less worries and psychic stress, and concluded that the new religions often serve as therapeutic groups for socially alienated youth.

Psychiatrist Marc Galanter's several excellent papers reveal positive aspects of participating in large communal groups. His study of Unification Church members used a number of personality inventories, which revealed: "Affiliation with the Unification Church apparently provided considerable and sustained relief from neurotic distress. Although the improvement was ubiquitous, a greater religious commitment was reported by those who indicated the most improvement" (Galanter, et al, 1979:168). His research on the Divine Light Mission led to similar conclusions (Galanter and Buckley, 1978:690): "The diversity of specific psychological symptoms alleviated here is notable. A decline was reported in symptoms affected by behavioral norms, such as drug taking and job trouble; it was also found in subjectively experienced symptoms, such as anxiety, not readily regulated." Galanter's fascinating and controversial 1978 paper propounded a biologically-based "relief effect", deriving from interaction of the human organism with features of the communal setting of the new religious groups. Galanter has recently integrated and up-dated his position with an interesting and provocative book (Galanter, 1989b), as well as edited a volume for the American Psychiatric Association on the topic of cults (Galanter, 1989a).

***

The earlier review of personality and psychiatric assessment of members of new religions led me to conclude (Richardson, 1985:221):

> The personality assessments of these group members reveal that life in the new religions is often therapeutic instead of harmful. Other information suggests that these young people are *affirming* their idealism by virtue of their involvement in such groups. Certainly there is some "submerging of personality" in groups which are communal or collective, simply because they do not foster the individualistic and competitive lifestyle to which we are accustomed, particularly in American society. However, there is little data to support the almost completely negative picture painted by a few psychiatrists who have been involved in the controversy over new religions.

New Research

A number of new research reports by psychologists have appeared since the review several years ago. I will select some that seem most interesting, particularly from a legal perspective, or which relate directly to some examined in the earlier paper. Included will be follow-up research done on the Jesus Movement group I and others studied in the 1970s (Taslimi, et al. 1991), as well as research done on the Rajneesh group in Oregon (Latkin, et al., 1987; Latkin, 1987, 1990; Sundberg, et al., 1990, 1991), and the much-publicized Hare Krishna (Ross, 1983a, 1983b, 1984, 1985; Weiss, 1987; Weiss and Comprey, 1987a,b, and c; Weiss and Mendoza, 1990; Poling and Kenny, 1986). Both the Rajneesh and Hare Krishna groups have been involved in considerable controversy and litigation (Richardson, 1990, 1991), making an examination of that research especially relevant, since I discuss legal ramifications of findings about mental health of participants in new religions in the last section.

a. Jesus Movement Group

The Jesus Movement organization studied extensively in the 1970s, referred to as "Shiloh", has since disbanded, with former members going many different directions. A number moved into conservative, non-denominational churches, including particularly Calvary Chapel, the group out of whence it first evolved (Richardson, et. al., 1978; Richardson, 1994a). Cheryl Taslimi, a former Shiloh member, recently completed a master's thesis based on follow-up research on Shiloh members, under the direction of Ralph Hood, psychologist at the University of Tennessee at Chattanooga. She administered the Adjective Check List —which we had also used in the early 1970s— to former members of Shiloh who had been a member at least one year between 1968 and 1978. As indicated, our earlier conclusion was that the pattern found, while quite functional within the communal context, appeared maladaptive for more normal living situations. While aware of problems associated with using instruments normed in one setting for analysis in markedly different ones, nonetheless we raised questions about the long-term efficacy of a life style that produced (or attracted) what we called "dependency-prone", passive, noncompetitive personalities. If participants were ever expected to return to a more normal life, would adaptations to communal living have long-term effects, carrying over into situations where such adaptations would be dysfunctional. Or would Shiloh members "recover" from this personality pattern, and be able to function in more normal, noncommunal settings? Cheryl Taslimi's research was designed to gather data relevant to this important question.

Taslimi's study involved mailing to a list of 468 former members (some of whom were not eligible for inclusion, based on a minimum one year participation criterion). She obtained 101 usable responses (56 males, 45 females), including only three who had been assessed back in the 1970s. Results were compared with (1) those from the Simmonds, et. al. work in 1972, (2) a normative sample of college students, and (3) a normative sample of adults. There are some interesting clustering of results when considering the individual scales within the ACL, but Taslimi concludes (1991: 309): "There is an overwhelming tendency for the subjects ... to demonstrate group scores like those of normative samples, in sharp contrast to the results of the 1972 studies [by Simmonds]." She adds (1991:309): "Clearly if any general trend towards relative 'maladaptivity' existed in the past, and if earlier findings were representative of all members of Shiloh, this phenomenon has not persisted, as least as demonstrated in these common personality characteristics." In short, the results indicate that these former members of Shiloh have apparently adapted adequately to life in noncommunal settings, to the extent indicated by their ACL response patterns.

b. The Rajneeshees

The followers of Bhagwan Shree Rajneesh, a world-wide movement with communities on all five continents, established a community in eastern Oregon in 1981, after serious problems associated with the large central ashram in Poona, India led Rajneesh to shut down the Poona operation and move to America (Carter, 1987). The group purchased a 64,000 acre ranch, and built a small city they called Rajneeshpuram, attracting thouands of followers there. By 1985 there were four to five thousand people residing at the new site, a development which aroused considerable controversy, leading to many legal battles with the state of Oregon and others (Richardson, 1990). The Oregon group disbanded in 1985, after the arrest of some leaders, including the Bhagwan and his chief associate Ma Sheela, on criminal charges.

Because this controversial group was not examined in the earlier review, it is particularly valuable to be able to discuss results of serious scholarly research on the group's participants. Several social scientists studied the Rajneesh group while in Oregon, including some psychologists from the University of Oregon (Latkin, et al., 1987; Latkin, 1987, 1990; Sundberg, et al., 1990, 1991). This team administered a set of instruments to most participants there in October, 1983 (635 of about 800 completed all instruments), as well as a follow-up survey of 150 of 200 randomly selected from the original 635 (only 100 randomly selected instruments of the 150 returned were analyzed for reporting in Latkin, et al., 1987). The instrumentation focused on demographic, personal background and attitudes, and psychological well-being information. Latkin (1987), in his dissertation, reported another set of responses of some 232 participants to a number of personality inventories, some of which are also discussed in Latkin (1990); Sundberg et al. (1992) reported results of administering the California Psychological Inventory to 67 members; and Sundberg et al. (1991) reported on administrations of the Thematic Apperception Test to Rajneesh members who had been high achievers prior to participating, as well as to a matched sample of nonparticipants in new religions. Because participants in this group differed in important ways from "typical" participants in new religions (Richardson, 1985), some demographic and background information should be presented.

Respondents to the Latkin et al. survey were 54% female, average age of 34 years, and 46% male, average age of 35. Seventy-four per cent were married, and 65% said they were living with their spouse. Twenty-five per cent had children, and 11% said they were living with them at

Rajneeshpuram. Eighty-eight per cent had been "sannyasins" (initiated members) at least two years, with 49% saying "five years or more;" 63% said they were living in another Rajneesh center prior to coming to Oregon. Forty per cent said they first heard of Rajneeshism from friends, 30% said they read books or listened to tapes of Bhagwan, and 10% said they visited a Rajneesh center to first learn about the Bhagwan. The mean length of time spent as a sannyasin was 6.9 years, with 2.5 years average time living on the Oregon ranch. Ninety-one per cent were white, and their prior religious background was varied — 30% Protestant, 27% Catholic, 20% Jewish, 14% "none", 4% Hindu or Buddhist, and 4% "other." Only 40% characterized themselves as religious prior to becoming a sannyasin.

Education level and orientation revealed by the Oregon team's research were particularly interesting, with ninety-five per cent graduating from high school, and 64% with a college degree. A random sample of 100 showed that 24% had a master's degree, while 12% had a doctorate of some sort. The area of academic degree for those with a bachelor's, master's, or doctorate were: arts and humanities, 27%; social sciences, 33%; natural sciences and math, 10%; and professional, 10%. Self-reported political orientation was quite skewed, with only 2% saying they were conservative: the rest were radical (11%), very liberal (31%), somewhat liberal (20%), and "neither liberal nor conservative" (36%). When asked about income earned in a year prior to joining, only 16% said less than $10,000, while 19% said they had earned over $40,000. Forty-eight per cent said they came from cities of over 100,000, with 35% from ones of over a half million.

The typical sannyasin at Rajneeshpuram is, therefore, considerably different from the typical member of one of the other controversial new religions. Sannyasins are older, much better educated, more family oriented, from a more financially successful background, and more politically liberal than participants in most of the groups that have been researched. A similar pattern of background characteristics was found in an earlier study of 300 sannyasins in the Poona community in 1980, which revealed that members were overwhelmingly from "occupations either of a creative kind, or in which their main role is service to others, particularly of a human development kind" (Wallis and Bruce, 1986: 201). Sociologist Lewis Carter's study of the development of the Oregon community also noted unique characteristics of members (1987:163):

> Some writers...make the mistake of assuming that Rajneesh recruitment

> follows the pattern of groups like the Hare Krishnas and Children of God...Rajneesh are almost uniformly older and at later stages in their lives before turning to the movements, and rather than chance recruitment by strangers,... Sannyasins indicate active pursuit of Rajneesh training after referral by friends. Some have been drawn by advertised therapies. Most have traveled widely and report earlier experiments in other religions and therapies.

These unique personal characteristics of sannyasins must be considered when interpreting the data on psychological well-being gathered by the Oregon researchers. Also, certain features of Rajneesh philosophy and organizational style —particularly their approach to sex roles— are relevant. As Latkin (1987) and Goldman (1988) note, the Rajneesh group emphasized flexible gender roles, and had a disproportionate number of women in managerial roles and in jobs —such as operating construction heavy equipment— usually reserved for males. This "androgynous" philosophy and practice could be expected to influence results of personality assessment, and such was the case, as Latkin's (1987) dissertation especially demonstrated. Also, the Rajneesh community was very open and loving, according to all reports. Latkin (1987:147 calls it an "affect-oriented society." The expression of emotions was encouraged and practiced. As Latkin notes, "This community-wide sanctioning of emotional expressiveness departs from American society's usual attitudes toward emotions."

The team of psychologists from the University of Oregon administered more standardized assessment instruments to Rajneesh members than has been given to any other new religion's participants. Latkin et al. (1987) reported results of inventories on perceived stress (Cohen et al., 1988), social support (Cohen and Hoberman, 1983), self-esteem (Rosenberg, 1965), and depression (Radloff, 1977). They also asked for self-assessed life satisfaction before and after becoming a sannyasin.

The latter measure revealed that life satisfaction ratings of members were extremely high, with 82% choosing the last level on a nine point scale. The reports of life satisfaction prior to becoming a sannyasin showed only 5% in the last level, with most grouped in the middle of the nine point scale. This is self-report data, taken from current members, which means results may be subject to some "biographical reconstruction" (Berger, 1967) and a selection bias, but nonetheless, the data show high levels of current satisfaction for those responding.

The Cohen et al. (1988) Perceived Stress Scale was designed to tap unpredictability, uncontrolability, and overload experiences in the lives of those being studied. The Rajneesh mean was significantly lower at 15.22 (N = 79, SD = 7.64) than the mean of 23.34 (N = 543, SD = 7.62) for a normative sample, indicating much lower levels of perceived stress among sannyasins.

Cohen and Hoberman's (1983) Interpersonal Support Evaluation List is made up of forty true-false statements developed to measure perceived social resources. The Rajneesh sample had a mean of 37.91 (N = 78, SD 1.51), compared to a normative sample mean of 36.5 (SD 7.4), indicating that the Rajneesh group perceived slightly higher levels of social support, with much less variation. (Latkin, et al. admit that the test is subject to ceiling effects, because the top score possible is 40.)

The 20 item Center for Epidemiological Studies Depression Scale used by Radloff (1977) focuses on depression symptoms over the past week. Rajneesh participants had a mean of 5.86 (N = 86, SD = 5.55), indicating significantly less recent depression than several normative samples, for which Radloff reports means from 7.94 to 9.25 (SDs from 7.53 to 8.58, N = 4996).

Rosenberg's 10 item Self Esteem Scale was developed to measure global feelings about the self (Rosenberg, 1965). The Rajneesh mean was 35.71 (N = 87, SD = 5.53), compared to means of 29.82 reported by Yancey, et al. (1972) (N = 1179, SD = 4.43). The higher mean score indicated higher self-esteem for Rajneesh group members.

The authors of the 1987 report suggested caution when interpreting their results because: (1) use of self-report data; (2) instruments having different meanings in different cultures; and (3) confounding of results because Rajneesh philosophy emphasizes the positive. They might have added that small Ns on some scales also raise concern.

Latkin (1987) included results from several other inventories, directly chosen to allow testing of hypotheses about effects of the Rajneesh philosophy and practice concerning sex roles. A Self-Consciousness Scale developed by Feigenstein et al. (1975) and revised by Kernis and Reis (1981) was administered, as was a slightly revised Coping Scale from Moos et al. (1982), the Cohen-Hoberman Inventory of Physical Symptoms (1983), the Job Diagnostic Index from Smith et al. (1969), a modified version of Wrightsman's Assumptions about Human Nature Scale (1974), and the Personal Attribute Questionnaire developed by Spence and Helmreich (1978) to measure gender role orientation. Latkin also asked some separate questions about values, as well as administered the Rosenberg Self-Esteem Scale and the Depression Scale referred to earlier, along with obtaining considerable other data from demographic and personal background questionnaires. Latkin did indepth interviews with 25 sannyasins, as well. Note that Latkin gathered his data shortly *after* the Bhagwan and Ma Sheela left the Oregon commune, a factor that apparently impacted some results.

Detailed results of all the instrumentation used by Latkin cannot be given here. However, I will summarize some of his conclusions germane to the issue of mental health of members. Of particular interest are results of the Personal Attribute Questionnaire designed to show gender role orientation. Both males and females scored higher on the Femininity Scale than on the Masculinity Scale, which means they valued positive, usually-feminine attributes more than they valued positive, usually-male attributes. Latkin examined the sixteen specific items on which males and females differed significantly, and found some startling results on the four items with significant differences (Latin, 1987:72): "Males reported themselves to cry and have hurt feelings significantly more than women reported these attributes. On the other hand, women had higher scores on feelings of dominance." Males also ranked slightly, but significantly, higher on "feelings of superiority."

The Fenigstein Self-Consciousness Scale contains three subscales: Private Self-Consciousness focusing on internal thoughts and feelings; Public Self-Consciousness attending to perceptions of self as a social object; and Social Anxiety, which deals with being ill at ease or uncomfortable in presence of others. The Rajneesh sample scored significantly below normative means on the Public and Social Anxiety subscales, while scoring significantly above on the Private Self-Consciousness scale. Thus, respondents seemed more introspective, but less concerned about other's opinions of themselves, and less socially anxious than normative samples.

A discussion of the results from the Fenigstein Self-Consciousness Scale and the Rosenberg Self-Esteem Scale adminstered as part of the dissertation study (Latkin, 1987) are presented in Latkin (1990). Scores for the Rajneeshees on the Self-Esteem Scale were nearly as high as the earlier use of the instrument reported in Latkin, et al. (1987) — the mean was 33.4 (N = 210, SD 3.9). These data, coupled with those just reported on the Self-Consciousness Scale, suggest (Latkin, 1990:91): "The score on Private Self-Consciousness accords with the movement's belief that self-exploration is a legitimate and respectable avocation, but it contradicts the stereotypical notion that members of new religions or cults are easily persuaded."

I will not fully discuss results of administering the Wrightsman

Assumptions about Human Nature Scale, and its relationship to other scales reported in Latkin (1987). However, results from one particular item, designed to indicate locus of control orientation, is relevant. That item is, "Our success in life is pretty much determined by forces outside our control." Ninety-three per cent of the 226 sannyasins who responded disagreed with that statement, suggesting a strong internal locus of control orientation.

Scores on the Depression Scale were elevated considerably compared to the earlier administration repoted in Latkin et al. (1987), with a mean of 12.96. Latkin attributes this to the fact that the Bhagwan and Ma Sheela had left the community and encountered considerable legal difficulties within the past year, which was a very traumatic event for sannyasins. This interpretation is supported by responses to the Coping Scale, which asks respondents to list a stressful event that occurred during the past year, and describe their reactions to it. The majority of sannyasins listed the Bhagwan's departure and related events.

Sundberg et al. (1990) presented results from administering the California Personality Inventory to 67 Rajneeshees (34 females and 33 males). They found male and females scoring patterns to be quite similar, with especially high scores on the Independence and Flexiblity scales of the CPI. The paper also reported an analysis in terms of Gough's (1987) new structural system of interpreting CPI scores. That system categorizes individuals based on three variables (Sundberg, et al. 1990:10): "Role (internalizing or detached vs. externalizing or involved), Temperment (norm favoring vs. norm doubting), and Realization (low-to-high levels of self-perceived relaization, or competence)." Gough has proposed four types of individuals —Alphas, Betas, Deltas, and Gammas— depending on their categorization on the three variables, and Sundberg, et al. (1990:11) claim that 25% of respondents in the general population fall into each of the four categories. The Rajneesh group of 67 included only two who were not either Gammas (57%) or Deltas (40%), which means that only two were "norm-favoring", while 75 were "norm-doubting." Gammas are described as follows (1990:11): "adventurous, clever, headstrong, progressive, and rebellious." Deltas are (1990:11-12): "more private and internally oriented and are described by the following terms: preoccupied, quiet, reserved, sensitive, and worrying."

Sundberg et al. (1990:15) stated: "Compared with most people on CPI norms, Rajneeshees showed considerable ability, social poise, and absence of rigidity, and at the same time, a strong dislike for conventional forms and rules." They speculate, however, that the demise of the group might have derived from the lack of balance in personality types, suggesting that any group, in order to survive, "requires some conventional norm-favoring participants" (1990:16).

Latkin's (1987) rich discussion of his results is well worth studying, as are the other papers from this research on the Rajneesh, but we have sampled enough results to draw a few conclusions. First, the data reported in the 1987 study (gathered prior to the departure of the Bhagwan), although involving small Ns on some key scales, supports the position that sannyasins were living in a very positive atmosphere that contributed to a strong self concept. Data from the later study (Latkin, 1987) also supports that general conclusion, with the caveat that loss of the leader was a traumatic event, which apparently influenced responses on the Depression Scale dramatically. However, even in the face of the loss of the Bhagwan, the philosophy of the group was evident in the results, especially concerning gender roles. Thus, this much-maligned group appeared to be succeeding to some extent in changing traditional approaches to gender in America society. That is no mean feat, and should be recognized by those who would only focus on the negative aspects of the Rajneesh experience in Oregon. The Sundberg, et al. results also suggests that most members were strong, well-focused personalities (even if the group may have needed some other personality types in order to survive).

The Rajneesh group had built a strong, loving community which most members apparently found very satisfying. The sannyasins were able to act out their philosophy and express their emotions without fear of retribution, except by the greater society. The group may have simply attracted the type of person described in the inventories, of course, which would undercut the view that the community developed and promoted a unique, loving and supportive, less male-dominated philosophy. Given the length of time that most respondents had been sannyasins, it is apparent that even if the group only attracted such people, the organization and philosophy of the community fostered such individuals and allowed them to continue along that path of human development.

c. Hare Krishna

The Hare Krishna group has been the focus of a great deal of psychological research since I did my review in the early 1980s. One book has appeared reporting results of a major personality assessment effort (Poling and Kenny, 1986), Arnold Weiss has done a dissertation out of which a number of papers have come (Weiss, 1987; Weiss and Comprey, 1887a, b, and c; Weiss and Mendoza, 1990); and Michael Ross has produced four papers out of his research on an Australian Hare Krishna group (Ross, 1983a and b, 1985a and b). I will select some of the more important aspects of these reports to summarize.

Ross (1983a) reports results from administering the MMPI, Goldberg's (1972) General Health Questionnaire, and the Eysenck Personality Inventory (1975) to the entire population of a Melbourne, Australia Hare Krishna temple. The 42 members, who averaged 1.5 years in the movement, were found to be within the normal range on all tests. Ross also presented the MMPI results to two outside assessors, who (1983a:418) "...found no associated elevation of related scales that would permit an assessment of psychopathology." Ross concluded (1983a:418): "Clearly, the argument that Hare Krishna devotees are individuals who suffer from psychopathology, as some investigators have claimed, cannot be supported on the basis of the present evidence." He adds that the longer one was a member, the more conventional the responses, the less anxious the respondents, and the less they felt socially alienated. Ross says of the behavioral changes brought about by participation, such as cutting the quite high levels of drug use prior to joining (1983a:418): "(T)his history of abstinence after joining the movement must rate as one of the more successful rehabilitation programs." He offered other strong conclusionary statements, based on his research (1983a:419-420):

> (T)hese devotees appeared extremely well adjusted... Most still visited their families and were visited by them;... In short, the popular view of Hare Krishna devotees as brainwashed and maladjusted individuals who have been snatched from their families was shown to be fallacious. ... Deprogramming and other actions against these individuals and their right to practice a particular religion cannot be justified on the grounds that they have been "brainwashed." ...Those researchers who base conclusions on their perceptions of movements rather than on clinical and psychometric evaluation of members of each organization are in danger of exonerating the bad or condemning the normal.

Ross (1985) reports a follow-up administration of the MMPI to 25 of the 42 members four years later. He says that the changes experienced, with one exception, were well within the normal range, and were beneficial rather than harmful. The one exception was increased anxiety on the part of the 25 members.

***

Poling and Kenny (1986) presented findings based on an application of the Jungian-based, Myers-Briggs 162 item personality assessment instrument (Myers, 1962) to 93 members from four different temples in the U.S. (Dallas, Philadelphia, Carrier, MI, and San Diego), which represented about 90% of the fully initiated members at these temples. They also administered the Rokeach Dogmatism Scale (Rokeach (1960) to 29 individuals at three temples.

Poling and Kenny were addressing two questions: why do some young people join Hare Krishna, and why do some persevere in their affiliation? To gain answers to these questions, the authors engaged in a large study of the Krishna, including: (1) an analysis of Krishna beliefs and ritual behaviors, using a Jungian framework; (2) extensive field work and participant observation at eight temples around the country, supplemented by biographical questionnaires, personality assessment, and indepth interviews, and (3) administration of the aforementioned personality assessment instruments reported in their 1986 book.

Phase one of the research led to the following conclusion (1986:i): "(1) Krishna, ISKCON's deity, may be viewed as a symbol of transformation stemming from man's collective and unconscious strivings toward transcendence; and (2) consciousness of Krishna is developed in ISKCON by redirecting sexual impulses and desires for sense gratification into devotional services involving sensory-emotive rituals." Phase two of the research led to the conclusion that "the devotees we observed displayed a high degree of homogeneity in terms of background, lifestyle, and personality traits." They describe the typical ISKCON preconvert as follows, based on their work and that of others (1986:1):

> ...a socio-economically advantaged family background; an early socialization process characterized by discord as well as an identity crisis prior to membership in ISKCON; an orientation toward being a world-saver; a rejection of parental authority and value system coupled with the need for a strong, male authority substitute; extensive use of drugs prior to joining ISKCON; a tendency to view the material world as devoid of meaning and reality, a vegetarian diet and a tendency to seek a new self-identity in non-traditional, Asian religions.

Phase three of the research used the Meyers-Briggs inventory to categorize individuals into one of 16 different personality types. The 16 types are combinations of four basic attributes — thinking versus feeling, sensing versus intuiting, introversion versus extraversion, and judging versus perceiving. "Thinking" is primarily intellectual and ideational, with an emphasis on logic and rationality. "Feeling" is the emotive or evaluative function that brings a subjective element to judgments. "Sensing", according to Poling and Kenny (1986:44), "promotes awareness of literal facts or sensory representations of tangible events and objects." "Intuition" involves perception through unconscious processes that are more irrational in character. "Introversion" refers to a focus on thoughts, feelings, perceptions, ideas, and fantasies, in contrast to "extroversion", which directs awareness to tangible entities external to the observer. Introverts are more reflective and socially withdrawn, while extroverts tend to be outgoing, and interested in others. "Judging" refers to a preference for an ordered and structured lifestyle, contrasted to "perceiving, which indicates a preference for a more spontaneous, experientially-oriented, and unstructured lifestyle. The latter pair of attributes was added to Jung's theoretical scheme by Meyers (1962).

Considerable homogeneity was found among the 93 Krishna devotees who took the Meyers-Briggs inventory. Forty per cent of those taking the test were classified as "ISTJ", which means they were introverted, sensory, thinking, and judging. Another 26% were classified as "ESTJ", which means they were extraverted, sensory, thinking, and judging. Thus 66% were classified as sensory, thinking, and judging. When looking at what percentages chose items classifying them on the separate attributes, the dominance of the STJ pattern stands out. Eighty-two per cent were classified as sensory, 78% as thinking, and 90% as judging (55% chose introversion). This startling pattern was interpreted by Poling and Kenny to mean that considerable selection had taken place to have such a concentration of a unique personality type within Krishna. They point out that only one out of 23 females in an earlier study (Meyers and Meyers, 1980) was of the ISTJ pattern which characterized 40% of the Krishna females tested. They also report administration of the inventory to samples of 29 Catholic high school females and 52 members of the Unitarian Church, which resulted in quite a different spread of personality types than those found with the Krishna sample.

Poling and Kenny say (1986:63): "It is our contention that the high frequency of sensing types among our ISKCON subjects validates the presence of the sensate orientation initially identified through other sources of information including interviews, direct observation, and previous scholarship." They describe the ISTJ personality as (1986:62), "painstaking, hardworking, systematic, and thorough", "often remarkably dependable", "stable,...seldom enter(ing) into endeavors impulsively", and "very hard to distract or discourage." The authors' explanation of why senates are attracted is quite provocative (1986:108):

> We view ISKCON devotees as highly sensate-oriented pleasure seekers who perceive themselves as constantly in danger of falling victim to sense gratification as an end in itself.
> ...(O)ur contention is that ISKCON devotees: (1) are preoccupied with the sensing process; and (2) are using thinking and judging to structure or control the sensate function. This explains the apparent paradox between the rejection of sense pleasure on the mundane level and its acceptance on the transcendent level.

Poling and Kenny note (1986:118) that, "ISKCON's categorical condemnation of the use of intoxicants of any kind (including caffeine) indicates a sensate preoccupation." They discuss the strict dietary rules as another indicator of controlling sensate pleasures. Most importantly, the redefinition and strict regulation of sexual behavior is viewed as a manifestation of the sensate preoccupation of devotees.

"Thinking" and "judging" help control the sensate impulses that plague ISKCON members. Major characteristics of the thinking function are (1986:127): "(1) the tendency to think in clear cut dichotomies stressing true vs. false...; (2) the tendency to accept one's own truth as absolute, coupled with the corresponding tendency to make errors with confidence; and (3) the tendency to value principles over persons." This style can mean that devotees, when dealing with outsiders, are argumentative and confrontational. "Judging" has as major features (1986:135): "(1) the tendency to conform to proper standards; (2) sustained effort in terms of projects; (3) a passion for a decisive, purposeful, planned life with a high degree of purposeful, self-regimentation and the acceptance of routine; and (4) a high degree of intolerance regarding the beliefs and lifestyles of others, coupled with dogmatic thinking." The latter point about dogmatic thinking is also evidenced by scores on Rokeach's Dogmatism scale, administered to 29 devotees at three temples (we are not told why the small N). ISKCON members had a mean of 191 (SD = 22.3), which was about two standard deviations above the normative mean of 142 (SD = 27.9) for college students reported in Rokeach (1960).

The authors note (1986:152): "the remarkable correspondence

between the predispositional factors of persons who join ISKCON and the structural factors of ISKCON itself." They refer to ISKCON as a "specialized institution in that its therapeutic techniques are designed solely for sensates" (1986:154). This unique organization attracts and reinforces a new identity in devotees, who change from a materialistic sensate to a more spiritual one. Poling and Kenny characterize ISKCON interestingly (1986:170): "From 1967 to approximately 1975, ISKCON functioned as a voluntary detoxification unit for countercultural, drug-addicted youth with a 'world-saver' mentality and a tendency to seek new identity in religion.... Later, from 1975 to the present, ISKCON functioned ...as a rehabilitative program analogous to Alcoholics Anonymous. Individuals who had been successfully detoxed were now rehabilitated."

Poling and Kenny close their book with a discussion of the so-called "brainwashing-deprogramming" controversy. They admit that their work might be viewed as supportive of the brainwashing idea, since it identifies a strong set of predispositional factors that indicate susceptibility to certain types of religious influence. However, they point out that their study does not support the brainwashing notion in terms of the element of coercion, which they define (1986:163) as "physical incarceration and mind control." They cite the ease with which devotees leave the movement, and the fact that there are large numbers of ex-devotees (more than there are members), and state (1986:164): "if ISKCON has employed brainwashing and mind-control techniques, these have been very unsuccessful." They also note that, although becoming a member was easier and more haphazard earlier in the movement's history, later a lengthy probationary period was instituted. Such a recruitment process does not resemble what most mean when they talk of brainwashing.

In answer to the two questions posed initially by the authors (who joins and who stays), the conclusion is that sensate personalities are attracted to the organization because of its unique features, and some of those who join remain for a time, because of what the organization does for them. No one is coerced into joining, or kept a prisoner once they have joined.

***

Arnold Weiss has produced significant research on Krishna devotees, through his dissertation (Weiss, 1985) and subsequent publications. His study included an assessment of the personality characteristics (Weiss and Comprey, 1987b) and personality factor structure of Krishna followers (Weiss and Comprey, 1987c), and a comparison of followers with psychiatric outpatients and "normals" (Weiss and Comprey, 1987a), all using the Comprey Personality Scales (Comprey, 1970a and b, 1980). He also has presented (Weiss, 1987) results of administering the Rand Corporation's Mental Health Inventory developed by Ware (Ware, et al., 1979; Veit and Ware, 1983), as well as results from relating an "Acculturation Scale" to the CPS and MHI data (Weiss and Mendoza, 1990).

All these reports are based on a sample of 186 devotees and 40 "sympathizers" (most of whom were in the process of becoming devotees), who averaged about 30 years of age. The 226 respondents represent about 5% of all Krishna followers in the United States at the time (Weiss, 1987:33). The 132 males and 94 females who volunteered for testing averaged 8.6 years in the Krishna movement. Marital status was: eighty-nine single, 101 married, 21 divorced, 10 separated, 3 cohabiting, and 2 widows. One hundred twenty-eight claimed no prior religious affiliation, 40 said they were Catholics, 20 were Protestant, 14 other Christian religions, 11 Jewish, and 11 from various Eastern religions. They came from temples in San Diego, Washington, D.C., Pennsylvania, with about 40% from Los Angeles. One hundred-sixteen had some college, 22 had bachelor's degrees, 10 had some graduate training, and 7 had graduate or professional degrees. One hundred eighty-eight were white, 13 were black, 9 were asian, 5 were hispanic, with 11 unclassified. Thirty-three were from lower socio-economic status origins, with 97 from the middle class, and 96 from the upper middle and upper classes (Weiss and Comprey, 1987c).

The 180 item Comprey Personality Scales measure eight personality traits or constructs, including (1987b:400-401):

1. Trust vs. Defensiveness (T). High scores indicate a belief in the basic honesty, trustworthiness, and good intentions of people.
2. Orderliness vs. Lack of Compulsion (O). High scores are characteristic of careful, meticulous, orderly, and highly organized individuals.
3. Social Conformity vs. Rebelliousness (C). Individuals with high scores accept society as it is, resent nonconformity in others, seek the approval of society, and respect the law.
4. Activity vs. Lack of Energy (A). High-scoring individuals have a great deal of energy and endurance, work hard, and strive to excel.

5. Emotional Stability vs. Neuroticism (S). High-scoring persons are free of depression, optomistic, relaxed, stable in mood, and confident.
6. Extraversion vs. Introversion (E). High-scoring individuals meet people easily, seek new friends, feel comfortable with strangers, and do not suffer from stage fright.
7. Masculinity vs. Femininity (M). High-scoring individuals tend to be rather tough-minded people who are not bothered by blood, crawling creatures, vulgarity, and who do not cry easily or show interest in love stories.
8. Empathy vs. Egocentrism (P). High-scoring individuals describe themselves as helpful, generous, sympathetic people who are interested in devoting their lives to the service of others.

Two additional scales —a Validity (V) scale and a Response Bias (R) scale— are included to detect distorted responding and faking.

Results of the CPS administration to Krishna followers, when factor-analysized to discern the personality structure of followers (Weiss and Comprey, 1987c), revealed that CPS personality dimensions found appropriate for use with diverse groups also described the Krishna well, with one exception. That exception was the Social Conformity scale, on which Krishna scores displayed score variance only one-third that of norm groups of males and females. Failure of this factor to emerge was interpreted as deriving from the conformity requirements within the group, which in turn led to more homogeneity with respect to this characteristic than with most other groups. Weiss and Comprey (1987c:327) conclude, however:

> The most surprising outcome... was not that the factor structure of personality underlying the CPS for Hare Krishna diverged from that for other groups but rather that it was so similar...What the present results show is that individuals in this Hare Krishna population subgroup, a minority United States culture possessing divergent habits, life style, and other characteristics, nevertheless can be described with respect to the same set of personality dimensions as that which previously has been found to be appropriate for use with what would be considered more typical individuals in the United States and other countries.

The assessment of personality characteristics (Weiss and Comprey, 1987b) revealed a number of significant differences, particularly for males, who differed on eight of the scales (R,T,O,C,S,E,M, and P). Krishna males were higher than the norm on O, C, S, E, and P, but below the norm on T and M. However, all scores were within the defined normal range (Comprey, 1980), except for the score on O (Orderliness vs. Compulsiveness), which was 1.44 SD above the normal group mean. Thus the male profile can be described as low on Trust and Masculinity, and high on Orderliness, Social Conformity, Emotional Stability, Extroversion, and Empathy. Also, males were higher on Response Bias, compared to the norm group. Krishna females differed from the norm group only on Trust and Orderliness: they were significantly below the norm for Trust, and significantly above (1.18 SDs) on Orderliness. Only scale O for females was out of the defined normal range, however.

The finding of a strong "compulsivity trait" among Krishna followers of both sexes (stronger with males) is called the "hallmark trait of the Hare Krishna personality" by Weiss and Comprey (1987b:406). Nearly 23% of the sample (including 27% of the males) scored at the extreme range on the O scale. Comprey (1980:22) has described the compulsive personality as:

> very meticulous, compulsive people who are,highly organized, conscientious, punctual, neat and tidy. They are driven to complete tasks, feel compelled to correct errors, and often fall prey to obsessive behavior. Many individuals with moderately high scores on this scale are highly productive persons who capitalize on their obsessive-compulsive inclinations to accomplish amazing feats...Unfortunately, this behavior in adult life may have some negative side effects on their overall adjustment.

Weiss and Comprey speak directly to whether this trait is a debilitating mental disorder, under the rubric of the Diagnostic and Statistical Manual III (American Psychiatric Association, 1980). They note that elevated scores on the O scale accompanied by high C scale scores (Conformity) has been suggested (Comprey, 1980:65) as characteristic of the "compulsive personality disorder" of the DSM-III. However, they point out that Krishna followers are not out of the normal range on the C scale; although males are significantly higher than the norm on C, they do not have enough extreme scores to fit the disorder's profile.

Weiss and Comrey discuss the congruence between the structured Krishna lifestyle and the results of the CPS application. Their discussion mirrors that of Poling and Kenny, whose classification of most Krishna followers as Judging and Thinking, and as highly Dogmatic, parallels the Weiss and Comprey finding of compulsivity as a dominant trait. The differences between Krishna males and females is indicative, Weiss and Comprey suggest, of more complex role requirements placed on Krishna males, who must practice their demanding religion, while also interfacing with the world to keep Krishna enterprises functioning.

In another paper Wiess (1987) presented an assessment of the mental health of the Krishna sample, using the Rand Mental Health Inventory, a measure of psychological distress and well-being. The 38 item, self-report inventory contains correlated subscales measuring Mental Health, Psychological Distress, Psychological Well-Being, Anxiety, Depression, Loss of Behavioral/Emotional Control, General Positive Affect, Emotional Ties, and Life Satisfaction.

Weiss concluded that the Krishna samples (by sex) generally compared favorably with the normative samples on mental health. No significant differences were found between Krishna women and the normative sample on any of the nine subscales of the MHI. Krishna males were higher on three of the nine scales — Psychological Well-Being, General Positive Affect, and Loss of Behavioral/Emotional Control, the latter of which was attributed to a Type I error (Weiss, 1987:29-30). Krishna males were found to score better than females on several of the subscales, a finding that was also noted with the normative samples, although Krishna women were somewhat less unhealthy, as measured by the MHI, than were women in the normative sample.

Weiss proposed a "positivity effect" for Krishna males, who showed the unusual pattern of being comparatively higher on Psychological Well-Being and General Positive Affect, but without lower Psychological Distress scores (1987:32):

> This male group responded as if happier, exhibiting more positive affect and behavior, and appearing to be more satisfied with their lives, and yet reporting anxiety, depression, and other unhappy feelings that were not different from those of normative men... Speculations are that this unusual effect may have arisen from a positiveness that Hare Krishna men derive from their religious experiences and life style or that it may represent an intentional "high" that they have fostered within themselves, perhaps unconsciously, to justify their religious position.

The conclusion drawn from this study is (Weiss, 1987:33): "Psychological distress and well-being of Hare Krishna do not differ significantly from that of the U.S. general population men and women, respectively, as measured on the Mental Health Inventory, with the exception of the "positivity effect" for Hare Krishna males." They also add (and mention in Weiss and Comprey, 1987a:722) that "the estimated rate of mental disorder of this Krishna sample was not significantly different from that of American society as reported by the National Institute of Mental Health in 1984."

Weiss and Comprey (1987a) adds to this picture of mental health normality, with a sophisticated treatment of CPS scores using a "stanine analysis" as part of comparing the Krishna sample with a well-studied psychiatric sample and a normative sample. Details will not be given here; however, a summary will give the flavor of results (1987a:721):

> Outpatients exhibited multiple pathologic signs of reduced daily functioning, compulsive personality disorder, and general emotional maladjustment. Hare Krishnas, except for their hallmark personality characteristic, a strong compulsivity trait, scored within the normal psychological range. Reduced trust in society was exhibited in many members although the average trust was normal.

The final paper by Weiss (Weiss and Mendoza, 1990) uses the MHI and CPS to evaluate mental health and personality differences in acculturation among Krishna members. Design and validation of the Acculturation Index, which is a measure of religiosity pertaining to the Krishna belief system and practices, is detailed in Weiss' dissertation (1985:73-93). The 53 item AI scale was designed to tap degree of immersion into the Hare Krishna religion. Scores on the CPS and MHI subscales were treated separately as dependent variables in a multiple regression analysis. The Krishna samples (by sex) were trichotomized by choosing the extreme thirds on the Acculturation Index for comparison purposes.

No association was found between scores on the AI and length of time in Hare Krishna (1990: 181). Some interesting relationships were found when relating the CPS and MHI subscales to AI scores; however, an overall summary statement from Wiess and Mendoza (1990:173) summarized their conclusions:

> Personality traits were mostly invariant with acculturation, and those traits on which the Hare Krishna differed from the norm group may be prerequisite to membership rather than being its consequences. Mental health was also largely invariable with acculturation, except that greater degree of acculturation was associated with greater subjective well-being.

In short, Weiss and Mendoza seem to be saying that the Hare Krishna movement attracts a certain type of person, and then encourages them to be more of that type of person, which causes those who remain to feel better about themselves. The authors also report that males fare slightly better in this analysis than females, as particularly shown by High AI males scoring significantly higher than Low AI ones on all five positive attribute subscales of the MHI, indicating better mental health (1990:177).

These findings have implications, discussed by Weiss and Mendoza (1990:180), for the anti-cult position "that greater cult involvement (as measured by higher acculturation) is associated with decreased mental health, as feared by some (Conway and Siegelman, 1982), and that less acculturation is more likely to be associated with normal mental health." Weiss and Mendoza state: "Our results suggest the contrary. High AI groups for both genders reported significantly greater well-being than did their respective MHI norms, while not reporting significantly less distress than did the norms (a positivity effect). Also, low AI group scores on a few subscales were significantly lower then were the MHI norms."

Summary Statement of Results

I see no reason to modify the conclusion statement from the earlier review. Indeed, the statement can be made even stronger, based on the thorough and sophisticated research that has been done, particularly by the University of Oregon team and by Weiss and his associates. The Rajneesh group had developed a lifestyle with more emotional openness and more gender equality than exists in normal life, and some quite well-educated and relatively high status people have chosen to be a part of that lifestyle. This seems the case particularly for some women. The Hare Krishna have developed a rigorous, but apparently satisfying lifestyle for a few people, attracted by the very attributes that bring criticism from some detractors. Male Hare Krishna members seem to fare particularly well, in spite of their "compulsivity." The Shiloh group members, who had displayed traits that might have been dysfunctional in normal society, have apparently overcome possible problems and adapted quite well to their new noncommunal lifestyles.

Conclusions and Legal Implications

In some papers directed at the mental health community since the earlier review, Brock Kilbourne and I have attempted to explain why someone might decide to participate in new religions, how that process might work, and to what consequences. In one (Kilbourne and

Richardson, 1985), we developed the concept of the "social experimenter role", based on a more positive interpretation of Robert Lifton's "Protean Man" concept. We proposed that people engaging in a seeking behavior which might be characterized as a "conversion career" should not necessarily to be viewed negatively in today's world. The search to define and improve oneself should be treated, not as frivolous behavior, but as a meaningful activity with many positive features.

In another paper (Kilbourne and Richardson, 1986), we posited the notion of the "communalization of religion", as a way of explaining what some young people may have been seeking in new religions. Keep in mind that many of these youth have distant, if not severed, relationships with their families, and they may be searching for surrogates. The "communalization" notion was developed in contrast with Thomas Luckmann's famous "privatization" of religion concept, used in his discussion of the growing prevalence of "invisible", noncommunity-oriented religion in modern society. Plainly, many youth do not want their religion to be invisible: they want and need a community in which to develop their human potential. That need for community may be met, at least for a time, by one of the newer religions.

In a third paper (Kilbourne and Richardson, 1988), we offered a social psychological model of healing based on similarities between communal new religions and therapy situations. We assumed that many participants in new religions did so for reasons that could be broadly defined as seeking healing, even if this motivation was not at a conscious level. We built our model of healing on an earlier paper (Kilbourne and Richardson, 1984), which discussed a number of commonalities between psychotherapies and new religions. In the 1988 effort, we discussed (1) the healer role, (2) the role of healee, and (3) the underlying "deep structure" of healing, and focused in the complementarity of the healer and healee roles, as well as process of healing itself within therapeutic and religious groups. This 1988 paper can be viewed as a social psychological counter to the socio-biological healing model proffered by Galanter (1989b), based on his extensive research on new religions. Although the models differ markedly, both are based upon a clear understanding that participation in the new religions quite often serves an ameliorative function for the participants.

***

Thus, it appears clear that those who would claim that new religions are tricking people into joining, deceiving them into remaining a participant, and contributing to the disintegration of their personality and mental health by virtue of the experience, have no support in the findings reported herein, as well as some other analyses that have been done. The groups studied seem to attract certain types of people, who exercise their volition in joining and affirm themselves through the experience, if they choose to remain. Most do not stay for long (which in itself undercuts the position of the anti-cultists), but few seem harmed by the experience, and many seem to enjoy and gain from their time in the groups.

Given these results and conclusions, the question of why such a controversy rages about participation in new religions is worth addressing. I have discussed reasons for the controversy in other papers (see particularly Kilbourne and Richardson, 1984, and Richardson, 1989), and will not repeat that analysis here. Suffice it to say that people involved in such research have different goals and interests at stake, different disciplinary and ideological perspectives, including important contrasts in methodology. These differences have contributed greatly to the arguments about new religions.

What is most troublesome about the controversy is that is has spilled over into the legal arena, from almost the beginning of the new religions' phenomenon in America. Some parents of participants have attempted to gain legal conservatorships over their children (no matter the age of said children) by having them declared incompetent by virtue of their decision to be involved in a new religion, and damage allegedly done to them by the group. This has often been done to facilitate "deprogramming" of the young member. Some former members of new religions and their parents have taken legal action against their former membership group, seeking damages for the time they spent in the group, as well as for the harm that was supposedly done to them while there. These developments have attracted growing attention from social scientists, legal scholars, religionists, and others (Bromley, 1983; Robbins, 1985; LeMoult, 1983; Shapiro, 1983; Kelly, 1983; Bromley and Richardson, 1983; Richardson, 1991).

Legal scholars and religionists focus attention on issues of religious freedom — a truly important concept within the American context. Social scientists have attended most to the claims being made within the legal arena about some of the issues discussed herein. Social scientists, religionists and others have found common interest in debunking testimony supporting certain new torts that are being promoted, using the vehicle of "cults" or new religions.

These new torts go by names like "brainwashing", "mind control", "coercive persuasion", and "thought reform", which are stand-ins for traditional torts like false imprisonment, fraud, and intentional infliction of emotional distress. These "new torts" are now being applied within religious contexts, especially those involving new religions. Thus, a freely made decision to join a religious group may get defined in a legal action as "brainwashing" or "thought reform", and a decision to stay in a group may be defined as a result of "coercive persuasion" or "mind control." This may sound strange, or even unbelievable to some, but such cases are being won by those proposing the novel scientific theories. Experts have been found who will testify to such theories, as applied to participation in new religions, and the legal system has sometimes accepted the theories wholeheartedly. Juries have awarded damages in the millions of dollars in a number of cases, a development with very detrimental effects on some new religions. I cannot detail these cases here (see Richardson, 1991 and 1994b and Anthony, 1990), but must report that the situation is very troublesome.

While there is some room for hope that the situation will not deteriorate further, that is not certain. Thus, it appears that the legal arena will continue to have issues such as the mental health and personality attributes of new religion participants discussed, with important consequences for individuals and the religions involved. Social scientists who are concerned about the continued misrepresentation of research results in the legal arena need to continue their vigilance. This is a new and different role for many of us, but it is a role that must be played. We must attempt to educate judges and juries about the findings of relevant research, instead of allowing a few self-proclaimed experts to enter testimony that badly misrepresents or completely ignores the psychology of religion research tradition. And, most of all we must continue to produce good research, such as that detailed in this paper, so that the task of educating those in the legal system will be made easier.

REFERENCES

American Psychiatric Assocition. (1980). *The Diagnostic and Statistical Manual*. 3rd edition revised. Washington: D.C.: American Psychiatric Association.

Anthony, D. (1990). Religious movements and brainwashing litigation: Evaluating key testimony." In T. Robbins and D. Anthony (Eds.), *In Gods We Trust* (pp. 295-344). New Brunswick, NJ: Transaction.

Anthony, D., Robbins, T. and McCarthy, J. (1980). Legitimating repression. *Society*, 17, 39-42.

Barker, E. (1981). Who'd be a Moonie? A comparative study of those who join the Unification Church in Britain. In B. Wilson (Ed.), *The Social Impact of New Religious Movements*. New York: Rose of Sharon Press.

Beckford, J. (1978). Accounting for conversion. *British Journal of Sociology*, 29, 249-262.

Berger, P. (1967). *The Sacred Canopy*. New York: Doubleday.

Bromley, D. (1983). Conservatorships and deprogramming: Legal and political prospects. In D. Bromley and J. Richardson (Eds.), *The Brainwashing/Deprogramming Controversy* (pp. 267-293). New York: Edwin Mellen.

Bromley, D. & Richardson, J. (Eds.) (1983). *The Brainwashing/Deprogramming Controversy*. Toronto: Edwin Mellen Press.

Brown, L. (1985). *Advances in the Psychology of Religion*. New York: Pergamon Press.

Carter, L. (1987). The "new renunciates" of the Bhagwan Shree Rajneesh: Observations and identification of problems of interpreting new religious movements. *Journal for the Scientific Study of Religion*, 26, 148-172.

Cohen, S. & Hoberman, H. (1983). Positive events and social supports as buffers of life change stress. *Journal of Applied Social Psychology*, 13, 99-125.

Cohen, S., Kamart, T., & Mermelstein, R. (1988). A global measure of perceived stress. *Journal of Health and Social Behavior*,

Comprey, A. (1970a). *Comprey Personality Scales*. San Diego: Educational and Industrial Testing Service.

Comprey, A. (1970b). *Manual for Comprey Personality Scales*. San Diego: Educational and Industrial Testing Service.

Comprey, A. (1980). *Handbook for Interpretations for the Comprey Personality Scales*. San Diego: Educational and Industrial Testing Service.

Conway F. & Seigleman (1982). Information disease: Have cults created a new mental illness? *Science Digest*, 90, 88-92.

Derks, F. & van der Lans, J. (1982). The post-cult syndrome: Fact or Fiction? Paper presented at Conference of Psychologists of Religion, Catholic University, Nijmegen, The Netherlands.

Eysenck, H. (1975). *Manual of the Eysenck Personality Questionnaire*. London: Hodder & Stoughton.

Feigenstein, A., Scheier, M., & Buss, A. (1975). Public and private self-consciousness: Assessment and theory. *Journal of Consulting and Clinical Psychology*, 43, 522-527.

Galanter, M. (1978). The "relief effect": A sociobiological model of neurotic distress and large group therapy. *American Journal of Psychiatry*, 135, 588-591.

Galanter, M. (1980). Psychological induction into the large-group: Findings from a modern religious sect. *American Journal of Psychiatry*, 137, 1574-1579.

Galanter, M. (1989a). *Cults, Faith Healing, and Coercion*. New York: Oxford University Press.

Galanter, M. (Ed.) (1989b). *Cults and New Religious Movements*. Washington, D.C.: American Psychiatric Association.

Galanter, M. & Buckley, P. (1978). Evangelical religion and meditation: Psychotherapeutic effects. *Journal of Nervous and mental Disease*, 166, 685-691.

Galanter, M., Rabkin, R., Rabkin, F. & Deutsch, A. (1979). The "Moonies": A psychological study of conversion and membership in a contemporary religious sect. *American Journal of Psychiatry*, 136, 165-169.

Goldberg, D. (1972). *The Detection of Psychiatric Illness by Questionnaire*. London: Oxford University Press.

Goldman, M.S. (1988). The women of Rajneeshpuram. *Center for the Study of Women Review*, 2, 18-21.

Kelly, (1983). Deprogramming and religious liberty. In D. Bromley and J. Richardson (Eds.), *The Brainwashing/Deprogramming Controversy* (pp. 309-318). New York: Edwin Mellen.

Kernis, M., & Reis, H. (1981). Self-consciousness, self-awareness, and justice in reward allocation. Unpublished manuscript.

Kilbourne, B. & Richardson, J. (1984). Psychotherapy and new religions in a pluralistic society. *American Psychologist*, 39, 237-251.

Kilbourne, B. & Richardson, J. (1985). Social experimentation: Self process or social role? *International Journal of Social Psychiatry*, 31, 13-22.

Kilbourne, B. & Richardson, J. (1986). The communalization of religious experience in contemporary religious groups. *Journal of Community Psychology*, 14, 206-212.

Kilbourne, B. & Richardson, J. (1988). A social psychological analysis of healing. *Journal of Integrative and Eclectic Psychotherapy*, 7, 20-34.

Kuner, W. (1983). New religions and mental health. In E. Barker (Ed.), *Of Gods and Men: New Religious Movements in the West* (pp. 255-263). Macon, GA: Mercer University Press.

Latkin, C. (1988). Rajneeshpuram, Oregon — An exploration of gender and work roles, self-concept, and psychological well-being in an experimental community. Doctoral dissertation, University of Oregon, Eugene Oregon.

Latkin, C., Hogan, R., Littman, R. & Sundberg, N. (1987). Who lives in utopia? A brief report of the Rajneesh research project. *Sociological Analysis*, 48, 73-81.

LeMoult, J. (1983). Deprogramming members of religious sects. In D. Bromley and J. Richardson (Eds.), *The Brainwashing Deprogramming Controversy* (pp. 234-257). New York: Edwin Mellen.

Moos, R., Cronkite, R., Billings, A., & Finney, J. (1982). *Health and Daily Living Form Manual*. Stanford, CA: Stanford University School of Medicine.

Myers, I. (1962). *The Myers-Briggs Type Indicator*. Palo Alto, CA: Consulting Psychologists Press.

Myers, I., & Myers, P. (1980). *Gifts Differing*. Palo Alto, CA: Consulting Psychologists Press.

Nicholi, A. (1974). A new dimension of the youth culture. *American Journal of Psychiatry*, 131, 396-401.

Nordquist, T. (1978). *Ananda Cooperative Village: A Study in the Beliefs, Values, and Attitudes of a New Age Religious Community*. Uppsala University: Religionshistoriska Institutionen Monograph Series.

Poling, T. & Kenny, J. (1986). *The Hare Krishna Character Type: A Study in Sensate Personality*. Lewiston, NY: Edwin Mellen.

Radloff, L. (1977). The CES-D scale: A self-report depression scale of research in the general population. *Applied Psychological Measurement*, 1, 385-401.

Richardson, J. (1980). Conversion careers. *Society, 17, 47-50.*

Richardson, J. (1982). Conversion, deprogramming, and brainwashing. *The Center Magazine*. 15, 18-24.

Richardson, J. (1994a). Calvary Chapel: Modern miracle of church growth. Forthcoming, Syzygy.

Richardson, J. (1990). New Religions on trial. The Oregon Experience. Paper presented at annual meting of the Pacific Sociological Association, Spokane, WA.

Richardson, J. (1991). Cult/brainwashing cases and the freedom of religion. *Journal of Church and State*, 33, 55-74.

Richardson, J. (1994). Legal Status of New Religions. Forthcoming, Social Compass.

Richardson, J. (1989). The psychology of induction. In M. Galanter (Ed.), *Cults and New Religious Movements*. Washington, D.C.: American Psychiatric Association.

Richardson, J., Stewart, M. & Simmonds, R. (1979). *Organized Miracles*. New Brunswick, NJ: Transaction Books.

Robbins, T. (1985). Government regulatory powers over religious movements: Deviant groups as test cases. *Journal for the Scientific Study of Religion*, 24, 237-51.

Rokeach, M. (1960). *The Open and Closed Mind*. New York: Basic Books.

Rosen, A. & Nordquist, T. (1980). Ego developmental level and values in a yogic community. *Journal of Personality and Social Psychology*, 39, 1152-1160.

Rosenberg, M. (1965). *Social and Adolescent Self-Image*. Princeton, NJ: Princeton University Press.

Ross, M. (1983a). Clinical profiles of Hare Krishna devotees. *American Journal of Psychiatry*, 140, 416-420.

Ross, M. (1983b). Mental health and membership in Hare Krishna: A case study. *Australian Psychologist*, 18, 128-129.

Ross, M. (1984). Problems with research on Hare Krishna Devotees. American Journal of Psychiatry, 141,144.

Ross, M. (1985). Mental health in Hare Krishna devotees: A longitudinal study. *American Journal of Social Psychiatry*, 4, 65-67.

Shapiro, R. (1983). Of robots, persons, and the protection of religious beliefs. *Southern California Law Review*. 56, 1277-1318.

Shupe, A. & Bromley, D. (1980). *The New Vigilantes*. Beverly Hills, CA: Sage.

Simmonds, R. (1978). Conversion or addiction: Consequences of joining a Jesus Movement group. In J. Richardson (Ed.) *Conversion Careers*. Beverly Hills, CA: Sage.

Simmonds, R., Richardson, J., & Harder, M. (1976). "A Jesus Movement group" An Adjective Checklist assessment. *Journal for the Scientific Study of Religion*, 15, 323-337.

Singer, M. (1979). Coming out of the cults. *Psychology Today*, 12, 72-82.

Skonovd, N. (1983). Apostasy: The process of defection from religious totalism. In D. Bromley and J. Richardson Eds.), *The Brainwashing/Deprogramming Controversy* (pp. 91-105). Toronto: Edwin Mellen.

Smith, P., Kendall, L., & Hulin, C. (1969). *The Measurement of Satisfaction in Work and Retirement*. Chicago: Rand McNally.

Spence, J. & Helmriech, R. (1978). *Masculinity and Femininity: Their Psychological Dimensions, Correlates, and Antecedents*. Austin: University of Texas Press.

Sundberg, N., Latkin, C., Littman, C., & Hagen, R. (1990). Personality in a religious commune: CPIs in Rajneeshpuram. *Journal of Personality Assessment*, 55, 7-17.

Sundberg, N., Goldman, M., Rotter, N., & Smyth, D. (1992). Personality and spirituality: Comparative TATs of high-achieving Rajneeshees. *Journal of Personality Assessment*, 59, 329-339.

Taslimi, C., Hood, R., & Watson, P. (1991). Assessment of former members of Shiloh: The Adjective Checklist 17 years later. *Journal for the Scientific Study of Religion*, 30, 306-311.

Ungerleider, T. & Wellisch, D. (1979). Coercive persuasion (brainwashing), religious cults and deprogramming. *American Journal of Psychiatry*, 136, 279-282.

Veit, C. & Ware, J. (1983). The structure of psychological distress and well-being in the general population. *Journal of Consulting and Clinical Psychology*, 51, 730-742.

Wallis, R. & Bruce, S. (1986). *Sociological Theory, Religion, and Collective Action*. Belfast: Queen's University.

Ware, J., Johnston, S., Davies-Avery, A., & Brook, R. (1979). *Conceptualization and Measurement of Health for Adults in the Health Insurance Study*. Volume 3, *Mental Health*. Santa Monica,CA: Rand Corporation.

Weiss, A. (1985). Mental health and personality characteristics of Hare Krishna devotees and sympathizers as a function of acculturation into the Hare Krishna movement. Doctoral dissertation, California School of Professional psychology, Los Angeles. *Dissertation Abstracts International*, 46, 8b.

Weiss, A. (1987). Psychological distress and well-being in Hare Krishna. *Psychological Reports*, 61, 23-35.

Weiss, A. & Comprey, A. (1987a). Personality and mental health of Hare Krishna compared with psychiatric outpatients and "normals." *Personality and Individual Differences*, 8, 721-730.

Weiss, A. & Comprey A. (1987b). Personality characteristics of Hare Krishna. *Journal of Personality Assessment*, 51, 399-413.

Weiss, A. & Comprey (1987c). Personality factor structure among Hare Krishna. *Educational and Psychological Measurement*, 47, 317-328.

Weiss, A. & Mendoza (1990). Effects of acculturation into the Hare Krishna on mental health and personality. *Journal for the Scientific Study of Religion*, 29, 173-184.

Wrightsman, L. (1974). *Assumptions About Human Nature: A Social Psychological Approach*. Monterey, CA: Brooks/Cole.

Wuthnow, R. (1976). *The Consciousness Reformation*. Berkeley, CA: University of California Press.

Wright, S. (1983). Defection from new religious movements: A test of some theoretical propositions. In D. Bromley and J. Richardson (Eds.) *The Brainwashing/Deprogramming Controversy* (pp. 106-121). New York: Edwin Mellen Press.

SECTION 2. THEORY-GUIDED RESEARCH

CHAPTER 8
A MODEL OF SEQUENTIAL DEVELOPMENT OF RELIGIOUS ORIENTATION AS A CRITERION OF MENTAL HEALTH

Pawel Socha

I. Problem of the developmental perspective of religious orientation.

The concept of religious orientation has been the most popular basis for the measurement of the qualitative aspects of individual religion. It was developed by G.W. Allport (1950), and G.W. Allport and J.M. Ross (1967), as the intrinsic and extrinsic dimensions. Briefly, extrinsic religious orientation describes a tendency to use religion instrumentally, as the *means*, for need satisfaction. Intrinsic religious orientation describes an entirely autotelic tendency or motive to *live* one's religion, therefore this orientation is considered the more mature religious orientation ("good and bad religion", see objections by L.A. Kirkpatrick and R.W. Hood, Jr., 1990).

C.D. Batson (1976; Batson, Ventis, 1982) proposed the idea of *quest* religious orientation, which has complicated that clear distinction. Although the initial aim was to fulfill several gaps in the operationalization of Allport's mature religious sentiment by the Allport-Ross intrinsic orientation scale, the quest orientation started to challenge the former as an index of religious maturity. Several studies showed that quest positively correlates with characteristics of mental health (Batson & Ventis, 1982) and altruism (Batson & Ventis, 1982; Batson et al., 1988, 1989).

Batson and Ventis maintain that the quest religious orientation describes only the dimensionality of individual religion. Thus, it is invalid to treat religious orientations typologically, so one cannot say that somebody is —for instance— quest oriented or a "typical quester." R.D. Kahoe and M.J. Meadow (1981, Meadow, Kahoe, 1984) have proposed the opposite position, suggesting the developmental perspective of religious orientation dimensions. It does not explicitly mean that a person with a high score in the quest scale is the most religiously mature person.

II. Models of the developmental sequence of religious orientation.

Since the R.W. Hood Jr. (1985) critique of the "quest is best" supposition, and considering the growing awareness of the inevitability of normative presuppositions in psychological research (Kaplan, 1986; Kwilecki, 1988), the problem of a valid developmental perspective on religious orientations has become more complex. To solve this issue, I have considered the existing concepts of development of religious orientation in the works of Allport, Allport and Ross, Batson and Ventis, Meadow and Kahoe, Hood and Morris, and others. Then I have inferred the possible models of a developmental sequence of religious orientations. These models take for granted the presuppositions implied in the assumed outcome of a given sequence, which is —in most instances— the mature religious sentiment. The models are:

Model A (patterned on Allport-Ross concept):
Stage 1 —indiscriminate proreligious orientation,
Stage 2 —extrinsic religious orientation,
Stage 3 —intrinsic religious orientation,
Stage? —indiscriminate antireligious orientation. A question mark signifies an inability to make a correct classification of this stage — some results point out its more mature character than the "intrinsic" stage, while some others suggest the opposite.

Model B (patterned on Batson's quest and the Meadow-Kahoe concepts):
Stage 1 —extrinsic religious orientation,
Stage 2 —intrinsic religious orientation,
Stage 3 —quest religious orientation.

Model H (patterned on Hood's remarks on quest and intrinsic positions):
Stage 1 —extrinsic religious orientation,
Stage 2 —quest religious orientation (religious crisis),
Stage 3 —intrinsic religious orientation.

Model D (patterned on previous concepts and on the developmental principles of internalization, dialectic transformation, and disequilibrium, expressed also in J.W. Fowler's faith development theory):
Stage 1 —external religious orientation,
Stage 2 —doubting quest religious orientation (crisis quest orientation),
Stage 3 —indiscriminately proreligious orientation,
Stage 4 —doubting quest religious orientation (crisis quest orientation),
Stage 5 —internal religious orientation,
Stage 6 —quest religious orientation (mature quest, prophecy, unity of

quest and finding, unity of internal and external, etc.).

Theoretical criteria for assessing the validity of presented models of developmental sequence of religious orientation were:
(1) The principle of internalization. I assumed that the background for most of the religious orientations concepts is the psychological process of internalization, reflected in the trend from the external to internal and autonomous, subjective sources of one's —including religious— development. From this point of view, the Batson RLI scales, better than Allport-Ross scales, describe a shift from an external to an internal locus of personal development.
(2) The characteristics of mental health understood in terms of one's capacity to undergo further growth as a person and a member of society. I assumed that the indices of control attributions, emotional independence, and psycho-social competence would be the appropriate characteristics of mental health. I assumed, too, that in the same age range, about 18-20, individuals can display different levels of developments.

III. Research methods.

The issue of a possible sequential order in the development of religious orientation was investigated as a part of some research on the differences between autonomous (more mature) and nonautonomous (less mature) persons concerning their religiousness and world view (Socha, Latala & Filas, 1991; Socha, 1992).

The following methods were used to measure *religiousness* in this study:
(1) The Individual Religiousness Scale (IRS) (Latala & Socha, 1981), a Likert-type scale measuring religious attitude in terms of religious doctrine, religious morality, religious ritual, and religious organization. We consider this scale a measure of Roman Catholic orthodoxy.
(2) The Christian Religiousness Scale (CRS) (Socha, 1988, pp. 73-74), a Thurstone-type scale measuring religious attitude in terms of religion as a value, independent of one's religious affiliation (denomination or its rejection).
(3) Religious self-identification. This index is derived from item No. 10 of the IRS scale (not counted in the scale): "I am a believer."
(4) The Batson Religious Life Inventory (RLI) (Batson & Ventis, 1982). We limited this method to three scales: internal, external and interactional (here simply the quest scale). The scales have been

translated and validated for the Polish students population (Socha, Latala & Filas, 1990). We omitted the Allport-Ross scales because of the assumed internalization paradigm, and because of time restrictions.
(5) The index of the dynamics of individual religion. We administered an additional short questionnaire in which there was a question about the perceived dynamics of one's religion in the past. It allowed us to classify responses into categories, according to whether their religiousness —in their opinion— had changed in a more religious direction or in a less religious direction, or had not changed at all or persists in crisis.

The following methods enabled us to measure *mental health* in terms of psychological maturity:
(1) The "Ster" —an original technique for assessing the attribution of different categories of control (Socha, 1988; Socha, Latala & Filas, 1991). These were the attributions of self-control in terms of being able to influence on the self, the immediate social environment, society, the state, the Church, God, and fate (luck), and the attributions of influences of the above categories on one's self. In the next steps every subject attributed his or her influences on particular categories of the social environment (e.g. best friends, parents, teachers), and their influences on his or her self.
(2) The Emotional Dependence Scale (EDS) (Socha, 1983, 1988, Socha, Latala & Filas, 1991), a 45-item questionnaire (including the lie scale items) measuring emotional dependence. A low score in this scale was indicated emotional independence.
(3) The Sociometric Sheet of Autonomy Perception (SSAP), a sociometric measure of psychosocial competence through group members' ratings. An additional measure was a self-rating of one's psychosocial competence, using the same categories as in the peer ratings. We also compared self-ratings and peer ratings for each individual, in order to obtain an index of realistic self-esteem.

We administered the research instruments to 462 high school senior students from Krakow and its satellite towns. The scales were administered to groups of subjects (school classes) to make possible sociometric measurement with the SSAP technique.

IV. Analysis of the results.

Scores on the Batson RLI scales were first divided into high and low scores, according to the median. Following the IRS index of orthodoxy,

81 nonreligious or weakly religious subjects were excluded from the sample. Considering particular orientation one of the dimensions of religiousness, all the results were cross-tabulated. The patterns of cross-tabulation reflect the above models of the sequential development of religious orientation. **Tables 1 to 4** present the percentages of subjects put into the stage categories of models A, B, H, and D.
As one can easily notice, model A is not supported by the data.

I did not use the Allport-Ross scales; Batson's external scale measures the external sources of individual religion instead of the instrumental way of being religious. External scale correlates quite strongly with internal, and (in the American studies) more with intrinsicness than with extrinsicness. So the measurement of the extrinsic religious orientation —in its classical sense— was questionable here. Besides, the model based —more or less— on the Allport-Ross concept does not include the quest orientation, so it cannot be taken into account.

Table 1. Distribution of high (+) and low (-) results into stage categories reflecting model A of sequential development of religious orientation.

Scale	Categories (after the assumed sequence of stages)			
	1	2	3	?
External	+	+	-	-
Internal	+	-	+	-
% of results	70.4	1.1	22.4	6.1

Table 2. Distribution of high (+) and low (-) results into stage categories reflecting model B of sequential development of religious orientation.

Scale	Categories (after the assumed sequence of stages)					categ. outside model		
	1	2	3	4	5			
External	-	+	+	-	-	+	+	-
Internal	-	+	-	+	-	-	+	+
Quest	-	-	-	-	+	+	+	+
% of results	3.2	29.6	0.5	9.5	2.9	0.5	40.9	12.9

Most of the results do not fit into the assumed categories of models B and H: in model B, 54.9% of the results lie outside of the assumed sequence of stage categories, in model H, 83.9% of the results lie outside. On the other hand, in the case of model D there is a different situation. The distribution of results in model D covers 100% of categories. It also resembles a normal distribution curve (See **Figure 1**).

Table 3. Distribution of high (+) and low (-) results into categories reflecting model H of sequential development of religious orientation

Scale	Categories (after the assumed sequence of stages)							
	1	2	3	4	categories outside model			
External	-	+	-	-	+	+	+	-
Internal	-	-	-	+	-	+	+	+
Quest	-	-	+	-	+	-	+	+
% of results	3.2	0.5	2.9	9.5	0.5	29.6	40.9	12.9

Table 4. Distribution of high (+) and low (-) results into categories reflecting model D of sequential development of religious orientation.

Scale	Categories (after the assumed sequence of stages)							
	1	2	3	4	5	6	7	8
External	-	+	+	+	+	-	-	-
Internal	-	-	-	+	+	+	+	-
Quest	-	-	+	-	+	-	+	+
% of results	3.2	0.5	0.5	29.6	40.9	9.5	12.9	2.9

In order to make possible further verification of model D of the sequential development of religious orientation, I have limited its range of categories to four (from category 4 to category 7). The numbers in the rest of the categories appeared too small for statistical analyses. Therefore I have taken the next steps to apply model D, consisting of:
Stage category 4: external — internal (undifferentiated) religiousness;
Stage category 5: external — internal — quest (doubtful, undifferentiated) religiousness;

Stage category 6: internal (transformed after doubting) religiousness;
Stage category 7: internal — quest (doubtful) religiousness.

These are the most common types of religiousness among the our subjects. Thus, one may consider model D as verified to that extent.

The significance of the differences on measures of religiousness and personal maturity variables among these four stage categories of the sequential development of religious orientation was assessed by means of the t-test for differences between two groups. The following passages will show the results.

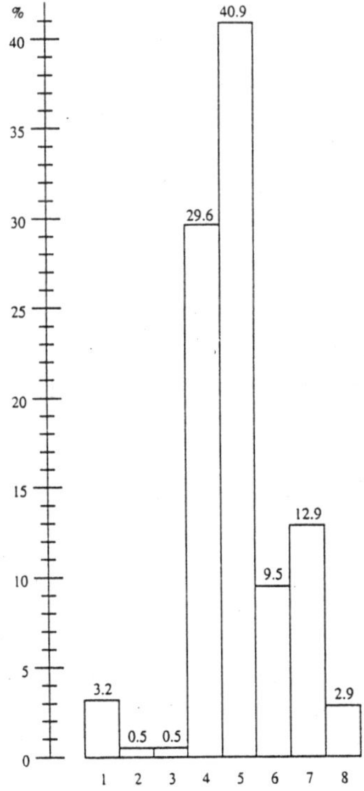

Fig. 1
Distribution of results in D model categories (after the assumed developmental sequence of stages of religious orientation), in percents. Total number of subjects N = 381.

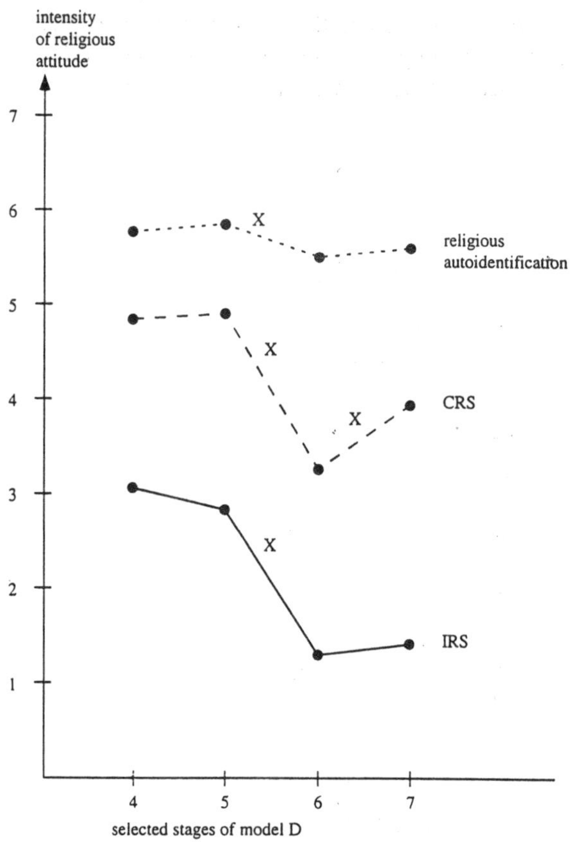

Fig. 2
Differences between the scores in the intensity of religious attitude variables for the stages of model D of sequential development of religious orientation. Letter "X" beside the given part of the plot points out the significant differences between two neighboring stages.

Stage categories of model D differ partly according to the intensity of religious attitude (Fig. 2). Particularly, a strong difference appears between stage categories 5 (external — internal — quest doubtful orientation) (See **Figure 2**) and 6 (internal orientation). That difference means, however, that the religiousness of the 6th stage category type has been lower, at least in terms of Roman Catholic orthodoxy. In the 7th (internal — quest) stage category, religiousness tends to be slightly stronger than in stage 6 (see the significant difference between the 6th and 7th stages in the CRS scale). There are also significant differences between the 6th and 7th stages in the IRS and self-identification variables. These differences indicate a less orthodox and still doubting religiousness.

Figure 3 shows differences between the selected stage categories of model D for the perceived dynamics of religiousness. Stage 6 seems to be different from the others. Subjects belonging to that category perceive their religiousness as less changing or as changing in a positive direction. Accordingly, comparing it with the stage 5 category, it shows significantly less crisis and nonreligious changes. Therefore, the internal religiosity appears to be stable, growing stronger, and more immune to crisis and weakening influences. (See **Figure 3**).

These influences had been perceived, however, by the persons belonging to the 5 th stage category (doubting undifferentiated religiosity). Stage category 7 has been less immune to crisis and antireligious influences. However, there is still no significant difference between it and category 6. At the same time —contrary to stage 6— this is a category of significantly more dynamic religiosity.

All the above confirm the relevance of religious orientation to perceived and also to real changes in individual religiousness. These allow us to figure out the development of religiosity throughout the selected stage categories of model D.

The distribution of the results on the scales measuring the intensity of religious attitudes, and also religious self-identification (Fig. 2) and religious dynamics (Fig. 3) suggests that it*would be more correct to change the order of the last two stage categories (6 and 7)*. Thus, the order of sequence of the development of religious orientation in terms of stage categories is as follows: *stage 4 - stage 5 - stage 7 - stage 6*. To stress the difference, in the following analysis the stages will be identified by Roman numerals: *stage 4 as I, stage 5 as II, stage 7 as III, and stage 6 as IV*.

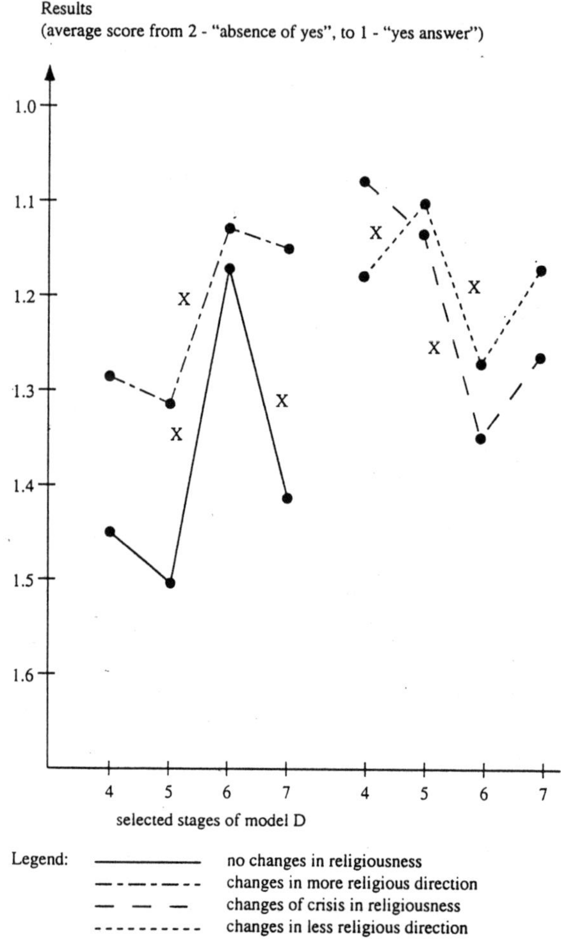

Fig. 3
Differences between the scores in the dynamics of perceived religiousness variables for the stages of model D of sequential development of religious orientation. Letter "X" beside the given part of the plot points out the significant differences between two neighboring stages.

One can figure out that perhaps before the quest orientation disappears (as it is present in the stage category 5 - now II), the external religious orientation must sufficiently diminish. It seems that the subjects passed over the external phase of their religiousness, and the doubting involved in that phase lost its role. If this way of thinking is correct, one can say that model D turns us partly back to R.W. Hood's ideas. It cannot be confirmed here, because the sample did not consist of fully adult persons. It is still possible that the subjects religiousness can further develop toward the more flexible, open, and existentially questing one, as well as an integrated and intrinsic one.

V. Verification of model D with psychological maturity variables.

The last step was to review the sequential order of religious orientation in model D in relation to the variables of psychological maturity. I computed the t-test values for each pair of neighboring stage categories (I and II, II and III, III, and IV) for these variables, and the "tau B" correlation coefficients for each of them (See **Table 5**)

Table 5. The differences between the neighboring stage categories of model D: t Student coefficient and tau B correlation coefficient for the whole variable of emotional dependence and the variable of religious development.

	Stage category					tau B
	I	II	III	IV	NonR	
Average sc.	5.21	5.07	4.24	4.25	3.98	-.179
"t"	0.715	3.418	-0.017			
p<	n.s.	.001	n.s.			.01

Legend: nonR = nonreligious persons
n.s. = nonsignificant difference

As Table 5 shows, there is only some evidence, namely correlations, to show that model D fits the distribution of emotional dependence scores (significant tau B). The only significant difference appeared between the II and III stages. This is insufficient for maintaining that as religiousness develops, independence increases. One could say, however, that growing out of the external position with the help of doubting has been confirmed with these data (See **Table 6**).

Table 6. The differences between the neighboring stage categories of model D: t Student coefficient and tau B correlation coefficient for the variables of control attributions of "Ster" technique and the sequence of religious development.

	Stage category					tau B
	I	II	III	IV	NonR	
Var:	SELF CAUSALITY					
Average sc.	4.82	4.87	5.10	4.86	5.14	-.030
"t"	0.239	-1.592	0.814			
p<	n.s.	n.s.	n.s.			n.s.
Var:	PARENTS CAUSALITY					
Average sc.	7.13	6.61	6.06	6.08	6.19	-.158
"t"	2.240	1.757	-0.047			
p<	.05	n.s.	n.s.			.01
Var:	FRIENDS, PEERS, GIRL-BOYFRIEND CAUSALITY					
Average sc.	5.39	5.25	5.24	5.22	5.20	-.017
"t"	0.888	0.032	0.083			
p<	n.s.	n.s.	n.s.			n.s.
Var:	TEACHER / RELIGION TEACHER CAUSALITY					
Average sc.	7.33	7.40	6.28	6.47	6.10	-.184
"t"	-0.466	5.043	-0.630			
p<	n.s.	.001	n.s.			

To be continued on the next page:

Table 6 continued:

	Stage category					tau B
	I	II	III	IV	NonR	
Var:	SOCIETY/STATE CAUSALITY					
Average sc.	6.79	6.61	6.30	6.66	6.38	-.067
"t"	1.007	1.258	-1.189			
p<	n.s.	n.s.	n.s.			
Var:	GOD/CHURCH CAUSALITY					
Average sc.	8.65	8.56	8.16	8.22	6.96	-.144
"t"	0.726	2.090	-0.195			
p<	n.s.	.005	n.s.			
var:	CASE/FATE/LUCK CAUSALITY					
Average sc.	7.41	6.87	7.75	7.33	6.76	.018
"t"	2.352	3.418	-0.017			
p<	.02	.001	n.s.			n.s.

Legend: nonR = nonreligious persons
n.s. = nonsignificant difference

Data presented in Table 6 show a quite complex picture of the relationships between model D and the "Ster" variables (these variables are the synthetic ones, developed as a result of taxonomic cluster analysis of the multiple character data of the "Ster" technique). Several variables —Parents Causality, Teacher/Religious Teacher Causality, God/Church Causality and Case/Fate/Luck Causality— appeared related to religious orientation development. These findings mean that most of their significant others had influenced the religious development of the subjects. The second regularity refers to the Case/Fate/Luck Causality variable, and suggests that dropping these attributions has something in common with the growth of the quest (doubting) religious orientation (stage II).

One can hardly explain all these findings. Generally, the diminishing influence of external causality seems to be connected with the development of religious orientation described by model D, particularly in transition from stage I to II and from stage II to III. There is no room here to show in detail how other synthetic variables of the "Ster" relate to model D. Briefly, they also show that the majority of differences within the ways of attributing the causality of different parts of one's world relate to the transitions between stages I and II, and stages II and III of model D.

The way classmates assess the psychosocial competence of their peers, which served here as an external criterion of one's psychological maturity, showed only a few significant relationships with the development of religious orientation (See **Table 7**).

Table 7. The differences between the neighboring stage categories of model D: t Student coefficient and tau B correlation coefficient for the variables of psychosocial competence measured with the sociometric technique SSAP and the sequence of development of religious orientation in model D.

	Stage category					tau B
	I	II	III	IV	NonR	
Var. I:	SOCIAL APPROVAL					
Average sc.	2.19	1.98	1.97	1.88	1.84	-.116
"t"		2.221	0.008	0.540		
p<		.05	n.s.	n.s.		.01
Var II:	POWER					
Average sc.	2.14	1.98	2.04	1.69	1.89	-.113
"t"		1.659	-0.460	1.895		
p<		n.s.	N.S.	n.s.		.04
Var III:	INTERPERSONAL KNOWLEDGE					
Average sc.	2.07	2.00	1.93	1.86	2.01	.010
"t"		0.738	0.471	0.460		
p<		n.s.	n.s.	n.s.		n.s.

to be continued on the next page:

Table 7 continued:

	Stage category					tau B
	I	II	III	IV	NonR	
Var IV:	TOLERANCE					
Average sc.	2.11	2.00	1.97	2.00	1.85	.059
"t"	1.173	0.220	-0.129			
p<	n.s.	n.s.	n.s.			n.s.
Var V:	INSIGHT IN THE CRITERIA OF ASSESSMENT OF PEOPLE USED BY THE OTHERS					
Average sc.	2.00	1.96	1.91	1.17	2.00	-.081
"t"	0.531	0.483	0.974			
p<	n.s.	n.s.	n.s.			n.s.
Var VI:	ALTRUISM					
Average sc.	2.14	2.04	1.81	1.88	1.86	-.122
"t"	1.090	1.842	-0.414			
p<	n.s.	n.s.	n.s.			.03
Var VII:	AUTOTELIC MOTIVATION					
Average sc.	1.93	1.98	1.85	2.02	2.01	-.006
"t"	-0.549	1.075	-1.080			
p<	n.s.	n.s.	n.s.			n.s.

to be continued on the next page:

Table 7 continued:

	Stage category					tau B
	I	II	III	IV	NonR	
Var VIII:	LEVEL OF ORGANIZATION OF ONES'S OWN ACTIVITY					
Avera-ge sc.	2.08	2.09	2.02	1.83	1.91	-.057
"t"	-0.099	0.532	1.121			
p<	n.s.	n.s.	n.s.			n.s.
Var IX	AUTORITY COMING FROM ONE'S OWN PSYCHOSOCIAL COMPETENCE					
Avera-ge sc.	2.18	2.03	2.06	1.91	1.86	-.090
"t"	1.643	-0.232	0.931			
p<	n.s.	n.s.	n.s.			n.s.

A relevant difference in social approval relates to stages I and II: Subjects with religious quest are more liked than those without it. There are also two significant correlations between the order of sequential development of religious orientation described in model D and two aspects of psychosocial maturity: Power and Altruism. These correlations suggest a positive relationship between the development of religious orientation and those characteristics of psychosocial competence: the more developed the religious orientation of the subjects, the more likely they will stay group leaders and behave in an altruistic way.

Finally, the sociometric criteria of psychosocial competence did not confirm the assumed relationship between the development of religious orientation and positive mental health. This relationship concerns only selected, though important, features of it.

There were no significant correlations or differences between the neighboring stage categories of model D and the variables of self-assessment on psychosocial competence (as it was measured additionally during the investigations with the SSAP technique). More promising seemed the level of realism of self-esteem, measured in terms of the relation of self-esteem to classmates' assessment with the use of the same psychosocial criterions. As Table 8 shows, there is no relationship between any of the stage categories and the index of realism of self-esteem (See **Table 8**).

Table 8. The differences between the neighboring stage categories of model D: t Student coefficient and tau B correlation coefficient for the variable of realism of self-esteem and the sequence of development of religious orientation in model D.

	Stage category					tau B
	I	II	III	IV	NonR	
Average sc.	4.56	4.29	4.51	4.38	4.25	-.025
"t"	1.156	-0.690	0.291			
p<	n.s.	n.s.	n.s.			n.s.

VI. Conclusion.

The aim of the research was to specify a possible model of sequential development of religious orientation, according to an original concept offered by G.W. Allport and developed further by others in terms of religious orientations: extrinsic, intrinsic and quest. Although in this study there were limited possibilities for the realizing of this aim (partly incomplete scales of religious orientations and non-longitudinal design of the measurement), I believe that the results may nevertheless be of interest to other researchers. The data showed the most likely sequence of religious orientation development.

Although the assumed relationships between the proposed model of sequential development of religious orientation appeared unequivocally, one is able to state that *in some aspects of mental health, understood in terms of psychological maturity, the proposed model D describes the ideal way for religious development*, at least in our population and culture. Converting this thinking, *one can propose the model D of sequential development of religious orientation as a possible criterion for assessing positive mental health*. Nevertheless, it is necessary to continue the empirical and methodological efforts to develop the validity of this model.

REFERENCES

Allport, G. W. (1950). *The individual and his religion, A psychological interpretation*. New York: Macmillan.

Allport, G. W. & Ross, J. M. (1967) Personal religious orientation and prejudice. *Journal of Personality and Social Psychology*, *5*, 432-443.

Batson, C. D. (1976) Religion as prosocial: Agent or double agent? *Journal for the Scientific Study of Religion*, *15(1)*, 29-46.

Batson, C. D. & Ventis, L. W. (1982). *The religious experience: A social-psychological perspective*. New York: Oxford University Press.

Batson, C. D. & Ventis, L. W. (1985). Misconception of quest: A reply to Hood and Morris. *Review of Religious Research*, *28*, 398-407.

Batson, C. D. et al. (1983). Religious prosocial motivation: Is it altruistic or egoistic? *Journal of Personality and Social Psychology*, *22*, 38-50.

Batson, C. D. et al. (1988). Five studies testing two new egoistic alternatives to the empathy-altruism hypothesis, *Journal of Personality and Social Psychology*, *5*, 52-77.

Hood, R. W. Jr. (1985). The conceptualization of religious purity in Allport's typology, *Journal for the Scientific Study of Religion*, *24*, 413-417.

Hood, R. W. & Morris, R. J. (1985). Conceptualization of quest: A critical rejoinder to Batson, *Review of Religious Research*, *26*, 391-397.

Kahoe, R. D. & Meadow, M. J. (1981). A developmental perspective of religious orientations dimensions, *Journal of Religion and Health*, *20*, 8-17.

Kaplan, B. (1986). Value presuppositions in theories of human development. IN: L. Cirillo & S. Wapner (Eds.), *Value presuppositions in theories of human development*. Hillsdale, New Jersey: Lawrence Erlbaum Associates, 81-103.

Kirkpatrick, L. A. & Hood, R. W. Jr. (1990). Intrinsic-extrinsic religious orientation: The boon or bane of contemporary psychology of religion? *Journal for the Scientific Study of Religion*, *29*, 442-462.

Kwilecki, S. (1988). A scientific approach to religious development: proposals and a case study, *Journal for the Scientific Study of Religion*, *27(3)*, 307-325.

Maslow, A. H. (1968). *Towards a psychology of being*, New York: Van Nostrand.

Maslow, A. H. (1971). *The farther reaches of human nature*, New York: Viking Compass Press.

Socha, P. (1983). *Zarys psychospolecznych uwarunkowan stosunku do religii* (An outline of the psychosocial determinants of the relations to religion). Ph.D. thesis, Jagiellonian University, Krakow, Poland.

Socha, P. (1988). *Religijnosc jako zrodlo zroznicowania osobowosci pod wzgledem autonomii* (Religiousness as a source of personality differentiation with regard to autonomy). Warszawa: ANS.

Socha, P. (1992). *Rozwoj orientacji religijnej i swiatopogladowej* (Development of religious and world view orientations). Krakow: Jagiellonian University Press.

Socha, P., Latala, A. & Filas, R. (1991). *Religijnosc osob autonomicznych i nieautonomicznych. Studium empiryczne* (Religiousness of the autonomous and nonautonomous persons. An empirical study), Krakow: Zaklad Wydawniczy "Nomos."

Tyler, F. B. (1978). Individual psychosocial competence: A personality configuration, *Educational and Psychosocial Measurement*, *38*, 309-323.

Waters, E. & Sroufe, L.A. (1983). Social competence as developmental construct, *Developmental Review*, *3*, 79-97.

CHAPTER 9
AN EXPERIMENTAL PERSPECTIVE ON RELIGION AS A THERAPEUTIC RESOURCE

L.B. Brown

While it is unlikely that any decision to make a psychiatric referral is now made simply on the basis of a patient's religious beliefs or actions, some people still think that being religious, or more commonly, belonging to a "cultic" minority religious group, is itself a sign of an almost psychotic irrationality. On the other hand, recent rules about equal opportunity, at least in Australia, preclude discrimination against anyone on the grounds of their age, sex, race, political opinion and "religious belief or absence of such belief."

Despite this constraint, there is a continuing "dance" (as Mansell Pattison put it) between psychiatry and religion. In the DSM IIIR (1987) Glossary, specific references to religious material are used to illustrate catatonic posturing, delusions, depression, incoherence, magical thinking, and "poverty in the content of speech". "Catatonic posturing", for example, refers to a patient who "may stand with arms outstretched as if he were Jesus on the cross", while grandiose delusions "may have a religious, somatic, or other theme". Other references to religion are found under schizotypal and histrionic personality disorders, and tangentially under "delusional (paranoid) disorder". This analysis emphasises the ambiguity of the secular implications of religion (Harned, 1958) and its expressive or instrumental "uses".

Religions can be rejected on a variety of grounds, including their alignment with paranoia, as when someone claims to have "heard the voice of God", although that is still an important way to find or express one's Christianity, or with depression when a person's religion is characterised by a sense of guilt (cf Prosen et al., 1983). Nevertheless, Ellis (1971) emphasised the psychological dangers of religious guilt and Chesen (1972) held the general view that religion could be hazardous to health. Those whose religion is focussed on an institutional tradition might, however, be less likely to be so closely aligned with its doctrines and practices that they would draw attention to themselves psychiatrically.

A contrasting psychiatric view is to be found in Robinson (1986) which, like the DSM IIIR, is published by the American Psychiatric Association, but stresses the therapeutic value of religion, with a note that "healing and religion have been separated only for a few centuries" (p. ix). Jerome Frank (1988) adopted a similarly positive stance in arguing for the "beneficial effect of shrines, religious healing, and other placebo effects (sic) in pharmaceutical and surgical treatments". It is also clear that "religious conviction" has a therapeutic role in providing supportive social networks that facilitate coping (Young and Dowling, 1987; Folkman and Lazarus et al, 1986), and that it can induce happiness (Argyle, 1987). In the same vein, Galanter (1990) suggests a "relief effect" in the "psychiatric impact of charismatic groups".

Earlier work I have been involved with showed that prayer, as an aspect of help seeking, forms part of a commonly available coping repertoire which, together with distraction, self-consolation, and affect reduction, can be used successfully to alleviate a depressive episode (Parker and Brown, 1982, 1986). A different set of studies has shown that while the responsibility for good outcomes or events can be assigned to God, bad outcomes are typically expected to be a responsibility of those directly involved with them (Lalljee, Brown and Hilton, 1990; Furnham and Brown, 1991). Such implicit patterns are in sharp contrast to the direct links that are expected between religious attitudes, beliefs or practices and personality traits, especially for those in "unusual" religions (cf. Larson et al., 1986). But Bergin's (1983) meta-analysis of 24 studies found little support for that opinion.

Prejudices about the psychiatric or "psychological" consequences of religion could, however, involve a generalised context effect that might be like the assumed madness of the English that Shakespeare refers to in Hamlet. In a conversation in Act V Scene I, the grave-digger says that if Hamlet does not recover his wits in England, "'tis no great matter", since "'Twill not be seen in him there. There the men are as a mad as he" (lines 149-150). As we have seen, an opposing view holds that religion can have an important role in maintaining mental health and social adjustment. Strong differences in the ways religions are assessed could therefore over-ride whatever the positive or negative consequences of religious commitment, belief, or practice might be.

That religiousness is not necessarily linked to psychiatric problems was shown by Kroll and Sheehan (1989) in a study of the religious beliefs, practices and experience of 52 psychiatric patients which "accord with national and local public poll results", from which they concluded that "religion is an important factor in most patients' lives." But to be able to identify the effects that religion might have it is important to clarify common expectations about the role of religious alignments in causing or resolving psychological disturbances, and prevailing attitudes to religious coping as a form of either personal or institutional control.

The present study.

Although I had initially planned to study the forms of religion that might warrant a psychiatric referral or diagnosis, preliminary work suggested that such decisions involve a range of moderators which include the nature of the illness, the social support that is available, and the patient's religious commitment. Furthermore, following Jones et al. (1971), differences in the judged usefulness of religion can be expected between the attitudes of those who are outsiders rather than insiders to it. Outsiders may disregard religious solutions because of the adverse effects they are assumed to have (especially on mental health), or because of a failure to understand what insiders take for granted about religious practices, when they draw on firm prejudices to identify the characteristicss of a "religious" person. Nevertheless, Gaston and Brown (1991) found that among both religious and non-religious individuals there is a strong bias to assign feminine characteristics to those described as "religous" and masculine characteristics to those who were simply described as "not religious", while Sprock et al. (1990) found that the personality disorders in DSM IIIR are strongly aligned with feminine characteristics.

The present study, based on answers to a set of 16 vignettes, was therefore designed to identify differences in the judgments that might be made by a large group of Australian University students about the usefulness of religious practices. It aimed to identify some of the contexts within which specific conclusions are drawn about the place of religion in helping a recovery from illness, by asking them about the appropriateness of two religious and two non-religious solutions after a differential diagnosis had been made between cancer, as a severe physical illness, and a mild psychological distress in which there was said to be "nothing wrong". (Referring to a diagnosis of cancer in this context has the advantage that it is both life-threatening and more categorical than most psychiatric diagnoses.)

The vignettes were modified from those developed in the U.S.A. by Lilliston who, in two separate studies, compared the effectiveness of three religious solutions against reading (as an informational and non-religious solution) for two diagnoses or problems. In the first study, Lilliston and Brown (1971) identified the target person as male, and they offered Church-going, prayer, and "involvement with a group emphasising intense emotional religious experience", as religious solutions. Although they found that adopting any of those religious solutions was less highly valued than an informational solution, the religious solutions were thought more reasonable for a life-threatening problem (cancer) than for the psychological problem. In their second study, which focussed on a female target, Lilliston, Brown and Schliebe (1972) found that the intensely emotional religious experience was valued less than either church-going or prayer, which were found to be "as effective as an informational solution."

The stimulus material for this Australian study was constructed to examine three factors: the sex of the target person as either a man or a woman, their diagnosis of cancer or a mild psychological distress and the solutions they adopted as "religious", by deciding either to go to Church regularly or to begin praying, or as "non-religious" when they contemplated suicide or decided to "read as much as they could about what was wrong with them". Lilliston's third religious solution (which had not worked well) was replaced by suicide to balance the religious and non-religious solutions, and because suicide was expected to be an important issue for the subjects who were religious. But suicide was rejected as a solution by nearly all these Australian students, although they approved of reading about what was wrong.

Each participant in the experiment was asked to evaluate only two vignettes from the full set of 16. Those two were selected so that each person was asked to react only to male or female targets, to both diagnoses and to one religious and one non-religious solution. The subjects were asked to rate each vignette they were given for how reasonable or effective the identified solution would be in dealing with the problem, whether the target person would need help from a "professional counsellor, such as a psychologist, social worker or psychiatrist", whether they would themselves be likely to act in the same way in that situation, and if anything else could be done that might be more successful. The form of the questionnaire is shown in Figure 1. (See **Figure 1**).

Figure 1: Showing a form of the questionnaire

A 42 year old middle class man (or woman, with appropriate gender changes throughout the text), married with two children, who had worked in car sales for 15 years, used to play golf and tennis in his spare time and enjoyed reading novels. Having felt unwell for about a month, he went to his G.P. who, after examining him, told him that he probably had cancer and referred him on to a specialist (or that he could find nothing wrong with him).

This man's initial reaction was to begin going to church (or to pray, consider suicide, or going to the library to read...) regularly, which was something he had not done since his childhood.

Please show how much you agree or disagree with each of the following reactions to what this man did, on the following scale:

Disagree strongly 1: 2: 3: 4: 5: 6: 7: 8: 9 Agree strongly

Score 1 if you strongly *disagree* with it through 5 if you might agree or disagree, to 9 if you strongly *agree* with it

A. He will probably need to seek help from a professional counsellor, such as a psychologist, social worker or psychiatrist.

Disagree strongly 1: 2: 3: 4: 5: 6: 7: 8: 9 Agree strongly

B. His approach to dealing with the anxiety generated by his problem is reasonable and will probably be effective.

Disagree strongly 1: 2: 3: 4: 5: 6: 7: 8: 9 Agree strongly

C. If I were in a situation like this man's I would most probably do what he did.

Disagree strongly 1: 2: 3: 4: 5: 6: 7: 8: 9 Agree strongly

Is there anything else he could have done that might be more successful?

Yes Don't know No

If you think he should do something else, list some of the things that could be more successful.

Data are available from 508 psychology students at the University of New South Wales, whose ages ranged from 17 to 53, with a mean of 21.6 (S.D. = 6.82). Each subject was asked about their sex and age, their religious denomination, how often they attended "religious services", the place of religion in their life, and how much "comfort" they received at Church, as well as whether they had a transcendental view of the world, and were pro- or anti-religious. The patterns of response for those characteristics are summarised in Table 1, which shows the levels of interest in religion in this diverse group of students. (See **Table 1**)

Table 1 Showing the sample's characteristics (in percentages)

		Male	Female	
1.	Sex	33 (n=167)	67 (n=341)	
2.	Age (not stated = 8)			
	Under 19	52	62	
	20 to 29	42	25	
	Over 30	6	13	
3.	Religious denomination (not stated = 23)			
	Catholic	28	24	
	Anglica or Orthodox	16	18	
	Protestant	5	6	
	Other[1]	35	39	
	Atheist or Agnostic	16	13	
	[1] Includes Christian unspecified, Buddhist, Moslem, and Other			
4.	How often do you attend religious services?			(not stated = 21)
	Never	23	18	
	Rarely	44	48	
	Once or twice a month	11	13	
	About once a week or more	22	21	
5.	What place does religion have in your life?			(not stated = 23)
	Not important	46	36	
	Quite important	34	43	
	Very important	20	21	

6. Regardless of whether you like the outcome, what percentage of the time would you actually receive comfort at church, in times of trouble and sorrow? (not stated = 10)

0 - 20%	51	50
21 - 40%	14	13
41 - 60%	8	11
61 - 80%	17	14
81 - 100%	10	12

7. To what extent is your own world view a transcendental or religious one? (9 point scale) (not stated = 5)

Low (1 - 3)	31	21
Medium (4 - 6)	31	33
High (7 - 9)	38	46

8. Position on a 9 point anti- pro-religious scale (not stated = 15)

Anti-religious (1-3)	23	18
Neither (4-6)	36	37
Pro-religious (7-9)	41	45

9. Religious commitment (summing items 4 & 5) (not stated = 23)

None (2)	16	16
Low (3-4)	46	47
Medium (5)	11	12
High (6-7)	24	25

When the scores for each participant's answers to questions about their religiousness were factor analysed (with a varimax rotation) across the whole sample, three factors with eigen values greater than 0.96 emerged. The first factor, which accounted for 58 per cent of the variance, involves religious commitment since all the religious variables except religious affiliation had loadings greater than 0.73 on it. The second and third factors each accounted for 11 per cent of the variance and were defined by religious affiliation and by age, with each of those variables loading 0.97 on its own factor. The subject independent variables therefore cover their age, sex, religious affiliation (as denomination) and religious commitment, with a score for religious commitment calculated for each subject by summing their answers to the questions about how often they attend religious services (on a four-step scale) and the importance of religion in their life (on three steps). Another set of independent variables covered the sex of the targets in the vignettes, the severity of their diagnosis, and the subjects' ratings of the specific solutions they were said to have adopted. Both sets of independent variables were entered into a step-wise regression analysis for each of the four separate dependent or outcome variables, which involved the effectiveness of the solution, whether the target would need further professional help, if the subject would do the same, and whether they suggested another solution. Scores on these outcome variables were calculated separately for each question as a deviation from the mean of the answers given by each participant to the two vignettes they received, to control for their interdependence. These sets of scores were therefore (raw V1) — (mean V1 + V2) = D1, and (raw V2) — (mean V1 + V2) = D2 (where V1 is the rating of the first vignette and V2 the rating of the second, with D1 and D2 the deviation scores).

Results

The broad perspective on the results, in Table 2 shows that suicide was the least effective solution but the one that most warrants help from a professional counsellor. It is also the one least likely to be followed by the subjects themselves. In answering the question about the need for "some other solution", a majority (67 per cent) identified a specific course of action, the most common being to seek a second opinion and to "live it up". No one offered another religious solution in answer to this question. (See **Table 2**)

Table 2 Showing the raw mean ratings over-all for each question for each vignette.

		Solutions			
Question	*Diagnosis*	Church	Pray	Suicide	Reading
1. Effectiveness of the solution	a. Cancer	5.20	4.82	2.95	5.86
	b. Nothing	5.38	4.49	2.72	3.86
2. Need professional help	a. Cancer	5.71	5.45	7.03	5.92
	b. Nothing	4.89	4.95	6.67	5.47
3. Would do the same	a. Cancer	4.27	4.81	2.94	6.32
	b. Nothing	4.13	4.14	2.49	2.88

4. Another possible solution	a. Cancer	1.47	1.60	1.30	1.62
	b. Nothing	1.53	1.44	1.27	1.23

Table 3 Multiple stepwise regressions on major predictors against each dependent variable.

Variables	*B*	SE_B	*Beta*	*T*
Effectiveness of the solution (R^2 = .508, N = 916)				
R commit. x R/NR solution	.370	.047	.583	7.95***
sex of subject x diagnosis	-.186	.028	-.191	6.66***
sex of subject x NR soln.	.213	.039	.154	5.39***
sex of subject x R soln.	.210	.039	.152	5.33***
R/NR soln.	-.857	.208	-.510	4.11***
sex of subject x R/NR soln.	.299	.102	.307	2.95**
sex of subject x diagnosis x NR soln.	-.104	.039	-.076	2.65**
sex of subject x diagnosis x R soln.	.103	.039	.075	2.62**
Constant -.003	.048	0.07		
Need to seek professional help (R^2 = .454, N = 917)				
R/NR soln. -.542	.045	-.357	12.07	***
sex of subject x diagnosis	-.146	.026	-.166	5.61***
NR soln. (reading or suicide)	-.330	.063	-.153	5.19***
R. soln. (church or prayer)	-.320	.063	-.149	5.06***
sex of target x diagnosis x R/NR soln.	.116	.045	.076	2.57*
Constant -.002.	.045	0.05		
Would do the same thing (R^2 = .515, N = 917)				
diagnosis (cancer or nothing)	-.359	.040	-.256	8.98***
R commit. x R/NR soln.	.334	.039	.632	8.65***
R/NR soln.	-.624	.102	-.446	6.09***
sex of target x diagnosis	.215	.040	.153	5.36***
NR soln. (reading or suicide)	.269	.057	.136	4.75***
R commit. x R soln.	.092	.021	.124	4.34***
diagnosis x R/NR soln.	.182	.040	.130	4.54***
sex of target x R/NR soln.	.171	.040	.122	4.26***
R commit	-.137	.040	-.101	3.44***
diagnosis x R soln.	.214	.056	.108	3.79***
denomination	.064	.028	.067	2.28*
sex of subject x diagnosis x NR soln.	.-.072	.033	-.063	2.19*
Constant	-.020	.150	0.13	

Another possible solution (R^2 = .620, N = 906)

diagnosis (cancer or nothing)	-.189	.015	-.328	12.44***
R commit. x R/NR soln..	065	.006	.302	11.48***
sex of target x R soln.	-.178	.021	-.219	8.28***
sex of target x diagnosis x NR soln.	-.171	.021	-.210	7.97***
sex of target x NR soluts..	.150	.021	.184	6.98***
sex of target x diagnosis x R soln.	-.092	.022	-.113	4.28***
sex of subject x church frequency	-.037	.008	-.133	4.78***
sex of subject x age	.004	.001	.113	4.02***
diagnosis x R soln.	.260	.078	.320	3.32***
sex of subject x diagnosis x NR soln.	-.112	.045	-.238	2.47*
sex of target	-.037	.015	-.065	2.46*
diagnosis x R/NR soln.	.034	.015	.059	2.22*
sex of target x NR soln.	-.032	.015	-.055	2.09*
R commit. x R soln.	.016	.008	.054	2.05*
Constant	.271	.041	0.01	

Note. SE_B = standard error of regression for B, and R = religious,

NR = non-religious, commit. = commitment, soln. = solution

*p < .05. **p < .01. ***p < .001.

A correlational analysis of the scores on the religious variables and the dependent (outcome) variables shows consistently strong relationships between the separate measures of religious commitment and the efficacy of Church-going and prayer (around .30), and whether the subjects would do the same themselves (around .50). Correlations around .20 (which were significant) between proposing another solution and the religious variables suggest that some other solution would be needed less when Church-going than when prayer was the chosen course of action. When those religious solutions were rated on nine-point Likert scales, the mean rated effectiveness over-all for Church-going was 5.29, and 4.65 for prayer. Reading about their condition, which most of the subjects said they would be likely to do themselves, was judged more effective for cancer (with a mean of 5.86) than when there was nothing wrong.

The only consistent age-related trend shows that older subjects said that any solution, but especially Church-going or prayer, would need "professional help", which suggests that they have given up the belief that those religious practices might have direct effects. This parallels Reik's (1955) theory that prayer involves three "stages", in praying first for "my will" to be done, then that "thy will" might be done, and later for "thy will to be done with my active help".

So far as sex is concerned, not only did the women subjects judge going to Church to be significantly more effective for the woman with cancer, they also identified with that solution themselves. The step-wise regression analyses showed significant interactions between the sex of the subjects and the sex of the targets for the effectiveness of the solutions, and between the sex of the subjects and the religious and non-religious solutions, with the females reacting more confidently both to the religious and the non-religious solutions. A three-way interaction between the sex of the subjects, the targets' diagnosis and the two religious solutions showed that, taken together, these effects support the consistent finding that women are more "religious" than men on all criteria, except for holding official positions in a Church (Brown, 1987, p. 132). Detailed results from the separate regression analyses are in Table 3. (See **Table 3**)

The effectiveness of the solution.

There was an over-all $F = 39.57$ ($p < .000$) that accounted for 51 per cent of the variance for the effectiveness of the solutions. The religious versus the non-religious solutions was a significant predictor (beta = .51, $p < .000$), although that factor interacted significantly with the religious commitment of the subjects (beta = -.58, $p < .000$), showing an explicit bias for those who are more religious to expect a greater effect for a religious solution. Although there were no significant interactions for the target's sex, the sex of the subjects and their advocacy of religious and non-religious solutions was significant. Furthermore, male and female subjects expected different effects from the separate solutions to each diagnosis, with the women expecting more benefit from the religious solutions for a diagnosis of cancer.

The need for further professional help.

The second regression analysis, against the need for additional help from a counsellor, had an overall $F = 47.2$, $p < .000$, and accounted for 45 per cent of the variance. It is clear that the non-religious solutions (suicide and reading) were thought to require more professional help than Church-going or prayer (beta = -.36, $p < .001$), as also would the woman with cancer.

Would the subjects "do the same thing?"

For this equation, with $F = 27.24$, $p < .000$, the subjects said they would be less likely to do the same thing when they were offered a non-religious, than when they had a religious solution (beta = -.45, $p < .001$). A significant interaction between the subjects' religious commitment and their preferred solutions (beta = .63, $p < .000$) shows that the more religiously committed preferred a religious solution for themselves. Moreover, the Catholics and Anglicans are more likely than other Protestants, or those in non-christian religious traditions to have said that they would do the same, when they were offered religious solutions.

Other solutions suggested.

The fourth multiple regression concerned whether or not "another solution" would be appropriate (with $F = 39.79$, $p < .000$), which again depended largely on the diagnosis (beta = .33, $p = .001$), with differences between the efficacy of the solutions adopted and the sex of the target. That some other solution would be needed when the diagnosis was cancer, but not when there was nothing wrong, supports the face validity of the data, since cancer is serious and warrants a broad approach to its treatment. Significant three-way interactions between the sex of the targets, their diagnosis and the solutions proposed have already been referred to and emphasise that the men suggested that something other than religion would be needed when there was nothing wrong.

The coherence of the results.

From a religious perspective, the consistent differences that have been found in the overall efficacy of religious and non-religious solutions following a differential diagnosis, show that the subjects were not driven to give those responses simply because of their religious commitment, since there were subtle differences in judgements about the efficacy of Church-going and prayer. When there is nothing wrong, prayer is more effective than Church-going, although prayer and Church-going were judged to be equally effective for cancer. While suicide and reading were thought to be equally (in)effective, reading would be better for cancer, with the difference between suicide and reading greater than that between Church-going and prayer. Those who contemplated suicide were expected to need professional help more often than those who had chosen to read, although those who decided to go to Church would also need more help than those who might have decided to pray. That the sex of the target or the subjects did not by itself predict any of the outcome judgements here is surprising, granted Lilliston's strong conclusion about sex differences, although that conclusion was reached from two separate studies. But my Table 3 shows that sex does have a complex effect on the results that is not restricted to its prejudiced link with religion.

In summary, whether religious or non-religious solutions were advocated depends on whether the targets had cancer or had nothing wrong with them. With a diagnosis of cancer, Church-going and prayer are equally effective, and although the non-religious solutions were judged less effective than the religious solutions, they would require more professional help. Those who are "religious" advocated the efficacy of Church-going and prayer, but not independently of the diagnosis. Suicide was, however, disapproved independently of the religiousness of the respondents.

Discussion.

The results from this study show a pattern which emphasises that individuals tailor their decisions about the efficacy of religious and non-religious solutions for specific diagnoses in a way that is consistent with their own religious commitment. The absence of significant main effects for any of the subject variables suggests that their answers were driven by widespread social attitudes to what is expected of religious and other solutions. This emphasises the primacy of social and contextual factors, and the importance of insiders' prototypic knowledge about when it is appropriate to use particular religious practices. The pattern of these results is reminiscent of Stark's (1990, p.386) remark that "humans are primarily rational creatures (and) ... when they do science correctly humans must respect the rules of logic and evidence that are hard-won fruits of their millennia of rationalism." Perhaps this also applies to religion, so that the links between religion and mental illness that I began with could reflect over-generalised attributions that reproduce the prejudices surrounding Western attitudes to religion, which are not checked often enough for their validity.

The results I have described show clear differences that reflect particular alignments with (or against) religion, and well-differentiated advocacies, with the more "religiously" committed more convinced about the efficacy of religious solutions, even if only in defined situations. That religious and non-religious groups (or individuals) try to constrain access to secular procedures or advice, and not only in medical domains, emphasises the potential for conflict between religious and other forms of knowledge. Bowker (1987, p.1) called those religious constraints "licensed insanities", and an "unacceptable face of religion" that typifies the bitter cultural, social, and personal conflicts which identify "religion" for many people.

The strands of argument that I brought together in building this study suggest the importance for any coping strategy of the specific contexts that can make particular solutions possible, and give meaning to them. While the study moved away from questions about religion and mental health, no religious perspective is carved from some amorphous psychic structure, since they are shaped by traditions that have, in their turn, helped to form those aspects of the secular world with which religion must interact. To withdraw from society into one's own spiritual community, as a solution for problems at the boundary between religious and secular domains, easily generates outsiders' suspicions about the equivalence of religiousness and mental illness, that could be fuelled by misinformation In a survey of 2,500 American women, for example, Shaver et al. (1980) found that those who had maintained the same religious affiliation all their lives were "healthy-minded", while converts had had "less religious childhoods, stronger adult religiousness and greater authoritarian tendencies". Witztum, Greenberg and Dasburgh (1990) found that similar dissatisfaction in a group in Israel had provided the impetus for them to change "their religious beliefs and life style". This group included "a large number of people who have been unstable for many years, who turned to orthodox Judaism in order to find tranquillity. Once the glow of arrival has abated, chronic problems re-emerge".

Although my data from this vignette study can not support exaggerated claims about how people might react when they must confront a diagnosis of cancer, they show that coping and the skills it requires tap an important facet of religion. A strong advantage of using a vignette methodology is the opportunity it gives to track a few parameters of religious responsiveness, showing for example, that prayer and Church-going, as major religious responses, are not aligned with a set of undifferentiated attitudes.

Further steps in the work I have reported might try to understand how it is that religion comes to be integrated into the lives of religious people, and why an apparently easy rhetoric about the usefulness of Church-going and prayer seems able to help maintain it. While we know too little of how religion is used as a therapeutic or coping device, Pargament's (1988) analysis of collaborative, deferring and self-directing religious styles of coping offers a model that would help to clarify how religious solutions are applied, once a diagnosis has been made and the existential abyss is to be confronted. Within this context we might remember that the ICD-9-CM's "V codes" refer to "factors influencing health status and contact with health services", which are primarily "psychological". Furthermore, "religious beliefs, and decisions based on personal value judgments about the advantages and disadvantages of the proposed treatment" is offered in DSM IIIR as a possible explanation for "non-compliance with medical treatment".

It seems that religions work for those who can accept them, although there is a further ambiguity in expecting internal, subjective or spiritual processes to support the external and institutional perspectives that themselves influence the members of a tradition, and which some hope to transcend.

Erik Fromm (1950) remarked that psychiatrists must be concerned with the truth of an idea — "otherwise they could not speak of a delusion or a paranoid system". The psychological truths of religion are "rational" as long as they are socially sanctioned and can pragmatically support what it is that they are expected to do (following Austin, 1962). This includes helping to alleviate the hazards of illness, whether it is severe and life-threatening or involves mistaken ideas about what might be wrong, which itself questions prejudices about the close alignment of religion with mental illness.

The balance between religious and secular solutions and their roles in any explanations that are offered present crucially important problems to us all, granted the respect, if not acceptance, religion is given in Western societies. Psychological or psychiatric, and sociological or religious explanations each capture something of the impact of the crises we face on our social and personal life, and mental or physical health. Furthermore, that different religious groups have disagreed so readily about the appropriateness or rationality of others' religious practices and claims or interpretations made heresy the traditional technique for dealing with religious deviance, through appeals to an accepted orthodoxy that would support an authoritative power to invalidate whatever was judged at the time to be heterodox (cf Deconchy, 1991). Charges of heresy are uncommon now, and a great deal that was once "deviant" is tolerated by many sections, if not by the whole of modern society. But modal responses still distinguish those who are religious from those who are not, and continue to make religious solutions attractive to those who are themselves "religious". The results of this study show, however, that such religious judgments are not global, either for those who do, or who do not claim a religion for themselves.

REFERENCES

American Psychiatric Association (1987). *Diagnostic and statistical manual of mental disorders* (Third Edition-Revised DSMIIIR). Washington, D.C. American Psychiatric Association.

Argyle, M. (1987). *The psychology of happiness*. London: Methuen.

Austin, J. L. (1962). *How to do things with words*. Oxford: Oxford University Press.

Bergin, A. E. (1983). Religiosity and mental health: a critical re-evaluation and meta-analysis. *Professional Psychology: Research and Practice*, *14*, 170-184.

Bowker, J. (1987). *Licensed insanities: religions and belief in God in the contemporary world*. London: Darton, Longman and Todd.

Brown, L. B. (1987). *The psychology of religious belief*. London: Academic Press.

Chesen, E. S. (1972). *Religion may be hazardous to your health*. New York: P.H. Wyden.

Deconchy, J. P. (1991). Religious belief systems: their ideological representation and practical constraints. *International Journal for the Psychology of Religion*, *1*, 5-21.

Ellis, A. (1971). *The case against religion: a psychotherapist's view*. New York: Institute for Rational Living.

Folkman, S., Lazarus, R. S., Gruen R. J., & DeLongis, A. (1986). Appraisal coping, health status and psychological symptoms. *Journal of Personality and Social Psychology*, *50*, 571-579.

Frank, J. D. (1988). Psychological and behavioral aspects of illness and treatment. *Revista Latinoamericana Psiocologia*, *20*, 45-65.

Fromm, E. (1950). *Psychoanalysis and religion*. New Haven: Yale University Press.

Furnham, A., & Brown, L. B. (1992). Theodicy: a neglected aspect of the psychology of religion. *International Journal for the Psychology of Religion* 2(1),37-46.

Galanter, M. (1990). Cults and zealous self-help movements: a psychiatric perspective. *American Journal of Psychiatry*, *147*, 543-51.

Gaston, J., & Brown, L. B. (1991). Religions and gender prototypes. *International Journal for the Psychology of Religion*. (in press).

Harned, D. B. (1958). *The ambiguity of religion*. Philadelphia: Westminster.

Jones, E. E., et al (1971). *Attribution: perceiving the causes of behavior*. Morristown N.J.: General Learning Press.

Kroll, J., & Sheehan, W. (1989). Religious beliefs and practices among 52 psychiatric inpatients in Minnesota. *American Journal of Psychiatry*, *146*, 67-72.

Lalljee, M., Brown, L. B., & Hilton, D. (1990). The relationships between images of God, explanations for failure to do one's duty to God, and involving God's agency. *Journal of Psychology and Theology*, *18*, 166-173.

Larson, D. B. (1986). Systematic analysis of research on religious variables in four major psychiatric journals, 1970-1982. *American Journal of Psychiatry*, *143*, 329-334.

Lilliston, L., & Brown, P. M. (1981). Perceived effectiveness of religious solutions to personal problems. *Journal of Clinical Psychology*, *37*, 118-122.

Lilliston, L., Brown, P. M., & Schliebe, H. P. (1982). Perception of religious solutions to personal problems of women. *Journal of Clinical Psychology*, *38*, 545-549.

Pargament, K. I. et al (1988). Religion and the problem solving process: three styles of coping. *Journal for the Scientific Study of Religion*, *27*, 90-104.

Parker, G. B., & Brown, L. B. (1982). Coping behaviours that mediate between life events and depression. *Archives of General Psychiatry*, *39*, 1386-1391.

Parker, G. B., Brown, L. B., & Blignault, I. (1986). Coping behaviours as predictors of the course of clinical depression. *Archives of General Psychiatry*, *43*, 561-565.

Prosen, M. (1983). Guilt and conscience in major depressive disorders. *American Journal of Psychiatry*, *140*, 839-844.

Reik, T. (1955). From spell to prayer. *Psychoanalysis*, *3*, 3-26.

Robinson, L. H. (ed). (1986). *Psychiatry and religion: overlapping concerns*. Washington, D. C.: American Psychiatric Press.

Shaver, P., Lenaver, M., & Sadd, S. (1980). Religiousness, conversion, and subjective well-being: the "healthy minded" religion of modern American women. *American Journal of Psychiatry*, *137*, 1563-1568.

Sprock, J., Blashfield, R. K., & Smith, B. (1990). Gender weighting of DSMIIIR personality disorder criteria. *American Journal of Psychiatry*, *147*, 586-590.

Stark, R. (1990). Response. *Journal for the Scientific Study of Religion*, *29*, 385-386.

Witztum, E., Greenberg, D., & Dasberg, H. (1990). Mental illness and religious change. *British Journal of Medical Psychology*, *63*, 33-41.

Young, G., & Dowling, W. (1987) Dimensions of religiosity in old age: accounting for variation in types of participation. *Journal of Gerontology*, *42*(4), 376-380.

Acknowledgement

Dr Gail F. Huon's advice has crucially shaped the analysis and interpretation of these results. Mr Paul Adamson carried out the preparation and analysis of the data, which were gathered by the Psychology I Tutors at the University of New South Wales, as part of the First Year Laboratory course in 1990.

CHAPTER 10
RELIGIOUS CONTRIBUTIONS TO THE PROCESS OF COPING WITH STRESS

Kenneth I. Pargament

As members of universities with interests in mental health and religion, we have our feet in three worlds — the worlds of research, clinical practice, and faith. Having only two feet, we find ourselves in a difficult position. So to help us stay on our feet, we must find theories and research in the religious area which are practically relevant to people who are struggling with problems.

Unfortunately, much of the theory and research in the area of religion is not particularly relevant to clinical practice. Of course this may be true of research more generally, which is largely nomothetic. Our research (and I include much of my own work here) has tended to focus on general questions. We ask, is religion good for your mental health? What types of faith are more mature? How does religion form, change, and grow? These are to be sure, important questions, but they do not speak to the people and the problems we see. The general questions we have asked speak about religion in the abstract, religion as a dispositional phenomenon, and religion as it applies to people in general.

But people in trouble grapple with specific life problems. Few come to a mental health setting complaining of their lack of faith development. Instead, they ask "How do I deal with the fact that I just lost my job? How do I handle my child who refuses to listen to reason? How do I make it through the day without feeling so tired and worn-out? How can I make this marriage of mine work?" Religion, when it is involved in this process, gets caught up in the nitty-gritty, the dirty details of life. William James put it this way: "The prince of darkness may be a gentleman, as we are told he is, but whatever the God of earth and heaven is, he can surely be no gentleman. His menial services are needed in the dust of our trials, even more than his dignity is needed in the empyrean" (James, 1975, p. 40). When religion is involved in the problems in life, there is little that is abstract or removed about it. Statements about how religion relates to mental health as a rule are not particularly helpful to the clinician, who rarely sees the rule and almost always sees the exceptions. The people we deal with live in particular contexts, cultures, times, and situations which in combination are quite exceptional.

Over the last several years, I've been interested in studying religion as it connects or fails to connect to ordinary people grappling with the most pressing situations of life. Here is where I think we have a lot to learn about faith, and here is where our research may be most useful to us as people concerned with helping others in times of stress. I'd like to describe some of what I've learned about religion and coping in this paper.

A Coping Framework

I think the concept of coping provides one way of linking theory and research in religion to the concrete problems of clinical practice. By coping I mean efforts to understand and deal with significant problems in life. Let me say a bit about coping before moving on to the role religion plays in the coping process.

The interest in coping grew out of a number of studies in which it was found that stressful events in and of themselves are not very good predictors of how an individual will behave. Descriptions of bereaved spouses, concentration camp survivors, and accident victims pointed to important differences in the ways people respond to these events. Some were shattered, others rebounded, and still others seemed to grow from their experience. What made the difference?

Theorists such as Richard Lazarus (see Lazarus & Folkman, 1984) said coping was the key — how the event was appraised and how the event was handled made the difference between a successful outcome and an unsuccessful one. And a large body of subsequent research has supported his claim. Is the event perceived as a threat or is it seen as a challenge? Does the individual feel that the event can be handled or does it take the person beyond his or her resources? Does the person deal with the problem directly or does he or she avoid it? These are some of the critical questions for coping.

Let me describe a framework of coping in just a bit more detail (Pargament, 1990). From a coping perspective, events do not simply happen to a passive person (See **Figure 1**). Each of us is engaged in a search for significance in life, and life events are viewed with significance in mind. They are anticipated, interpreted, and handled according to what the person values or finds most significant in life. Oftentimes we willingly subject ourselves stress to gain things of value. Coming to a conference can be stressful, yet it offers something of

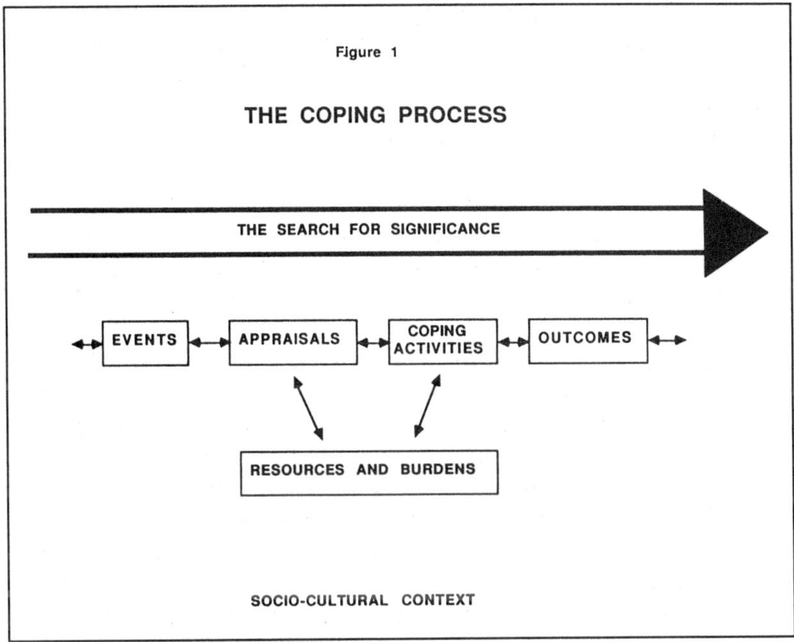

significance to us. Of course what is significant will vary from person to person. Perhaps that is why we can find someone like the eminent physicist Steven Hawking who, faced with a disease that leaves his body paralyzed, can say, "I'm fortunate that it left the thing I care about most unharmed, my mind".

If an event threatens the person with loss or results in harm to the things he or she cares about, the individual will engage in coping activities to minimize the loss or maximize the gain in significance in the situation. Exactly what the person will do will depend not only on the nature of the situation that is confronted but also on the nature of what he or she bring to coping. None of us come to coping empty-handed. This fact is overlooked in S-R models of stress-response. Each of us has a system of resources and burdens, and what we do when faced with stress is deeply affected by the resources and burdens we bring to coping. By resources and burdens I mean the general orienting system for living, which is made up of thoughts, feelings, relationships, attitudes, roles, and personality characteristics. In coping, we are limited only by the tools that are made available to us or that we make available for ourselves.

Out of this general orienting system, we form specific appraisals and coping activities for dealing with stressful experiences. Generally, we look for the most compelling activity among the alternatives that are available to us. The term "compelling" connotes cognition and affect. We cope not only in ways that make sense but also in ways that feel right.

As can be seen in Figure 1, the appraisals and activities of coping, drawn from the orienting system of resources and burdens, mediate the relationship between events and outcomes. What this means is that experienced outcomes have less to do with objective events than with how we deal with them.

Finally, it is important to underscore one other point. The entire coping process takes place in a larger cultural context. Events, appraisals, coping activities, resources, burdens, and outcomes are woven out of a greater cultural fabric. Although I have seen no data on it, my guess would be that members of different eastern European nations coped quite differently with their years under communist rule, in part because the nations carry different cultural histories and traditions, not the least of which is religion.

Within this framework of coping we can do micro-analyses of particular individual-situation encounters. We can also analyze many groups of such encounters. Or we can do comparative studies of the ways different groups or cultures cope.

This is a very quick and abbreviated review of a highly interactive framework. But let me reiterate why I think it is valuable. It describes what we so often see in mental health work: a collision between a person and a specific situation taking place against the backdrop of a larger cultural context. It is a framework that is relevant to theory, research, and practice, and I think it is particularly relevant to the study of religion. In the rest of my talk I would like to highlight a few things we are beginning to learn about religion and coping.

Religion is Commonly Called on as a Way of Dealing with Stressful Times

Crisis has played a central role in the religious experience of the most pivotal religious figures, Buddha, Confusius and from Isaiah, to Mohammed, Jesus and Luther. But it is also involved in the lives of ordinary people. Listen to some of the last thoughts of some people before their plane crashed on a farm in Iowa (Life Magazine, 1989).

> "After the flight attendant explained emergency landing procedures, we were left with our thoughts. That's when I began praying. I closed my eyes and thought, "Dear Lord, I pray that you'll guide the pilot's hands." I also thought that if God wanted to take my life, that it was O.K. with me. I was full of peace. Here I was sitting on the edge of eternity. I wasn't facing the end of my life."

> "I did what I needed to do to prepare to die. My thought at the time was that I wanted to be reborn into a family where I would be able to hear the teachings of Buddha. I'd done a lot of Buddhist meditation in my life, and this trained me to become one pointed in my awareness. I was totally focused on the brace position."

For most of these survivors, the disaster led to beliefs and feelings related to religion in one way or another. But not everyone turned to religion. One survivor said: "I don't believe there is a kindly Supreme Being who responds to people one on one. People ask me if I am still a nonbeliever after my life was saved. If everybody had had his life saved except the bad people on the plane, maybe I'd believe a little more. But that's not what happened. Mothers of young children died."

Empirical studies are consistent with these anecdotes. I have completed a review of this literature and found that the percentages of people who involve religion in coping range from about 30 percent to 90 percent depending on the population, the situation, and their social context. In short, religion is often called on in coping with difficult situations but not always. There are some atheists in foxholes. The key question isn't *whether* people turn to religion, but *when*.

Religious Involvement in Coping is Determined by Cultural, Social, Institutional, Situational, and Individual Dimensions

We asked several hundred members of mainstream congregations in the United States to describe the most serious negative life event they had experienced in the past year. We then asked them whether their religious beliefs, practices, or feelings were involved in dealing with the event in any way. Table 1 shows the significant predictors of religious involvement in coping (Pargament, Ensing, Falgout, Olsen, Reilly, Van Haitsma, & Warren, 1990) (See **Table 1**).

Table 1 PREDICTORS OF RELIGIOUS INVOLVEMENT IN COPING

Demographic		Religious dispositions		Religious coping styles	
Sex	.13***	Intrinsic	.39***	Collaborative	.34***
Age	n.s.	Extrinsic	-.15***	Deferring	.28***
Education	n.s.	Quest	n.s.	Self-directed	-.27***
Marital status	n.s.	Orthodoxy	.23***		
Income	n.s.	Experience	.32***		
		Loving God Image	.10*		
		Prayer	.30***		
		Attendance	.17***		
R^2 =.04		R^2 =.20		R^2 =.16	
Life events		**Appraisals**		**Congregational**	
Number of events	.13***	Causal: self	n.s.	Type of church:	(F=4.03)***
Months since event	n.s.	Causal: God's will	.17***		
Type of event	(F=5.14)***	Causal: chance	-.06		
		Causal: God's Punishment	n.s.		
		Personal health Threat	.12***		
		Cannot cope	.08*		
		Harm/Loss	.16***		
		Threat to others	.17***		
		Opportunity	.27***		
		Challenge	.22***		
		Can cope	n.s.		
		Accept	n.s.		
		Spiritual threat	.22***		
R^2 =.10		R^2 =.20		R^2 =.07	

As can be seen, religious involvement with a serious negative life event was predicted by several kinds of variables: demographic, religious dispositional, religious coping styles, the number and kind of life stresses the person had experienced, the individual's appraisals of the event, and the type of congregation they attended. Generally, people who were more intrinsically religious, who had a more collaborative religious coping style, and who felt more threatened, harmed and challenged by the event were more likely to turn to religion in coping. These results support the notion that people involve religion in coping when it is more available and more compelling than the alternatives.

So we find that religious involvement in coping is predictable, nested within layers of social, situational, and individual dimensions. Our findings are consistent with those of others such as Lawrence Brown and Bernard Spilka (Brown, 1966; Spilka, Shaver, & Kirkpatrick, 1985).

Situation-Specific Religious Coping Efforts are Identifiable

Most measures of religiousness focus on religion as a general disposition. We ask about generalized beliefs, practices, and orientations. Perhaps we are less sure how to measure religion at a more concrete, situation-specific level.

My students and I tried to see whether we could measure situation-specific religious coping efforts, that is, what people do with their religion in the midst of difficult life situations. We developed measures of religious appraisals, religious purposes in coping, and religious coping activities. We then asked the several hundred participants of our Project on Religion and Coping to indicate which religious coping efforts they used to deal with their significant negative life event (Pargament et al., in press).

In Table 2, you can see that people were able to identify the purposes that religion sewed for them in coping. Our factor analysis of these results yielded five factors: looking to religion for self-development, for spirituality, for resolution of problems, for sharing with others, and for emotional and behavioral restraint. In short, we found that people look to religion for different things. (See **Table 2**).

Let me give examples of two different purposes of religion (Pargament, Royster, Albert, Crowe, Cullman, Holley, Schaefer, Sytniak, & Wood, 1990). In one case, religion serves as a source of comfort and resolution for one elderly Mormon man who describes the death of his first wife in a car accident: "There was a big flatbed truck that had broken down, nobody around it, and we hit that thing going 70. It just took the top right off the car. She was killed instantly. There was a big gash on her wrist and it wasn't bleeding and I couldn't get any pulse. And I felt that I could lay my hands on her head and bring her back (referring to a religious custom in the Latter-day Saint church of healing the sick by "laying on of hands"). And a voice spoke to me and said: 'Do you want her back a vegetable? She's fine. She's all right.' And... to let her go. That voice was just as clear to me as though somebody spoke to me. And it was quite a comfort, really, because I knew she was all right. I guess, no, I think that a lot of times, death is not an enemy. It's a friend, really, especially when the person is suffering. At least she didn't have to suffer."

Table 2 FUNCTIONS OF RELIGION

	% Endorsement
SELF-DEVELOPMENT	
Help in feeling good about myself	76
Feeling more in control of my life	80
Help in improving myself as a person	79
SPIRITUAL	
Personal closeness with God	84
A sense of meaning and purpose in life	79
Feelings of hope about the future	90
RESOLUTION	
Help in solving my problems	80
A sense of peace and comfort	92
SHARING	
Help in expressing my feelings	85
A sense of closeness and belonging with other people	81
RESTRAINT	
Help in keeping my emotions or actions under control	87

Compare the comfort this man sought through his faith to the search for meaning and emotional control we find in a young Buddhist who has to deal with a psychiatric hospitalization of his brother. "When I discovered Zen Buddhism, I realized that all the things I was worrying about would come to pass away — would not be permanent... My seeing reality has made me place misfortunes into proper perspective. I do not blow out of proportion my brother's problem. I recognize that part of the problem is chemical and that it's only a matter of time... when it is discovered how to bring him to an equilibrium. I feel a lot of emotions. But I have them under better control. I know when to make them less important and when reason must override feeling".

That people look to religion for different things is one of our key findings. The simple distinction between living and using one's religion from the I-E literature doesn't do justice to the rich ways people involve religion in coping (Pargament, 1992). As Paul Johnson (1955) put it: "Purity of motive is often lauded as if superior to mixed motives. But all motives are mixed; the only purity is not simplicity but harmony of many co-ordinating motives in symphonic chords of ongoing purpose" (p. 214).

We were also able to measure religious involvement in the appraisals of difficult life situations (Pargament et al., 1990). As can be seen in Table 3, a majority of the participants believed that the recalled event was a reflection of God's will. Smaller numbers felt that the event was a punishment by God for their sins or that the event threatened them spiritually. So religion was clearly a part of the appraisals people made of their critical events. (See **Table 3**).

Table 3 APPRAISALS

	% Endorsement
RELIGIOUS APPRAISALS	
God's will	53
God's punishment	7
Threat to spiritual well-being	31
NON-RELIGIOUS APPRAISALS	
Caused by self	31
Caused by chance	41
Threat to personal health	39
Threat to well-being of other	57
Harm/loss	50
Opportunity to grow	82
Challenge to do something about situation	57
Accept the situation	89
Can cope with the situation	57
Cannot cope with the situation	36

And in Table 4, it can be seen that people were able to identify a variety of religious coping activities. (See **Table 4**). These dimensions were derived through factor analysis (Pargament et al., 1990). The Spiritually based factor stresses the individual's personal relationship with God throughout coping. Good Deeds is another religious response to the negative event, consisting of living a better, more religiously integrated life. Discontent is made of items that express anger or distance from God and the church, as well as uncertainly about one's faith. Religious

Support involves receiving support from the clergy and other congregation members. Plead includes pleas for a miracle, bargaining with God, and questions about why the event happened. And we made up a sixth scale called Religious Avoidance from items that divert the individual's attention from the problem through reading the Bible or focusing on the after-life.

Table 4 RELIGIOUS COPING ACTIVITIES SCALES

	% Endorsement
SPIRITUALLY-BASED	
Trusted that God would not let anything terrible happen to me	78
Experienced God's love and care	92
Realized that God was trying to strengthen me	80
In dealing with the problem I was guided by God	88
Realized that I didn't have to suffer since Jesus suffered for me	88
Used Christ as an example of how I should live	80
Took control over what I could, and gave the rest up to God	89
My faith showed me different ways to handle the problem	88
Accepted that the situation was not in my hands but in the hands of God	84
Found the lesson from God in the event	75
God showed me how to deal with the situation	88
Used my faith to help me decide how to cope with the situation	64
GOOD DEEDS	
Tried to be less sinful	69
Confessed my sins	69
Led a more loving life	81
Attended religious services or participated in religious rituals	80
Participated in church groups (support groups, prayer groups, Bible)	45
Provided help to other church members	56

to be continued on the next page:

Table 4 (continued)

DISCONTENT	
Felt angry with or distant from God	26
Felt angry with or distant from the members of the church	19
Questioned my religious beliefs and faith	27
RELIGIOUS SUPPORT	
Received support from clergy	48
Received support from other members of the church	63
PLEAD	
Asked for a miracle	46
Bargained with God to make things better	23
Asked God why it happened	56
RELIGIOUS AVOIDANCE	
Focused on the world-to-come rather than the problems of this world	47
I let God solve my problems for me	64
Prayed or read the Bible to keep my mind off of my problems	65

The scales of religious coping have acceptable internal consistency, and as can be seen, many of the items were commonly endorsed by people. We also found large differences among people in the ways they used religion in coping. I'm not saying this is the last word on religious coping measures. My guess is we would see different religious coping factors in different samples and cultures. But the important point here is that religion can be measured as a situation-specific phenomena.

Religious Coping Efforts are Predictors of Outcomes of Coping

In our Project on Religion and Coping, these situation-specific religious coping efforts significantly predicted three outcome measures: a measure of general psychological status (the GHQ), a measure of how the event turned out (General Outcome), and a measure of religious change as a result of the event (Religious Outcome).

Table 5 COMPARING THE PREDICTIVE POWER OF RELIGIOUS COPING, RELIGIOUS DISPOSITIONAL, AND NONRELIGIOUS COPING VARIABLES

	GHQ	General Outcome	Religious Outcome
R^2	R^2	R^2	
Religious Coping Variables (removing Religious Dispositional Variables)	.09	.26	.21
Religious Dispositional Variables (removing Religious Coping Variables)	.02	.03	.03
Religious Coping Variables (removing Nonreligious Coping Variables)	.03	.06	.26
Nonreligious Coping Variables (removing Religious Coping Variables)	.04	.09	.00

But it is possible that our religious coping measures add little above and beyond what we know from our more traditional dispositional measures of religiousness. To test whether religious coping measures add to our predictive power, we determined the unique predictive power of both religious coping measures and of more traditional dispositional measures of religiousness such as Intrinsic, Extrinsic, Quest, Religious Orthodoxy, and Religious Practices. The results are shown in Table 5. (See **Table 5**). The religious coping measures are *better* predictors of outcomes than our traditional measures of religious dispositions. So if we want to know something about how critical life events will turn out, it is more important to know something about how the person deals with that specific situation than his of her more general approach to life. Our findings fit with the model of religious coping efforts as mediators of the relationship between critical events, religious dispositional variables and outcomes (see also Pargament et al., 1992).

One other possibility important to consider is that religious coping efforts are simply a larger part of more general coping. For example, religious avoidance in coping could be simply a part of a more general avoidant coping style. If this were the case, then there would be little need to study *religious* coping efforts as a separate class of coping activities. To test whether religious coping is different in any way from more general coping, we compared the predictive power of our religious coping variables with some measures of nonreligious coping. As can be seen at the bottom of Table 5, both religious and nonreligious coping efforts have some unique predictive power (all of those R^2 are statistically significant). (See **Table 5**). While religious and nonreligious coping activities correlate with each other, each adds a piece to the puzzle. This only makes sense; religion isn't the full story in coping, but it does add an important dimension to it, one that has been overlooked in the general coping literature.

So we are starting to learn some important things about religion and coping:

— That people often but not always turn to religion in coping; when they do will depend upon a set of psychological, social, and situational factors that influence whether religious solutions to problems are available and compelling;

— That religious coping can be measured as a situation-specific phenomenon;

— That religious coping efforts are predictive of how critical events turn out, that they predict outcomes more strongly than our standard religious dispositional measures, and that they add something beyond what we know from nonreligious approaches to coping.

Implications of a Religion and Coping Perspective for Mental Health

What does all of this mean for mental health? From a coping perspective there can be no single key to effective coping. We simply cannot point to one factor alone as critical to good coping. For instance, who is to say that denial of a problem is not at times appropriate? In fact, there is evidence that denial plays a positive mental health role, particularly in the initial phases of crisis when the person needs some breathing space to mobilize his or her resources.

Who is to say that active problem-solving approaches, those that emphasize control and initiative are always good? For some problems and some situations, the most adaptive things to do may be to give up or hand control over to someone else, as in the case of the patient who gives up control to a physician.

Who is to say that having a good outcome is the key to good coping? Outcomes can be very misleading. What are we to make of people who struggle valiantly with injustice but fail in their struggle? Have they coped poorly? Or what about those who achieve positive outcomes through no efforts of their own or by stepping on other people's toes?

I don't think the key to good coping can be found in any one element. What is good for one person may not be good for another. What works in one situation may not work in another. What holds true in one culture may not hold true in another. The key to good coping lies in the whole process — how well the whole system works together. And let me briefly suggest a few criteria for evaluating the effectiveness of the coping process, focussing on the role of religion in this process. First, is the coping process *comprehensive*? Can it deal with the range of experiences the individual is likely to face or is it limited to only a few? Many religious systems are fair-weather friends. They provide support, meaning, and reassurance to the person as long as things are going well, but when the person encounters injustice, suffering, or loss, the system breaks down. After all, how could a loving God hurt one so badly? The person is left with a feeling that he or she is being punished but is not sure why or for what. These religions are ineffective in coping because they are not comprehensive. They are religions only for the healthy-minded, and yet this is a world of pain and suffering too.

Related to comprehensiveness is *flexibility*. Is the religious system malleable and flexible enough to deal with new situations, with social and personal change, or does it limit the capacity to generate new and innovative ways of thinking about problems?

Another key to effective coping is whether the process is *integrated*. Are the bits and pieces of the coping process unified and interconnected or are they fragmented and incoherent? There are several areas in the coping process where the elements may fit together or may not. For instance are the coping activities well-suited to the demands of the situation? Does the person stuck on the side of the road with a flat tire pray for God to change the tire or pray to God for the strength to change the tire?

Here is another kind of integration. Do the coping activities of the individual fit with the nature of the larger social system. I saw a woman in therapy who had lost her baby at six months of age. But she wasn't in therapy because of the baby. She was there because of conflict with her extended family. My client was a devout woman who strongly believed that her baby is in Heaven caring for her and her family. Her minister supported her in this view. My client insisted that her baby is still part of her family spiritually and wanted her family to acknowledge the presence of her child by talking about him, visiting his grave, and recognizing the anniversary of his death. The family was very uncomfortable with this. From their point of view, the baby was dead and her mother was refusing to accept reality. The problem here wasn't my client and it wasn't her family; it was a lack of fit between the pieces.

Finally, effective coping is benevolent and fruitful. It rests on a view of the universe benign enough so that we feel it's safe to venture out into the world and deal with problems. Visions of vengeful, wrathful Gods are generally inconsistent with this view. And effective coping is fruitful, in general leading to good things not only for the individual but for the larger community as well.

These criteria are not so rigid that they lock us into a fixed and uniform standard of effective coping for everyone. The form and content of comprehensiveness, integration, benevolence and fruitfulness can vary from person to person, situation to situation, or culture to culture. But the criteria provide some standards for evaluating effectiveness both within and across social settings, so we are not left with the problems of a completely relativistic point of view.

Conclusions

I hope this talk has provided a useful introduction into the psychology of religion and coping. Let me conclude by noting three reasons why I think this is a valuable perspective for our field:

First, the usefulness of the religion and coping perspective not only at the individual level of analysis but also at the situational and social levels, makes it well-suited to cross-cultural study.

Second, the perspective is important because it connects religious study to a significant body of research and theory within other areas of science: physiological, psychological, sociological, and anthropological. It raises important theoretical and empirical questions for further study.

Finally, this kind of study helps us to translate the often abstract concepts and beliefs of religion into practice. When we study religion and coping we are studying how religion comes to life in our most desperate situations. This is not a religion in the abstract or a religion removed from life. Because it connects to experience so immediately, it has clear implications for mental health practice. And more personally, it helps those of us with our feet in three worlds to keep our balance.

REFERENCES

Brown, L. B. (1966). Egocentric thought in petitionary prayer: A cross-cultural study. *Journal of Social Psychology, 68*, 197-210.

James, W. (1975). *Pragmatism*. Cambridge: Harvard University Press.

Johnson, P. E. (1955). *Psychology of religion*. Nashville: Abingdon Press.

Life Magazine (1989). *"Here I was sitting at the edge of eternity"*. 12(10), pp. 28-33, 38, 39.

Lazarus, R. S. & Folkman, S. (1984). *Stress, appraisal and coping*. New York: Springer.

Pargament, K. I. (1990). God help me: Toward a theoretical framework of coping for the psychology of religion. *Research in the Social Scientific Study of Religion, 2*, 195-224.

Pargament, K. I. (1992) Of means and ends. Religion and the search for significance. *International Journal for the Scientific Study of Religion, 2*, 201-229.

Pargament, K. I. Olsen, H., Reilly, B., Falgout, K., Ensing, O.S., & Van Haitsma, K. (1992). God help me (II): The relationship of religious exitations to religious coping with negative life events. *Journal for the Scientific* Study of Religion, 31, 504-513.

Pargament, K. I., Ensing, D. S., Falgout, K., Olsen, H., Reilly, B., Van Haitsma, K., & Warren, R. (1990). God help me (I): Religious coping efforts as predictors of the outcomes to significant negative life events. *American Journal of Community Psychology, 18*, 793-824.

Pargament, K. I., Royster, B. J. T., Albert, M., Crowe, M., Cullman, E. P., Holley, R., Schaefer, D., Sytniak, M. & Wood, M. (1990). A qualitative approach to the study of religion and coping: Four tentative conclusions. Paper presented at the American Psychological Association, Boston, Massachusetts, August, 1990.

Spilka, B., Shaver, P., & Kirkpatrick, L. (1985). A general attribution theory for the psychology of religion. *Journal for the Scientific Study of Religion, 24*, 1-20.

CHAPTER 11
RELIGIOUS VISIONS IN CONTEMPORARY SWEDEN

Antoon Geels

In all times and all cultures individuals have reported visions of a divine world, visions of religious figures like Muhammed, the goddess Kali, Jesus, or of different ghosts or demons as in Tibetan Buddhism. Within the last mentioned tradition there exist specific techniques in order to evoke visions, techniques which are legitimated by a conceptual framework about visions and how they can influence human beings, especially at the moment of death. Similar techniques exist in many other traditions. In most non-Western cultures those techniques are closely related to religious rituals (Goodman, 1987), e.g., shamanistic rituals. When the shaman is "possessed" by a divine being he "sees" the gods descending from their heavenly resort. Even the other main type of shaman, the soul-traveller, "sees" happenings of a divine nature, which can be transmitted to his environment.

The above mentioned examples of trained or evoked visions can be contrasted with what we can call spontaneous visions. A large group belonging to this category consists of the apparitions of the Virgin Mary, which are common in Catholic countries (see e.g. Christian, 1981; Carroll, 1986; Zimdars-Swartz, 1991). This group has perhaps most in common with the type of experiences I have been studying during the 1980s, i.e., religious visions in contemporary Sweden, reported by so-called ordinary Swedish citizens. Their experiences represent a sort of "popular" mysticism, as contrasted to a mysticism of the élite or monastic mysticism.

When planning this large project on religious visions I started from the conviction that it was necessary, from the psychological point of view, to study the experiences of living subjects. The results of such studies, I thought, could possibly shed new light on historical visions such as those reported by Hildegard of Bingen, Hadewych, Teresa of Avila, and many others. As a result of these considerations I planned my project in three phases: (1) An in-depth idiographic study of an internationally known swedish artist, whose paintings have been inspired by religious visions; (2) A nomothetic study of about 100-150 contemporary Swedish visionaries; and (3) A cross-cultural study, using contemporary and historical documents. Conclusions drawn from the first two studies could be applied to the cross-cultural investigation. The first two phases have been completed and are published in two monographs (Geels, 1989; 1991). In this article I will summarize the most essential parts of the method used and the main results obtained from the second study.

Religious visions and mystical experience

It is my opinion that religious visions belong to the study of mysticism. There are, of course, researchers who defend a different opinion, among them Walter T. Stace. Religious visions, Stace writes, do not belong in the category of mystical experiences because they "have the character of sensuous imagery" whereas mystical experiences are nonsensuous. Another reason, Stace continues, is that mystics themselves regard them as less important or even as an obstacle to spiritual maturity (Stace, 1960).

A similar argument can be found in a book written by another philosopher of religion — William J. Wainwright. Starting from a definition of mystical experience proper, i.e. unitary states, which are noetic, but lack specific empirical content, Wainwright concludes that visions and voices should be excluded from this category, especially because of their empirical content (Wainwright, 1981). In addition to this argument Wainwright mentions that a considerable number of scholars exclude visions from the field of mysticism (e.g. Underhill, 1926; Inge, 1969) This fact, however, is probably related to the first argument. In other words, scholars exclude visions from the scientific study of mysticism because some mystics exclude them from mystical experience proper. But to neglect visions for this reason is just as inappropriate as it is for a psychologist to neglect dreams for the dubious reason that the client regards them as trivial or meaningless (see Moore, 1978).

The above mentioned attitude is probably one of the main reasons why there exist so few psychological studies of religious visions. One of the major studies in the field is the monumental work of the swedish scholar Ernst Arbman (1963; 1968; 1970), who definitely places religious visions in the study of mysticism. He even goes as far as the following statement: "Mysticism may be said to be tantamount to visionary-ecstatic religious practice or religiosity" (1963, p. 547).

If one wishes to include visions in the study of mysticism, it is appropriate to present a definition of mysticism, or rather of mystical experience. The definition presented below was selected from a publication of Robert S. Ellwood (1980, p.29). The definition has been enlarged to some extent in order to cover a broader category of experiences. The additions are marked in italics:

> Mystical experience is experience in a religious *or a profane* context that is immediately or subsequently interpreted by the experiencer as encounter with *a higher or* ultimate divine reality in a direct, *according to the subject* nonrational way that engenders a deep sense of unity and of living during the experience on a level of being other than the ordinary. *This experience leads to far-reaching consequences in the individual's life.*

It is obvious that mystical experiences do not occur only in a religious context. Research reports mention for example experiences in nature (see e.g. Hay, 1982), or in prison (Koestler, 1954). These experiences can, from an ontological point of view, also be understood as an encounter with a higher dimension of reality. Similarly, the mystic or visionary can regard this experience as a nonrational experience, which does not prevent the scholar from adopting another opinion. That is the reason why I add the words "according to the subject" to the definition of Ellwood. Lastly, but perhaps most importantly, the consequential dimension of mystical experiences has often been neglected. That is why I add the phrase that "this experience leads to far-reaching consequences in the individual's life".

Considering this rather broad definition it is difficult not to include visions as a type of mystical experience. A religious vision is an encounter with, according to the subject, a divine dimension of reality, an encounter which has the characteristics of perception. With the expression "characteristics of perception" I mean that descriptions of these experiences often contain concepts that refer to one or more of the senses. Most often the visionary refers to visual perception, but also to auditive or tactile sensations. The last two categories mentioned are regarded as visionary out of theoretical considerations. In my opinion there exists a close relationship between the study of religious visions and the field of mental imagery within general psychology, an area of research which again attracts many scholars.

Method of data collection

By advertising in Swedish newspapers and with considerable aid from the media I came into contact with approximately 150 persons. About 100 of them decided to participate in the project which, as I explained to them, would take several years to accomplish. As a first step in our cooperation I asked them to write a short biography (about 6 pages), focusing on decisive positive and negative experiences during childhood, adolescence and, especially, at the time shortly prior to the religious vision. I call this part of my method a Critical Incident Biography (CIB). I also asked them to write down details of the contents of the vision, for example what Jesus or the angel looked like, and if he or she had seen something similar before.

I also sent the informants a questionnaire, focusing, among other items, on religious activity (church attendance, how often the informants pray, read the bible), their attitude towards the Bible (for example fundamentalistic, hermeneutic), their concept of God (personal-impersonal, transcendent-immanent), and their religious orientation as defined by Batson & Ventis (1982), i.e. means, end, or quest orientation.

A few months later I sent them the same questionnaire again, but now in the past tense. In an accompanying letter I asked the informants to sit down, relax, and to return, in their minds, to the time before the religious visions. I was interested in processes of change concerning religious activity, attitudes, concept of God, etc. I am well aware of the methodological complications involved in such a procedure. The alternative was to have nothing at all as a comparison.

First of all there are time aspects and factors from the psychology of memory. Some of the experiences described by the informants refer to events from several decades ago. An old lady wrote the following words in her first letter to me: "Tears still run down my cheeks when I write this, although it happened 50 years ago." The quotation is a good example of the intense emotional factor involved in these experiences. In this connection I was reminded of the so-called "intensity-of-affect-hypothesis", according to which there is a relation between the intense emotions at the time of the experience and the individual's memory of it (see Holmes, 1970; Pettersson, 1975, p.115ff).

An additional argument in favour of the above-mentioned procedure is that people who went through dramatic conversion experiences often divide their lives into a "before" and an "after", a circumstance which often leads to a reinterpretation of the lives before the experience (cf. Ullman, 1989). I have met the same phenomenon in my case studies. I would also like to add that people who have had intense religious experiences remember them very well and they usually know in which way their lives, attitudes, and values are being transformed.

Bearing these considerations in mind I decided to send out the second questionnaire. Almost all the informants, 91 in all, returned both questionnaires. Their ages were relatively high. No less than 43 informants were between 50-70 years old. Nineteen informants were older than seventy, while only fourteen informants were younger than forty. One informant refused to reveal his age. (With regard to the relatively high age cf. Hay, 1980, where a similar result is reported.)

The data were computarized with the aid of a program called StatView (MacIntosh). I chose to describe 35 cases in the form of short biographies (4-6 pages), integrating all the data gathered from letters, the CIB's and the questionnaires. All informants read my draft for approval. This way it was possible to study the visions in the biographical context. Inspired by the so-called "grounded-theory approach" developed by Barney G. Glaser & Anselm L Strauss (1967), I continuously compared the data and continued to work with the following categories: religious socialisation, relations with parents and the degree of psychological stress during childhood, adolescence and the adult life. All categories were, in accordance with this method, further divided into dimensions and qualities. The category of religious socialisation, for example, was divided in the dimensions of Sunday-school, religious socialisation in the parental home, at school, etc, dimensions which were further divided into the categories of weak, moderate, or strong religious socialisation.

The method used is accordingly of an inductive nature. The starting point is the collected material, which has been compared over and over again, leading finally to a theory which aims at integrating the results. From another perspective the method chosen can be characterised as a combination of qualitative and quantitative methods: a content analysis of case-studies and statistical analysis of the questionnaires. In my opinion this type of combination offers a lot of promises for the future.

Summaries of some case studies

Some of the results of this comparative analysis are the following relations between a weak, moderate, or strong religious socialisation and the type of vision. Ten out of thirty-five informants give evidence of a strong religious socialisation. Nine of them had visions of Jesus. Fourteen of the remaining informants exhibiting a weak or moderate religious socialisation had more abstract visions of light, force, or unity in nature. The rest of the thirty-five cases, eleven in total, either had visions of angels (4) or of Jesus (7).

The comparative analysis also showed that the most striking common denominator of the visionaries was a life-crisis, not primarily during childhood, but shortly prior to the religious vision. Only four out of thirty-five cases reported a crisis in their early childhood, while twenty-six informants experienced a strong crisis, and seven a moderate crisis during the time just prior to the vision. This strong relation between an acute life-crisis and the religious vision reminded me of a poem with the headline "Friend, in moments of devastation", written by the well-known Swedish poet Erik Axel Stagnelius:

> Therefore rejoice, o friend, and sing in the darkness of sorrow: The night is the mother of day, Chaos lives next to God.

This relation can easily be exemplified with summaries of a few case-studies.

First there is the case of Reidar, born in Norway in 1930, where he grew up during the German occupation of the country. In the year 1944, when he was fourteen years old, the Germans put him in a concentration camp just outside Oslo. When the war ended he stole a bicycle in order to return home to his parents, about a hundred miles to the north. He got caught by the police and from that time on he became criminal and spent many shorter and longer periods in prison. During the 60s he became involved in drugs, especially heroin, which he took for many years. During the summer of 1970 he reached the absolute low of his life. "The craving for heroin burnt in my body. I had blood in my urine and feces, and when I vomited there was blood." He finally came to a doctor who gave him only another month to live. Reidar decided to inject a final dose of heroin and then climbed up on the highest bridge in Gothenburg, Sweden, ready to jump. At this moment he both heard and saw Jesus:

> In front of me I saw the outline of a face. Was I hallucinating again? But the outline became more clear. I did not see clear features, but I saw that there was a crown of thorns on top of the head and that the hair was curly and shining gold. It sort of radiated light from it, and I saw two hands, the palms of which were wounded, stretched out to me. And I heard a voice, so soft and fatherly loving, as I have never heard before. "Reidar, Reidar", I heard. "You have tried everything in life. You have lost everything. There is nothing more left. The only thing you look forward to is to take your life. If you decide to do that, you will be lost eternally and there will be no memory of you. But you have forgotten to count with me. Put what is left of your life in my hands and I will heal and save you".

Reidar does not know how he managed to climb down from the bridge. From that moment on his life became organized. About a year and a half later he married and eventually the couple had two children. Reidar still visits prisons, but now as a pastor, preaching the gospel of Jesus.

The case of Mary is similar to that of Reidar. Mary was on the verge of suicide. Her search for the meaning of life, a world-view, eventually led to an acute crisis, which was wiped out in one stroke when she met Jesus in a vision. Suddenly she saw a way out of chaos. In Mary's own words:

> I was sitting quite relaxed, just in front of the house where I lived. I don't think there was any thought inside my head. It was a hot summer day and I could not see a cloud in the sky. Then I looked up in the sky and what did I see? A figure of Christ across the whole sky. Christ was standing there, straight-backed with his mantle folded around him. At his right side there was a big male lion with

> a huge mane, his paws kindly stretched out in front of him. The face of Christ was long and thin, with long, somewhat curly hair. Around his head I could see a halo (which I have never seen on any picture). It looked like strongly stretched triangles with their points upwards. When seeing this figure of Christ, he simultaneously turned himself to me and made a gesture with his right hand. It could only be interpreted in one way — follow me. The next second everything was gone.

There are many similarities between Reidar and Mary. Both had a negative relationship with their mother, both went through a difficult religious socialisation. But as distinguished from Reidar, Mary already during her years at school exhibited a strong concern for existential questions about life and death, searching as she was for a world-view. Jesus played an important role in her life during those years. In the case of Reidar, Jesus entered his life when Reidar was in prison, where he met a saved convict (prisoner). From a psychological point of view this means that it is no coincidence that Reidar and Mary had visions of Jesus, who played an important role in their earlier life.

Another interesting finding in the comparative analysis of these case studies is that a strong religious socialisation is not a necessary condition for a religious vision. Quite a few of the informants hardly received any religious education in their parental home. But their visionary experiences are, as we have seen, of a different kind, which I chose to call abstract or unstructured visions of, for example, light.

One can clearly notice these factors in the case of Agneta, who in a situation of psychological shock with "anxiety and thoughts of suicide" had a vision of light, which gave her intense feelings of joy. How should the experience be interpreted? "The concept of God didn't exist for me", she mentions. Her first interpretation was that it could be a manic psychosis. But when talking to a priest she understood that it was a religious experience. The most important words that came to her mind during the vision of light were "forgiveness" and "satisfaction", words that fit very well the type of crisis situation that she described.

My final example, belonging to the same category, is Alice. She was brought up in a small farm, was struck by tuberculosis in her early teens, got married — "the years free from sorrow". Then, in the middle of the 70s, the heavy years began. First her mother died. The firm trust in God, which her mother expressed, made a strong impression on Alice. About one year later her husband became ill, with a life-threatening illness. Alice refers to this period in her life as "the dark night of the soul", an expression borrowed from the great catholic mystic John of the Cross. Just like the 16th century mystic Alice had an immense experience of the absence of God. The day after her husband's death she felt as if she was not alone at home. At the same time she saw a light — "the good, warming light". Her understanding of this experience was that her husband now was in good hands.

Alice's interest in religion now increased. After eight years alone Alice had to face another crisis, this time with a cervical vertebra. At this time, late one evening in May 1985, she had her nature-mystical visionary experience, beautifully described in the following words:

> It was close to eleven in the evening when I happened to look out of the window. The sky was grey and cloudy and in the twilight everything was so calm and quiet. Behind their black, shining windows people already had gone to sleep, but from some windows a feeble light (svagt ljus) was shining.
> All my life I have lived in a sort of friendly relationship with trees and I confidentially share my existence with those birches and pines that grow outside my house.
> Suddenly my gaze was fixed on one of the pines, the trunk of which was concealed behind a house. I could only see the top of the tree, which shined flaming red in a strong glowing light. Fire-coloured flames of light sort of devoured the top of the pine-tree. Waves of light were visible around the top of the tree.
> From my window view I clearly saw the branches of the pine and it's needles looked strongly enlarged. They seemed to be self-shining and sparkling red. /—/
> I stood there, breathless and quiet, with my sight fixed on this pine-top, which really was burning of fire and heat — but without being consumed and charred into ashes.
> A feeling of total harmony flowed through me during these seconds, before the glowing, shining light slowly dissolved and disappeared. My whole being was in strong union with an undestructable, universal wholeness, where everything is eternal and immortal.

Life-crisis and visionary experience

The relation between crisis and intense religious experience is, of course, well-known within the psychology of religion, all the way from Starbuck and James to Ullman, who in a recently published study of religious conversion pointed at the same relation (Ullman, 1989). It is also well-known that the religious experience, during a few seconds of intense emotion, solves the situation of crisis. Now, my main question is if we can find out which psychological processes can be involved in these life-transforming experiences. I have some suggestions concerning this question and will return to them shortly.

In order to structure the comparative analysis of the 35 case-studies, I used the creativity analogy proposed by Batson & Ventis. The analogy differentiates between four phases:

1. Preparation; in our case especially the religious socialisation and the degree of psychological stress.
2. Incubation.
3. Illumination; that is the religious vision.
4. Verification; that is the new life, the transformed self.

I will present some short comments on these phases.

1. Preparation. The crisis can be regarded as the most important motivational basis for the religious visions. The most frequent motives mentioned by the informants are a need for love, often a compensation for a lack of motherly or fatherly love; a need for meaning, a longing for a world-view; a need of confirmation, for example of an earlier impression of divine presence; and a need of consolation in a difficult life-situation.

In the case of Hans we could notice stress connected with his father being absent during his childhood. The longing felt by Hans for his father and fatherly love is clearly expressed in his auditory experience in his adolescence, when he heard the words "I am your heavenly Father. I love you".

Another example is Anita, who in her early twenties experienced an existential crisis. Life was without meaning. Anita had always resisted the inner religiosity of her parents. Now, as an adult and mother, she was reminded of this religiosity in her parental home. Then, in a vision, she saw Jesus on the cross, and shortly thereafter a hand which gently lifted the symbolic image of her heart. For Anita these visions not only meant that Jesus existed but also that his essence was love, a view which she holds to this day. Her existential crisis dissolved; instead of chaos there was order, integration.

2. Incubation. In quite a few cases it was obvious that the informants went through a phase which W. James called "the psychology of self-surrender". In addition to this concept I observed a probable shift in cognitive style to a receptive mode (Deikman, 1971; 1976). In a majority of cases the religious visions occurred when the informant was alone and relaxed, for example when going to sleep or when waking up during the night, when taking a bath, etc. In other words: situations which promote a shift in cognitive style. Similar situations have been observed within the psychology of the creative process.

I will illustrate both the psychology of self-surrender and the shift in cognitive mode with a few very short examples. First there are the informants who were on the verge of committing suicide. The minutes and seconds just before a planned suicide are, of course, as close to a total surrender as one can come. Another informant, Ester, cried out: "Now, Jesus, I give you my whole joyless life". Immediately after this desperate cry she experienced the presence of Jesus. A further example is Berit, who after a long period of illness felt a newly awakened interest for religion and studied the Bible in order to find an explanation for her suffering. She became disappointed and came to the conclusion that there is no goodness in the whole world. In a fury she firmly closed the bible. Precisely at this moment she "saw" Jesus, who smiled at her.

The shift in cognitive style can be illustrated with the case of Åke. For him alone, a grey cloudy sky in January was transformed into "a strong yellow light". In the case of Mary, mentioned above, we noticed that the vision came to her in a situation of total relaxation, the direct opposite of her extremely distressed life. Alice woke up at night and saw a light in which Jesus appeared. The visionary experience answered her need of confirmation that Jesus is alive. Years of doubt were wiped out in a few seconds. Bertil was tired of his numerous attempts to try to achieve a personal revelation of Jesus, an expression of his need for confirmation of an earlier experience of salvation. He lay down on his bed in the monastery where he was temporarily staying, relaxed and stared at the cloth hanging above the wash-basin. Suddenly "the cloth started to come alive". Eventually, after a few minutes, Bertil continues, "I saw the contours of a face". Bertil immediately interpreted the experience as an apparition of Jesus. Now he finally had received the confirmation which for many years he had been striving for.

3. Illumination. I focused on four dimensions of the religious visions: the emotional, communicative, perceptual, and cognitive dimensions. As for the emotional dimension, feelings of intense joy, peace, security and love are dominant. The communicative qualities are good, as contrasted to classical mystical experiences, which are qualified by ineffability.

With regard to the perceptual dimension, the visual perceptions are dominant, sometimes in combination with auditory and/or tactile perceptions. Another important finding is a reported inhibition of external and internal stimulation during the vision. With regard to the cognitive dimension, I studied the informants' interpretations of the more or less structured vision content. I found that more abstract, unstructured experiences are more open for interpretation than structured experiences.

I will refrain from giving more examples, as the case studies cited above already, to a certain degree, illustrate these factors. It can be worth mentioning, however, that of all the fifty experiences quoted in the thirty-five cases (some of the informants had more than one experience) exactly half of them were of a visual type. Seven experiences were a combination of visual and auditory sensations, while only four experiences were purely of an auditory nature. The last category is tactile sensations, of which there are three, and a combination of tactile and visual sensation, of which there are two. Nine experiences were difficult to judge in accordance with the categories chosen.

4. Verification — the new life. As expected, the religious activites of the informants increased significantly after the vision. Those who went to church once a week or two-three times a month increased from 27% to 48%. Those reading the Bible with the same frequency increased from 21% to 47%, while private prayer in the same category increased even more, from 49% to 79%. It is interesting to note that private dimensions of religiosity such as prayer and Bible reading increase more than church-attendance. A plausible explanation for this difference is that intense religious experiences belong to the most personal experiences in a person's life.

With regard to the informants attitude towards the Bible, the fundamentalist attitude decreases from 45% to 36%, while the religious-hermeneutic attitude increases from 28% to 54%.

The questionnaire contained sixteen statements related to the concept of God. In the analysis of the answers I worked with two axes: personal-impersonal aspects and transcendent-immanent aspects. An example of an impersonal-immanent statement is the following: "God is the white light which is hidden in the things of the world". An example of a personal-transcendent statement is: "God is for me like a person, but tremendously lifted above earthly life".

It is perfectly clear that the last mentioned aspects decrease, in favour of the impersonal-immanent aspects of the God image. The results are statistically significant.

A final aspect of change in the informants religiosity concerns their religious orientation, as defined by Batson and Ventis (1982). As far as extrinsic orientation is concerned, the results are uncertain. Due to space limitations I cannot go deeper into this matter. The changes concerning the quest-orientation are of a minor nature and therefore certainly not statistically significant (this scale has been debated at great length and has now been revised). The changes in the intrinsic dimension, however, are statistically significant, as expected. It is perfectly clear that the informants, after their visionary experiences, live their religion and try to create a harmonious relation between religion and daily life.

The psychology of visionary experience

In an attempt to integrate the data (in accordance with the Glaser & Strauss approach) I presented a model of personality, based on ego-psychology. The model focuses on perceptual-cognitive processes, without neglecting primary process mechanisms. It is my conviction that the psychology of religion is in great need of new theoretical approaches to the study of religious visions. Below I will try to outline the main parts of the chosen model and the dynamic process which, according to my judgment, can be activated in religious visions.

Following Rothstein (1981), and in connection with developments in object relations theory, Epstein (1988) distinguishes between the representational and functional aspects of the ego. With the help of the former, the individual constructs a differentiated view of himself and the outside world. This subsystem can further be divided into object- and self-representations. The functional system consists of adaptive, defensive, mediating and synthetic functions.

The adaptive function is responsible for adaptation to reality. It has at its disposal a number of abilities or dispositions which are inherited, such as perception, memory, intelligence, and language. The ego psychologist of the forties and fifties spoke of the primary apparatus of the ego (Hartmann 1958).

The defensive function of the ego also in one way serves adaptation to the environment, more particularly to the psychological environment. In contrast to the former function, however, the ego's defense mechanisms are not inherited but acquired under the influence of the socio-cultural milieu. In earlier ego psychology this function was called the ego's secondary apparatus.

The mediating function corresponds to the classic psychoanalytic view of the ego-acting as a mediator between the id and the super ego, or between the id and the environment. An interesting function is the synthetic one, that is an "organ for equilibrium", which strives for balance in a constantly shifting psyche. We see here, in other words, that the psychoanalytic theorising of Freud has been carried considerably further. Epstein's model, here rather simplified, integrates among other things post-war advances, including object relations theory.

It thus emerges that the "I" is not identical with the ego. The "I" is rather one component in a composite structure. The "I" is described as "the self-representation as agent" (Rothstein). It is an active subject since "it sees itself as the one capable of activity", comments Epstein. The I is developed from the ego's continuous sensation of itself.

I tried to relate this model of personality to Hans-Carl Leuner's concept of the "autosymbolic representation of intrapsychic conflicts" (Leuner, 1977, 1978). According to Leuner, this psychological process is often activated in situations of extreme emotional stress. His results have been confirmed, amongst others, by Peter Slade & Richard Bentall in a recently published empirical study of hallucinations (1988). Bearing these theoretical concepts in mind, I am now in a position to summarize some of the results of this study.

The acute crisis prior to the vision leads to a situation of self-surrender or a cognitive shift to a receptive mode, through different situations of relaxation. Such a shift alters the normal balance or homeostasis within the complex ego-structure, which in turn leads to an inhibition or partial inhibition of adaptive, defensive, and mediating functions, in favour of an activation of the synthetic function. An inhibition of these functions simultaneously leads to a partial or total inhibition of the "self-representation", the experience of the I as an active subject. The synthetic function chooses that psychological process which is best suited for its goal: homeostasis, equilibrium. The religious vision establishes order in a chaotic system. Basically it could be a sort of adaptive process, similar to physiological processes such as sweating when the body is too warm and shivering when it is too cold. The psychological system also strives for homeostasis, order, which naturally can be attained in different ways. Religious visions can be understood as autosymbolic representations of intrapsychic conflicts, a dynamic process "chosen" by the synthetic function in order to establish homeostasis. It is striking that the content of the informants visions fit so well into their situations of chaos. The religious visions immediately establish order in chaos. In other words, religious visions, or object representations like Jesus or Angels are symbolic representations of order, as against chaos.

REFERENCES

Arbman, E. (1963, 1968, 1970). *Ecstasy or Religious Trance*. Three Vols. Stockholm: Norstedts Forlag.

Batson, C.D. & Ventis, W.L. (1982). *The Religious Experience: A Social-Psychological Approach*. New York & Oxford: Oxford University Press.

Carroll, M.P. (1986). *The Cult of the Virgin Mary*. Princeton: Princeton University Press.

Christian, W.A. (1981). *Apparitions in Late Medieval and Renaissance Spain*. Princeton: Princeton University Press.

Deikman, A. (1971). Bimodal Consciousness. *Archives of General Psychiatry*, 25, 481-489.

Deikman, A. (1976). Bimodal Consciousness and the Mystical Experience. In P. Lee (Ed.). *Symposium on Consciousness*. New York: Viking Press.
Ellwood, R. S. (1980). *Mysticism in World Religion*. Englewood Cliffs, NJ: Prentice-Hall.
Epstein, M. (1988). The Deconstruction of the Self: Ego and "Egolessness" in Buddhist Insight Meditation. The Journal of *Transpersonal Psychology*, 20, 61-69.
Geels, A. (1989). *Skapande mystik. En psykologisk studie av Violet Tengbergs religiösa visioner och konstnärliga skapande*. (Creative Mysticism. A Psychological study of Violet Tengberg's religious visions and artistic creations). Malmö: Plus Ultra.
Geels, A. (1991). *Att möta Gud i kaos. Religiösa visioner i dagens Sverige*.(Encounter with God in Chaos. Religious visions in contemporary Sweden). Stockholm: Norstedts Forlag.
Glaser, B. & Strauss, A.L.(1967) *The Discovery of Grounded Theory.Strategies for Qualitative Research*. Chicago: Aldine.
Goodman, F. D. (1987). Visions. In M. Eliade (Ed.) *The Encyclopedia of Religion*, Vol.15, pp. 282-288.
Hay, D. (1982). *Exploring Inner Space*. Harmondsworth: Penguin.
Hartman, H. (1958). *Ego Psychology and the Problem of Adaptation*. New York: International Universities Press.
Holmes, D. S. (1970). Differential Change in Affective Intensity and the Forgetting of Unpleasant Personal Experiences. *Journal of Personality and Social Psychology*, 15, 234-239.
Inge, W.R. (1969). *Mysticism in Religion*. London: Rider & Co.
Koestler, A. (1954). *The Invisible Writing*. Boston: Beacon Press.
Leuner, H. (1977). Guided Affective Imatery: An Account of its Development. *Journal of Mental Imagery*, 1, 73-91
Leuner, H. (1978). Basic Principles and Therapeutic Efficacy of Guided Affective Imagery (GAI). In J.L. Singer & K.S. Pope (Eds.), *The Power of Human Imagination*.
Moore, P.G. (1978). Mystical Experience, Mystical Doctrine, Mystical Technique. In S.T. Katz (Ed.) *Mysticism and Philosophical Analysis*.
Pettersson, T. (1975). *The Retention of Religious Experience*. Uppsala: Almquist & Wiksell International.
Rothstein, A. (1981). The Ego: An evolving construct. *International Journal of Psychoanalysis*, 62, 435-445.
Slade, P.D. & Bentall, R.P. (1988). *Sensory Deception. A Scientific Analysis of Hallucination*. London & Sydney: Croom Helm.
Stace, W.T. (1960). *Mysticism and Philosophy*. London: Macmillan
Ullman, C. (1989). *The Transformed Self. The Psychology of Religious Conversion*. New York: Plenum Press.
Underhill, E. (1926). *Mysticism. A Study in the Nature and Development of Man's Spiritual Consciousness*. London: Methuen.
Wainwright, W.J. (1981). *Mysticism. A Study of its Nature, Cognitive Value and Moral Implications*. Thetford.
Zimdars-Swartz, S.L. (1991). *Encountering Mary. From La Salette to Medjugorje*. Princeton: Princeton University Press.

SECTION 3 CLINICAL RESEARCH

CHAPTER 12
RELIGIOUS ORIENTATION, RELIGIOUS ACTIVITY AND MENTAL HEALTH.

Eystein Kaldestad

Martin and Nichols (1962) found that until 1962 in the research literature religious belief had been found to correlate with three MMPI scales. In a sample of 163 college students these expected personality correlates were in general not found. Sanua (1969) reviewed a number of recent studies pertinent to the common belief that religion is a basis of sound mental health and general well-being, and found no empirical support for the theory.

Lindenthal et al. (1970) found in a cross-sectional metropolitan random sample of 938 adults that a measure of psychopathology was found to be negatively correlated with church affiliation and with church attendance. The more psychologically impaired the individual, the more likely he was to attend church even less frequently in time of crisis than before. Psychopathology was positively correlated with reported prayer at times of life crisis. In 1971 Stark (1971) summed up the research literature at that time by stating that whether psychopathology was measured by clinical diagnosis of severe impairment or by more inclusive and less severe survey indices, there was a negative relationship with religious commitment. Indeed, psychopathology seemed to impede the manifestation of conventional religious beliefs and activities.

Kahoe (1974) found in a sample of 518 college students that intrinsic religious orientation was related to responsibility and internal locus of control, while extrinsic religious orientation was negatively related to the same. Heintzelman and Lawrence (1976) found in a sample of 82 students that their orthodox religiosity correlated significantly negatively with manifest hostility, and not significantly with anxiety and self-esteem.

Lea (1982) made an overview of the social scientific literature of the past two decades concerning the relationship between religion, mental health and social behaviour. He concluded that religiosity is negatively related to personal adjustment in students, but appears positively related to adjustment in the adult population, especially among the elderly. Batson and Ventis (1982) found that researchers had used seven measures of mental health. They reviewed 67 studies and found among these 37 negative relations between religion and mental health, and 15 positive and 15 neutral relations. Religious engagement gave negative results for personal competence and control, self-acceptance and self-actualization and for open-mindedness and flexibility. There was a negative correlation between religiosity and freedom from worry and guilt in young people, but a positive one for older individuals. For appropriate social behaviour and for personal identity there were no significant results. There was a strong positive correlation between religiosity and the absence of mental illness. The negative correlation between religion and positive measures of mental health is the result of extrinsic (Alpport & Ross, 1967) religious orientation. Both the intrinsic (Alpport & Ross, 1967) and quest orientation (Batson & Ventis, 1982) are positively related to positive measures of mental health. The intrinsic orientation is related positively especially to freedom from worry and guilt, and to personal competence and control. The quest orientation is positively related to openmindedness and flexibility. For absence of mental illness there were no data in relation to these three religious orientations.

Bergin (1983) found that a metaanalysis of 24 pertinent studies revealed no support for the preconception that religiousness is necessarily correlated with psychopathology, but it also showed only slightly positive correlation of religion and mental health. He suggested that it is not surprising that given the diverse measures of religion and the diverse criteria of mental functioning, results of correlating the two sets of factors yield a mixed picture.

Francis (1985) restricted himself only to those studies which were concerned with the quantitative study of personality and religion, and decided to adopt Eysenck's theory as the basis of the relationship between personality and religion. In two samples of 1088 and of 1715 subjects he and his coworkers found that religion was uncorrelated with neuroticism when sex differences were partialed out. They also found that in the first sample the introverts were more religious than the extraverts, but the proportion of variance accounted for was small. In the sample of 1715 subjects introverts were still more religious. The Eysenck Lie scale probably either measures a lack of insight or conformity to social rules and pressures. Francis et al. found that those who score high on the Lie scale tend to be more religious than those who score low on this measure.

Spilka, Hood and Gorsuch (1985) reviwed the empirical research literature and found that religion correlates equally well with evidence of both positive and negative adjustment for persons of all ages. Many studies reveal no relationship between religion and personal effectiveness. There is no evidence that religious persons become psychotic more or less frequently than those considered nonreligious. Research has further shown that a pattern of desirable personal and social characteristics is the lot of those who tend to be intrinsic and committed in outlook. The individual attributes of extrinsic and consensual persons, however, leave much to be desired. Spilka, Hood and Gorsuch concluded that despite the fact that a great deal of research on religion and mental disorder has been published, it is apparent that this work generally tends to be scattered, poorly conceived and carried out, and frequently lacks any coherent theoretical organization. Clearly, this is a fruitfull area needing much more rigorous examination.

Witter, Stock, Okun and Haring (1985) reported on a quantitative, meta-analytic research synthesis of 556 sources of the U.S. research literature, of which 28 contained religion/subjective well-being effect sizes. They found that religion was significantly, positively, related to subjective well-being. The relation between religion and subjective well-being was stronger for religious activity than for religiosity measures. The relation was stronger for samples of older than younger adults. The strength of the religion/subjective well-being relation had decreased over time. Religion accounted for between 2 and 6 percent of the variance in adult subjective well-being. Religion appeared to be less potent than eight other variables: income, occupational status, health, adjustment, lonliness, neuroticism, family satisfaction and work satisfaction. It was as potent as five variables: education, socioeconomic status composite, marital status, work status and social activity, and more potent than three other variables: age, gender and race.

Chamberlain and Zika (1988) reached two major conclusions: First, the relation between religiosity and subjective well-being, where it does occur, is positive but small. Second, it is clear that the relationship between religiosity and subjective well-being is variable, depending how these constructs are assessed. Perhaps the major outcome of this study is to emphasize that no absolute conclusions can be drawn about the religiosity-well-being relationship.

Donahue (1989) made the claim that future research should examine the cognitive structure and ramifications of religious belief, determine which belief structures are associated with which effects, and at least allow conservative/moderate/liberal delineations of Protestants. Watson, Morris and Hood (1989) maintained that the diversity of religious types in the population may present formidable challenges to anyone hoping to make cumulative research progress in documenting the psychological effects of religious commitment. Use of the Allport and Ross scales (1967) to identify types of religious orientation may prove invaluable in clarifying the constitution of samples. They found in a sample of 212 subjects that orthodox perspectives were associated with beneficial psychological effects.

Crawford, Handal and Wiener (1989) maintained that past studies often failed to test for a possible differential relationship between religion and mental health/distress as a function of sex. Highly religious females were significantly less distressed and manifested better psychological adjustment than medium and low religious subjects. In male subjects there was no significant relationship between subjects' degree of religiousness and mental health/distress.

Ross (1990) found in a telephone survey of a sample of 401 cases that those who believed strongly in their religion had lower distress levels than those who professed a weak belief. Those who rejected all religion also had low distress levels. Persons who participated in religion without religious conviction were in the worst condition psychologically.

Schwab and Petersen (1990) found in a sample of 164 subjects that the concept of "A wrathful God" was positively related to lonliness, and "A helpful God" on the other hand, showed a negative correlation with lonliness. Heskestad (1984) found in a sample of 73 surgical and 87 psychiatric patients no correlation between psychic morbidity and religiousness and religious upbringing. There was a weak negative correlation between psychiatric morbidity and religious integrity and religious stability.

Stifoss-Hanssen (1988) developed a scale for religious rigidity/flexibility and found in a sample of 56 hospitalized neurotic patients and 70 healthy subjects as controls that there was a significantly higher rigidity in the religiosity of the neurotic patients than in the religiosity of the control group.

Larson et al. (1986) made a systematic analysis of quantitative research on religious variables in four major psychiatric journals between 1978 and 1982. Of 2348 psychiatric articles reviewed, 59 included a quantified religious variable, most often a single static measure of religion. They concluded that a comparison with systematic analyses of religious research in psychology and sociology suggests that psychiatric research lacks conceptual and methodological sophistication in the religious area. The data suggest that the academic knowledge and skills needed to evaluate religion have not been absorbed into the psychiatric domain.

Robinson (1986) also made a systematic analysis of the same psychiatric journals for the same period and asked: Why does psychiatry so infreqquently evaluate religion, and when it does, why does it do so at such a substandard level of quality? She concluded that religious measures should be used more frequently in psychiatric research, and one should include multidimensional religiosity measures with acceptable reliability.

Kroll and Sheehan (1989) studied religious beliefs, practices and experiences of 52 psychiatric inpatients and found that patients with depressive and anxiety disorders tended to score lower than those with other diagnoses on a wide variety of indexes of religion. The authors concluded that religion is an important factor in most patients' lives and that individual inquiry and systematic research into this neglected area are both feasible and important.

As a conclusion one may maintain that in the research literature there seem to be few or no conclusive empirical research reports regarding the relations between religion, personality and mental health. As Bergin (1983), suggested it is not surprising that given the diverse measures of religion and the diverse criteria of mental functioning, results of correlating the two sets of factors yield a mixed picture.

Research questions.

The purpose of this study wass to add some more empirical knowledge of these questions to the already existing research literature. Are there important religious and personality differences between men and women? Which differences are there between sincerely believing Christians and those not so sincerely believing people regarding religious measures, personality variables and mental health? Which differences are there for the same variables between the healthy subjects and psychiatric patients? How important are the informants' parents' Christian belief, the informants' gender, age, education, personality type and psychiatric symptoms for their religious orientation, religious activity, christian belief and morality? How important are religious orientations of the intrinsic, extrinsic and quest type for the informants' religious activity, Christian belief and morality?

Material and methods.

Seventy healthy persons from the staff and 88 nonpsychotic psychiatric inpatients at the psychiatric hospital Modum Bads Nervesanatorium answered a questionnaire with 358 items.

Since some of the items in the questionnaire were meaningfull only for believing Christians, subjects that answered strongly disagree to the item: I am a believing Christian, were excluded from the material to be analyzed. Those who answered strongly agree to this item, were put into the "wholly believing group", and those who answered either partly agree, unsure/neutral or partly disagree to this item, were called the "partially believing group". All the Ss were Protestants, mostly Lutherans.

In addition to demographic questions the subjects reported about their parents' Christian beliefs and about their own religious activity. The parents' belief was scored from five to one, and their scores were averaged: sincerely believing 5, positive attitude 4, neutral 3, do not know 2, negative 1. The informants' religious activity score was from six to zero based upon their participation in divine services and religious meetings, interest for religious programs in TV and radio, religious articles in papers and the weekly press, how often they pray and how often they read the Bible.

Then there were items randomly distributed from eight different questionnaires: Allport & Ross Intrinsic Scale (nine items) and Extrinsic Scales (11 items) (Allport & Ross, 1967), Batson & Ventis' Quest (Interactional) Scale (six items) (1982), Batson & Ventis' Doctrinal Orthodoxy Scale (12 items) (1982), Kaldestad's Liberal Belief Scale (eight items) (1992), Woodrum's Moral Conservatism Index (five items) (1988a,b), Kaldestad's Humanistic Morality Scale (eight items) (1992), Stifoss-Hanssen's Religious Rigidity/Flexibility Scale (39 items) (1988). All these questionnaires were scored on a Likert scale ranging from 5 = strongly agree, 4 = partly agree, 3 = unsure, neutral, 2 = partly disagree to 1 = strongly disagree. Then there came 11 items from the LAM Scales of Hunt (1972) with answers scored as literal, antiliteral or symbolic. As a measurement instrument for mental health were used the SCL-90 (Derogatis, Lipman, & Covi, 1973) with 90 psychiatric symptoms scored from zero to four, and for personality and character Torgersen's Basic Character Inventory (Lippe & Torgersen, 1984; Torgersen, 1980) with 136 items scored yes or no, and the scores put together in quantified subscales for oral, obsessive and hysterical character types, with scores from zero to eight.

The development of Norwegian versions of the scales was described in two previous articles (Kaldestad, 1991, 1992), where the conceptual and discriminating validity, internal consistency as measured with Cronbach's alpha, and the factor structure of the scales and their intercorrelations were presented (See **Tables 1 and 2**). The eight items of Kaldestad's Liberal Belief Scale were reversed and put together with the 12 items from Batson & Ventis' Doctrinal Orthodoxy Scale to form a combined Orthodox-Liberal Belief Scale, where high scores indicate a high degree of orthodox belief and low scores indicate as high degree of liberal belief. In the same way the eight items of Kaldestad's Humanistic Morality Scale were reversed and put together with the five items from Woodrum's Moral Conservatism Index to form a combined Christian-

Humanistic Morality Scale, where high scores can be interpreted as high degree of conservative Christian moral attitudes and low scores can be interpreted as high degree of humanistic morality attitudes.

Table 1. Cronbach's alpha and average inter-item-correlations for the Likert scales (n= 158).

Scale	Cronbach's alpha	Mean inter-item-correlat.
Intrinsic Scale	0.854	0.392
Extrinsic Scale	0.709	0.183
Quest (Interactional) Scale	0.498	0.145
Doctrinal Orthodoxy Scale	0.954	0.652
Liberal Belief Scale	0.743	0.269
Moral Concervatism Index	0.681	0.292
Humanistic Morality Scale	0.796	0.322
Orthodox-Liberal Scale	0.929	0.418
Christian-Humanistic Scale	0.824	0.253

Two-tailed two-sample T-tests of the scores on the scales between the "wholly believing group" and the "partially believing group", between the two sexes, and between healthy subjects and psychiatric patients, were performed.

Stepwise multiple regression analyses were performed with scores on Intrinsic, Extrinsic and Quest (Interactional) Scales, and score for religious activity, scores on the Orthodox-Liberal Belief Scale and the Christian-Humanistic Morality Scale as dependent variables, and as independent variables: parents' Christian belief, informants' gender, age (years), education (years), scores on oral, obsessive and hysterical character subscales of the Basic Character Inventory, and SCL-90 GSI score.

A second type of stepwise multiple regression analyses used scores for religious activity, Orthodox-Liberal Belief and Christian-Humanistic Morality as dependent variables, and as independent variables used scores on Allport and Ross' Intrinsic and Extrinsic Scales and Batson & Ventis' Quest (Interactional) Scale.

Table 2. Pearson's correlation coefficients among scores of the belief and morality scales (n= 158).

	Orthodox	Liberal	Conserv	Humanist	Ortholib	Christhum
Orthodox	1.000	-0.637	0.536	-0.697		0.721
Liberal		1.000	-0.438	0.708		-0.681
Conserv			1.000	-0.511	0.548	
Humanist				1.000	-0.769	
Ortholib					1.000	0.775
Christhum						1.000

Explanations: Orthodox = Batson & Ventis' Doctrinal Orthodoxy Scale. Liberal = Kaldestad's Liberal Belief Scale. Conserv = Woodrum's Moral Conservatism Index. Humanist = Kaldestad's Humanistic Morality Scale. Ortholib = Kaldestad's Orthodox-Liberal Belief Scale. Christhum = Kaldestad's Christian-Humanistic Morality Scale.

Results.

Women had significantly less education, less believing parents, less orthodox belief and more humanistic morality than men (See **Table 3**). The "wholly believing" group had significantly more believing parents, higher intrinsic, higher orthodox, higher conservative Christian morality scores, higher religious activity, but lower SCL-90 GSI score, lower BCI oral score, lower extrinsic, lower quest, lower liberal, and lower humanistic morality scores than the "partially believing" group (See **Table 4**).

The psychiatric patients had significantly higher SCL-90 GSI score, higher BCI oral and obsessive scores, and higher extrinsic and quest scores, but less education and lower BCI hysterical score than the healthy persons (See **Table 5**).

Table 3. Two-tailed two-sample T-tests between 52 men and 106 women (n= 158).

Variable	Men		Women		Sign.probabil.
	Mean	SD	Mean	SD	p
Age (years)	41.67	9.76	41.41	11.03	0.882
Education (years)	15.27	4.11	13.56	3.50	0.007 **
Parent's belief	4.24	1.00	3.88	0.97	0.030 *
SCL-90 GSI score	0.85	0.68	0.85	0.73	0.981
BCI oral score	3.61	1.96	3.92	1.96	0.355
BCI anal score	5.10	1.44	5.04	1.39	0.801
BCI hyster. score	3.60	1.47	3.84	1.59	0.368
Intrinsic score	3.53	0.74	3.39	0.95	0.366
Extrinsic score	2.45	0.64	2.54	0.64	0.396
Quest score	2.83	0.75	2.83	0.65	0.990
Orthodoxy score	4.33	0.80	4.01	0.98	0.043 *
Liberal score	3.26	0.86	3.45	0.80	0.168
Christian morality s.	3.23	1.02	3.13	0.94	0.555
Humanistic morality	3.38	0.83	3.69	0.81	0.024 *
Orthodox-liberal s.	3.70	0.73	3.43	0.84	0.050 *
Christian-human s.	2.86	0.79	2.62	0.75	0.074
Religious activity	2.58	1.02	2.31	0.91	0.101

* = $p < 0.05$. ** = $p < 0.01$. *** = $p < 0.001$.

Stepwise multiple regression (See **Table 6**) shows that parents beliefs significantly increased the informants' intrinsic score, religious activity, and their orthodox-liberal and Christian-humanistic morality scores, and reduced their extrinsic and quest scores. The variance explained by their parents beliefs varied from 4.5 to 18.2 %. BCI oral score and age increased their extrinsic score and together with parents beliefs explained a variance of 20.5 %. SCL-90 GSI score increased their quest score, and explained 12.5 % of the variance.

Table 4 Two-tailed two-sample t-tests between 80 "partially believing" and 78 "wholly believing" subjects (n = 158).

Variable	Part. believ. probability		Wholly believ.		Sign.	
	Mean	SD	Mean	SD	p	
Age (years)	41.58	11.19	41.41	10.02	0.923	
Education (years)	13.61	3.76	14.65	3.75	0.082	
Parents' belief	3.76	0.96	4.24	0.98	0.002	**
SCL-90 GSI score	1.02	0.75	0.67	0.64	0.002	**
BCI Oral score	4.26	1.92	3.37	1.91	0.004	**
BCI Obsessive score	5.07	1.51	5.04	1.30	0.897	
BCI Hysterical score	3.64	1.58	3.89	1.52	0.309	
Intrinsic score	2.85	0.76	4.04	0.53	0.000	***
Extrinsic score	2.87	0.51	2.14	0.55	0.000	***
Quest score	2.96	0.55	2.70	0.78	0.016	*
Orthodoxy score	3.49	0.90	4.77	0.31	0.000	***
Liberal Belief score	3.79	0.62	2.98	0.81	0.000	***
Moral Conservatism s.	2.82	0.89	3.52	0.91	0.000	***
Humanistic Morality s.	4.03	0.63	3.14	0.76	0.000	***
Orthodox-Liberal s.	2.98	0.71	4.07	0.45	0.000	***
Christian-Human. s.	2.30	0.62	3.11	0.68	0.000	***
Religious activity	1.81	0.75	3.01	0.73	0.000	***

* = $p < 0.05$. ** = $p < 0.01$. *** = $p < 0.001$.

Stepwise multiple regression (See **Table 7**) shows that intrinsic score increased, and extrinsic and quest scores reduced the informants' religious activity, with an explained variance together of 61.7 %. Intrinsic score increased and extrinsic score reduced the orthodox-liberal score, with an explained variance together of 61.1 %. Intrinsic score increased and quest score reduced their Christian-humanistic morality score, with an explained variance together of 51.9 %.

Independent variables with non-significant F ratio and B-coefficient are not mentioned in the Tables 6 and 7.

Table 5 Two-tailed two-sample t-tests between 70 healthy persons and 88 psychiatric patients (n = 158).

Variable	Part. believ.		Wholly believ.		Sign. probability	
	Mean	SD	Mean	SD	p	
Age (years)	42.46	12.14	40.73	09.19	0.325	
Education (years)	15.17	3.57	13.29	3.76	0.002	**
Parents' belief	4.11	0.91	3.90	1.05	0.186	
SCL-90 GSI score	0.29	0.23	1.29	0.66	0.000	***
BCI Oral score	2.46	1.39	4.90	1.64	0.000	***
BCI Obsessive score	4.79	1.22	5.27	1.51	0.032	*
BCI Hysterical score	4.42	1.41	3.24	1.45	0.000	***
Intrinsic score	3.47	0.92	3.41	0.86	0.676	
Extrinsic score	2.31	0.62	2.68	0.62	0.000	***
Quest score	2.67	0.65	2.95	0.69	0.011	*
Orthodoxy score	4.15	0.98	4.10	0.90	0.744	
Liberal Belief score	3.44	0.78	3.35	0.86	0.485	
Moral Conservatism s.	3.03	0.88	3.27	1.02	0.129	
Humanistic Morality s.	3.51	0.88	3.65	0.78	0.299	
Orthodox-Liberal s.	3.51	0.84	3.52	0.79	0.954	
Christian-Human. s.	2.70	0.78	2.70	0.76	0.966	
Religious activity	2.47	0.98	2.34	0.93	0.412	

* = $p < 0.05$. ** = $p < 0.01$. *** = $p < 0.001$.

Discussion.

That the women had less education than the men was as expected, especially for the older women. This trend is changing in our society for younger women. The other differences between women and men may be a result of the sampling process, and may not be representative for the christians in Norway.

Table 6 Stepwise multiple regression analyses for 70 healthy persons and 88 psychiatric patients (n = 158). Independent variables, parents' belief, respondents' gender, age (years), education (years), SCL-90 GSI score, scores on Basic Character Inventory for Oral, Obsessive and Hysterical personality types.

Dependent variable	Independent var.	Sign. F	R squared	B coeffic.
Intrinsic	Parents' belief	0.001	0.073	0.240
Extrinsic	Oral BCI	0.000	0.134	0.120
	Parents' belief	0.000	0.180	-0.128
	Age	0.000	0.205	0.010
Quest	SCL-90 GSI score	0.000	0.125	0.360
	Parents' belief	0.000	0.170	-0.147
Religious activity	Parents' belief	0.001	0.067	0.248
Orthodox-Liberal	Parents' belief	0.000	0.124	0.288
Christian-Humanist.	Parents' belief	0.000	0.182	0.330

The differences between the "wholly believing" and the "partially believing" group were as expected for the intrinsic, extrinsic, quest, orthodox, liberal, conservative Christian and humanistic scores, and may be interpreted as a positive confirmation of the discriminating validity of these scales. The differences between these groups in the informants' parents religious beliefs, SCL-90 GSI score and BCI oral score, tell us that the more sincerely believing peoples have had more sincerely believing parents, and are themselves more mentally healthy with a more mature personality than the less sincerely believing group.

As expected the psychiatric patients had higher SCL-90 GSI score, and BCI oral and obsessive scores, and lower BCI hysterical score than the healthy persons. The psychiatric patients had more psychiatric symptoms and less adequate personality than the healthy persons. The psychiatric patients also had higher scores on the Quest and Extrinsic Scales than the healthy subjects. Psychiatric patients use their religion for personal and social interests more than the healthy subjects do.

Psychiatric patients also seem to be less secure in their Christian belief than the healthy subjects. That psychiatric patients also had lower education than the healthy subjects may be a result of the sampling process, since the healthy subjects were persons from the well-educated staff of our hospital.

Table 7 Stepwise mltiple regression analyses for 70 healthy persons and 88 psychiatric patients (n = 158). Independent variables: Intrinsic, Extrinsic and Quest scores.

Dependent variable	Independent var.	Sign. F	R squared	B coefficient
Religious activity	Intrinsic	0.000	0.571	0.730
	Extrinsic	0.000	0.606	-0.233
	Quest	0.000	0.617	-0.158
Orthodox-Liberal	Intrinsic	0.000	0.568	0.593
	Extrinsic	0.000	0.611	-0.293
Christian-Humanis.	Intrinsic	0.000	0.460	0.582
	Quest	0.000	0.519	-0.272

In multiple regression analysis one may choose the dependent and the independent variables from theoretical considerations of which variables affect other variables. Although explained variance does not necessarily imply a causal relationship between the independent variable and the dependent variable, one may be inclined to think in that way.

Trait variables that exist before the state variable, may be interpreted as independent variables with the last mentioned state variable as dependent variable. Intrinsic, extrinsic and quest orientations probably are mostly trait variables, but also to some degree state variables. Psychiatric illness and immature personality reactions may influence the extrinsic and quest orientations.

Since the intrinsic, extrinsic and quest orientations are religious, motivational variables, it seems likely that these orientations may influence religious activity, belief and morality. One would, however, be on theoretically safer ground if one used only religious activity and SCL-90 GSI score as dependent variables, since these variables are typical state variables, and in the same regression equation use earlier and prevailing trait variables as independent variables.

In our regression analyses the most significant finding was that the informants' parents' religious belief explained so much of the variance of the informants' scores on the Intrinsic, Extrinsic, Quest, Orthodox-liberal and Christian-humanistic Scales and on the religious activity. A Christian upbringing seems to be very influential in determinging individual religiosity. High extrinsic score was associated with oral character traits and increased with age. An oral person probably is dependent and seeks personal comfort and social security through the religion. And with older age one probably also seeks more of these goals than younger peoples.

High quest score was associated with higher SCL-90 GSI score. Peoples with psychiatric symptomatology seem to be more doubting and undetermined in their christian belief, and are perhaps more occupied with existential musing than more healthy persons.

The effects of intrinsic, extrinsic and quest attitudes on religious activity were as expected. The intrinsic type of person also is the more religiously active person. There is harmony between religious orientation and religous activity. The extrinsic person is more occupied with getting something with the help of his religious engagement than with doing something himself. The person with quest attitude perhaps is so occupied with doubt and musing that less interest is left for religous activity.

As Batson and Ventis (1982) pointed out, there is an association between intrinsic orientation and orthodox belief. The more intrinsic are also the more orthodox. And the more extrinsic are also the more liberal. However, in this material extrinsic orientation does not seem to have such an effect.
Researchers throughout the world ought to cooperate in developing standard measuring instruments for religiosity, personality, mental health and pathology, so that the empirical results could be summed up in a quantitative meta-analysis of the relations among these variables.

REFERENCES

Allport, G. W., & Ross, J. M. (1967). Personal religious orientation and prejudice. *Journal of Personality and Social Psychology, 5,* 432-443.

Batson, C. D., & Ventis, W. L. (1982). *The religious experience. A social-psychological perspective.* New York: Oxford University Press.

Bergin, A. E. (1983). Religiosity and mental health: A critical reevaluation and meta-analysis. *Professional Psychology: Research and Practice, 14,* 170-184.

Chamberlain, K., & Zika, S. (1988). Religiosity, life meaning and well-being: some relationships in a sample of women. *Journal for the Scientific Study of Religion, 27,* 411-420.

Crawford, M. E., Handal, P. J., & Wiener, R. L. (1989). The relationship between religion and mental health/distress. *Review of Religious Research, 31,* 16-22.

Derogatis, L. R., Lipman, R. S., & Covi, L. (1973). SCL-90: An outpatient psychiatric rating scale - preliminary report. *Psychopharmacology Bulletin, 9,* 13-28.

Donahue, M. J. (1989). Disregarding theology in the psychology of religion: some examples. *Journal of Psychology and Theology, 17,* 329-335.

Francis, L. J. (1985). Personality and religion: theory and measurement. In: *Brown LB. Advances in the psychology of religion.* Oxford: Pergamon Press.

Heintzelman, M. E., & Lawrence, A. F. (1976). Relationship between religious orthodoxy and three personality variables. *Psychological Reports, 38,* 756-758.

Heskestad, S. (1984). Religi¢sitet og mental helse: En empirisk unders¢kelse. (Religiosity and mental health: An empirical study). *Nordisk psykiatrisk tidsskrift. (Nordic Journal of Psychiatry), 18,* 353-361.

Hunt, R. A. (1972). Mythological-symbolic religous commitment: The LAM scales. *Journal for the Scientific Study of Religion, 11,* 42-52.

Kahoe, R. D. (1974). Personality and achievement correlates of intrinsic and extrinsic religious orientations. *Journal of Personality and Social Psychology, 29,* 812-818.

Kaldestad, E. (1991). Intrinsic, Extrinsic and Quest Scales. Development of Norwegian versions. In: *Klinisk religionspsykologi.* Religionspsykologiska skrifter 7. Uppsala: Uppsala University Press.

Kaldestad, E. (1992). Questionnaires for doctrinal belief and morality. *Journal for Empirical Theology, 5,* 70-84.

Kroll, J., & Sheehan, W. (1989). Religious beliefs and practices among 52 psychiatric inpatients in Minnesota. *American Journal of Psychiatry*, 146, 67-72.

Larson, D. B., Pattison, E. M., Blazer, D. G., Omran, A. R., Kaplan, B. H. (1986). Systematic analysis of research on religious variables in four major psychiatric journals, 1978- 1982. *American Journal of Psychiatry, 143,* 329-334.

Lea, G. (1982). Religion, mental health and clinical issues. *Journal of Relgion and Health*, 21, 336-351.

Lindenthal, J. J., Myers, J. K., Pepper, M. P., & Stern, M. S. (1970). Mental status and religious behaviour. *Journal for the Scientific Study of Religion*, 9, 143-149.

Lippe, A. V. D., & Torgersen, S. (1984). Character and defense: Relationships between oral, obsessive and hysterical character traits and defense mechanisms. *Scandinavian Journal of Psychology, 25,* 258-264.

Martin, C., & Nichols, R. C. (1962). Personality and religious belief. *Journal of Social Psychology, 56,* 3-8.

Robinson, L. H. (1986). *Psychiatry and religion: Overlapping concerns.* Washington, D.C.: American Psychiatric Press, Inc.

Ross, C. E. (1990). Religion and psychological distress. *Journal for the Scientific Study of Religion*, 29, 236-245.

Sanua, V. D. (1969). Religion, mental health, and personality: A review of empirical studies. *American Journal of Psychiatry*, 125,97-107.

Schwab, R., & Petersen, K. U. (1990). Religiousness: Its relation to lonliness, neuroticism and subjective well-being. *Journal for the Scientific Study of Religion, 29,* 335-345.

Spilka, B., Hood, R. W. Jr., & Gorsuch, R. L. (1985). *The psychology of religion. An empirical approach.* Englewood Cliffs, N.J.: Prentice-Hall, Inc.

Stark, R. (1971). Psychopathology and religious commitment. *Review of Religious Research*, 12, 165-176.

Stifoss-Hanssen, H. (1988). *Rigid religiosity and mental health: An empirical study.* Paper presented at the XXIV International Congress of Psychology, Sidney, Australia, August 1988.

Torgersen, S. (1980). Hereditary-environmental differentiation of general neurotic, obsessive, and impulsive hysterical personality traits. *Acta Genetica Medicae et Gemellologiae*, 29, 193-207.

Watson, P. J., Morris, R. J., & Hood, R. W. Jr. (1989). Sin and self-functioning, part 4: Depression, assertiveness and religious commitments. *Journal of Psychology and Theology, 17,* 44-58.

Witter, R. A., Stock, W. A., Okun, M. A., & Haring, M. J. (1985). Religion and subjective wellbeing in adulthood: A quantitative synthesis. *Review of Religious Research, 26,* 332-342.

Woodrum, E. (1988a). Moral conservatism and the 1984 presidential election. *Journal for the Scientific Study of Religion, 27,* 192-210.

Woodrum, E. (1988b). Determinants of moral attitudes. *Journal for the Scientific Study of Religion*, 27, 553-573.

CHAPTER 13
A RELIGIOSITY SCALE BASED ON QUEST THEORY: DEVELOPMENT AND APPLICATION TO THE MENTAL HEALTH PROBLEM[1]

Hans Stifoss-Hanssen[2,3] & K Gunnar Götestam[2]

There are many views about the relationship between religion and mental health, based on clinical experience, but few have studied these relations empirically. Psychodynamic writings based on case studies have given important contributions to the discussion of the problem (Freud 1940-52, Rizzuto 1979, Meissner 1984, etc.), but these studies suffer from their linkedness to individual biographies and therefore yield no sufficient basis for generalization. Another way would be to explore the field with the use of modern psychological research design, using quantitative methods. These methods, however, primarily serve to falsify certain hypotheses and make others probable, and they do not usually enable conclusions about cause and effect.

Batson and Ventis box-score analysis (1982) is very informative, and their contention that the motivational dimension of religiosity seems to be the most interesting variable to explore if one wants to relate data on religion to to mental health or illness (Batson & Ventis 1982, pp. 211). In the present study the concepts mean - end and quest religiosity were therefore utilized, having both the theoretical assumptions and the validated scales in mind. It is taken into account that these theories and scales build upon a wide range of previous research (Allport & Ross 1967, Allen & Spilka 1967, Hoge 1972), and Strommen et al.'s (1972) work was also included.

---

[1] The research project has been supported by the Medical Faculty, University of Trondheim, Modum Bads Nervesanatorium Research Institute, and the Norwegian Council for Mental Health.

[2] Department of Psychiatry and Behavioural Medicine, University of Trondheim and Östmarka Hospital, Trondheim, Norway.

[3] Modum Bads Nervesanatorium Research Institute, Vikersund, Norway.

Using a scientific procedure on these grounds is, however, not without problems. These concepts and scales have some limitations, as far as their reliability is concerned, but more important, a transference into the Norwegian field of religiosity is not without problems (see for instance Heskestad 1984, and Kaldestad 1990).

With the indicated limitations in mind, the aim with the present study was to develop and apply a Rigid Religiosity Scale (RR Scale) to two different samples, one with neurotic patients, and one "normal" group. Furthermore, the scale should be refined, by factor analysis, to recalculate the sample on the basis of a revised RR Scale.

METHODS

Subjects

The questionnaire was answered by two different samples (first sample from a previous study, and second sample in the present study). There were two types of subjects, one group consisting of hospitalized, neurotic patients ($n_1=56$, $n_2=88$, response frequency 72%), recruited among in-patients at the Modum Bad Nervesanatorium, and the other being a "normal" control group ($n_1=70$, $n_2=70$, response frequency 74%), recurited from the staff and clergy at the same clinic. The sex distribution was in the first sample patients 22/34 (M/F) and "normals" 12/57, and in the second sample patients 33/55 and "normals" 19/51.

Questionnaires

Religious Rigidity: Including new items based on the idea behind the scales mentioned above, and consciously adapting this to what we conceived as the Norwegian religios tradition and culture, a new questionnaire was developed. Some items were more or less directly translated, in particular the six quest items that were translated and fully applied (Batson & Ventis 1982).

The original questionnaire consisted of six dimensions (five dimensions and 39 items shown in the Appendix, the sixth dimension with 11 items consitutes the LAM scale, see Hunt 1972, and Stifoss-Hanssen 1994b) was considered as a measure of rigid (vs flexible) religiosity.

The questionnaire was designed with items to be responded to on a five-point scale (strongly agree - strongly disagree, scored as 0-4 or 4-0 dependent on the direction of the item).

Religios rigidity has earlier been shown with the first sample in a previous study, which resulted in the Rigid-Flexible Religiosity Scale (RFR-39; se Appendix).

Psychiatric Symptoms: SCL-90 is a 90 item five point rating scale including nine different symptom dimensions (see Table 2), made for psychiatric outpatients (Derogatis, Lipman & Covi 1973). It has a high consistency, and is wellknown to be a valid instrument for neurotic psychiatric patients.

Table 1. Results of Factor analysis

Item	*Factor I Rigidity*	*Factor II Flexibility*	*Factor III Concretion*	*Factor IV Creativity*
ASS9	7864			
ASS3	7247			
COM5	7161			
COM2	6938			
COM6	6707			
COM4	6091			
ASS2	5505			
COM7	5414			
ASS12	4929			
ACC2		6712		
ACC7		6416		
ACC3		6087		
ACC4		5838		
ACC6		5689		
ACC5		5469		
COM8		5395		
SYM5		-4821		
SYM4		-4172		
SYM1			6826	
SYM2			6744	
ACC1			5592	
ASS6			5391	
COM3			5220	
SYM3			5165	
SYM6			5152	
ASS11			3826	
ASS10				-7687
ASS8				-6510
ASS1				-6131
ASS7				5201
ASS5				4678
ASS4				-3919
COM1				3284

Procedure

For the patients the questionnaires were distributed in a hospital setting and preceded by a brief instruction, and answered within this setting. The questionnaires given to the "normal" subjects was also accompanied by a similar instruction.

The first sample was in the present situation used for a factor analytic approach, and the new structure was then tested on the second sample.

Preliminaries

In the previous study, the aim was to look for differences in religiosity between the groups, or more exactly to test the hypothesis that the patients had a more "rigid" form of religiosity than the controls. This hypothesis was confirmed, and some significant group differences in the theoretically conceived dimensions of items were found as well (Stifoss-Hanssen 1994a). All the items in RFR-39 are shown in the Appendix.

However, the results indicated that the instrument did not have sufficient homogeneity. Our construct "Rigid Religiosity" seemed not to exist in the material in an evenly distributed way. The construct was therefore reconsidered, and the RFR-39 was subjected to a factor analytic approach, followed by a second test on the second sample.

Factor analytic revision of the scale

A series of factor analyses were computed (Norušis 1986) using Principal Component Analyses with Varimax rotation, where dimesions seemed rather consistent, mainly aggregating in a couple of factors.

LAM items: The LAM scale items were all accumulated under the main factor (Rigidity, see Table 1), but we have sofar not found any direct connection between LAM and mental pathology (Stifoss-Hanssen 1994b). It was therefore decided to leave that dimension out in further analyses in the present study, and rather to look at the LAM-data more effectively in other connections.

Quest Items: The quest items did not separate between patients and controls. Furthermore, the factor analysis spread them over all factors, with quite low loadings. This finding is confirmed by Kaldestad (1990). The quest items are interesting as a background, some of our items seem to cover the theoretical intention behind quest, which is complexity, doubt and tentativeness (Batson & Ventis 1982 p. 149), although in a negative formulation. The factor might thus be said to describe "absence of quest attitude".

On the background of this reasoning, it was decided to limit further analyses to the remaining four dimensions. We finally chose a four factor

PCA solution (explaining 47.1% of the variation), shown in Table 1.

Rigid Religiosity Factor: First of all, the analysis yielded one factor, composed of items from the two theoretical dimensions "complexity-simplicity" (COM) and "assertiveness-permissiveness" (ASS).

From the Factor analysis, a new RR-9 Scale was therefore developed from this Rigidity factor, which had a satisfactory homogeneity (Cronbachs alpha .77). It consists of the following nine items:

7. My faith makes everything easy to understand (COM2)

8. According to my religios convictions, I have to think carefully before I allow myself to indulge in something I feel attracted to (ASS2)

9. I feel that I ought to devote myself to other people's needs because of the demands of my religios convictions (ASS3)

17. It is important for me that all elements of my personal faith fit together (COM4)

22. It is important for me to maintain harmony at all times, especially in relation to those who share my faith (COM5)

26. When I realize that I disagree about religios matters with someone I care about, I try to avoid thinking about it (COM6)

30. I believe that God stands behind everything that happens, even the evil (COM7)

31. My faith makes me cautious (ASS9)

38. When I am going to decide whether something is morally wrong or not, I usually check whether it is in conflict with my rules of life (ASS12)

Other Factors: The other three factors, containing 9, 8, and 7 items respectively, seemed less conceptually homogenous. These factors may be denominated (II) Flexibility, (III) Level of Concretion, (IV) Creativity.

RESULTS

The SCL-90 questionnaire confirmed that there was a clear difference in psychopathology between the groups (see Stifoss-Hansen 1987).

A check on the first sample showed a significant group difference for Factor I, with 1.92 for patients and 0.92 for "normals" ($t=7.60$, $p<.001$).

On the second sample, the corresponding values are 1.84 for patients and 1.19 for "normals" ($t=6.24$, $p. <.001$).

None of the other factors gained significant differences between the groups, neither in the "old", nor in the second sample.

Correlations and regression analyses: There were high correlations between Factor I and the different subscales of SCL-90, both in the "old" and in the second sample (see Table 2). In addition there was a few significant correlations with other factors in the first sample (see Table 2).

A series of regression analyses were performed on the second sample with the group variable (patients vs "normals") as dependent variable. The results show a significant effect for age, but not sex. Further there was a significant result for Factor I and IV, but not for Factor II and III (Table 3).

Table 2. Correlations between factors and psychiatric symptoms (decimal points omitted)

Factors	*SOM*[1]	*OCD*	*SEN*	*DEP*	*ANX*	*HOS*	*PHO*	*PAR*	*PSY*
First sample									
F 1	496	572	516	461	521	282[2]	382	571	555
F 3								209[3]	218[3]
F 4							187[3]	275[2]	
Second sample									
F 1	478	488	436	468	465	181[3]	416	415	349

[1] SOM=Somatization, OCD=Obsessive-compulsive symptoms, SEN=Interpersonal sensitivity, DEP=Depression, ANX=Anxiety, HOS=Hostility, PHO=Phobic anxiety, PAR=Paranoid ideations, PSY=Psychoticism.
[2] Significant on 1% level. [3] Significant on 5% level (all other correlations significant on 1 ‰ level).

Table 3. Results of forward regression analyses in second sample

Variables	*Beta*	*t*	*p*
Dependent variable: Group			
Independent variables			
Factor 1 (Rigidity)	.444	7.43	.0001
Factor 4 (Creativity)	-.077	2.76	.0065
Age	-.041	2.55	.0119

DISCUSSION

The present type of study should be replicated in order to improve both method and hypothesis testing. A further collection of data on a larger scale (400 respondents), and an interwiev study based on the main questions of the questionnaire is planned.

A main future effort will be to discuss our scale's similarities and possible compatibility with the means-end-quest scales. These scales have been the main inspiration and source, and the theory behind quest is particularly interesting. But at the same time, our scales are not only a translation and our factors are new. In what way the present research can be a complement to the means-end-quest research is an open question. Maybe it can even serve as a correction to the present research, or maybe it is totally separate.

Some empirical answers will be sought, in the further investigation in collaboration with Kaldestad (1994). Kaldestad applies a new questionnaire as well as the original means-end-quest items. Since our data collections are fully comparable, we have the possibility to test the connection empirically. This is also part of our future plan.

The main achievements so far is the application of empirical religios motivation research to a Scandinavian (Norwegian) sample, a general contri-bution to the development of motivational factors and a suggestion as to what kind of religiosity is linked to mental pathology. This last aspect was originally the main goal, and in the future it will be tried to approach cause-effect relationships. So far, we are in the same place as Batson and Ventis (1982), that is, we have given a description of a kind of religiosity and linked it to psychopathology. We have not answered their question: "When we find religion associated with various attitudes and behaviors, is this because religion produced these attitudes and behaviors or simply because it reflects them?" (1982, p. 305). However, we agree with Batson and Ventis when they assume that religion is a cause, at least in many people's lives at many times, although it is still left to be shown scientifically.

This assumption is also undoubtedly in line with the beliefs of clergy and lay workers of religion, who would like to make this a cause for a beneficial effect.

Summary

In a previous study, a Rigid-Flexible Religiosity Scale (RFR-39) differentiated between a psychiatric patient group and a "normal" comparison group. This scale was factor-analysed, and a shorter version of this rigidity scale (RR-9) gave similar differences with another sample of patients and "normals". It is concluded that religios rigidity is a reliable and valid characteristic of religiosity, which has increased occurrence in psychiatric patients.

REFERENCES

Allen, R.O. Spilka, B. (1967): Committed and consensual religion: A specification of religion-prejudice relationships. *Journal for the Scientific Study of Religion,* **6**: 191-206.

Allport, G.W. Ross, B. (1967): Personal religious orientation and prejudice. *Journal of Personality and Social Psychology,* **5**: 432-443.

Batson, C.D. and Ventis, W.R. (1982): *The Religious Experience: A Social-Psychological Perspective.* New York: Oxford University Press

Derogatis, L.R., Lipman, R.S. and Covi, L. (1973): SCL-90: An outpatient psychiatric rating scale. *Psychopharmacology Bulletin,* **9**: 13-28.

Freud, S. (1940-52): *Gesammelte Werke 1-17.* London: Hogarth Press.

Heskestad, S. (1984): Religiösitet og mental helse. En empirisk undersökelse (Religion and mental health: An empirical study). *Nordic Psychiatric Journal,* **38**, 353-361.

Hoge, D.R. (1972): A validated intrinsic religious motivation scale. *Journal for the Scientific Study of Religion,* **11**: 369-376.

Hunt, R.A. (1972): Mythological-symbolic religious commitment: The LAM scales. *Journal for the Scientific Study of Religion,* **11**: 42-52.

Kaldestad, E. (1990): Intrinsic, extrinsic and quest scales. Development of Norwegian versions. Proceedings from Second Nordic Symposium of Psychology of Religion. Religionspsykologiska Skrifter (Studies of Psychology of Religion) no. 8. Uppsala: Uppsala University.

Meissner, W.W. (1984): *Psychoanalysis and Religious Experience.* New Haven CT: Yale University Press.

Norušis, M.J. (1986): *SPSS/PC+ for the IBM PC/AT.* Chicago IL: SPSS Inc.

Rizzuto, A.M. (1979): *The Birth of the Living God. A Psychoanalytic Study.* Chicago IL: University of Chicago Press.

Stifoss-Hanssen, H. (1987): Religiös rigiditet og mental helse (Religious rigidity and mental health). O Wikström (Ed): *Religionspsykologi nu* (Psychology of religion at present). Religionspsykologiska Skrifter (Studies of Psychology of Religion) no. 1. Uppsala: Uppsala University.

Stifoss-Hanssen, H. (1994a): Rigid religiosity and mental health: An empirical study. L B Brown (Ed): *Religion, Personality and Mental Health,* New York: Springer Verlag, 1994, pp 138-143.

Stifoss-Hanssen, H. (1994b): Hermeneutic and motivational aspects of religiosity: Symbolic reinterpretation (LAM) and rigid religiosity related to mental health. Submitted to *International Journal for the Psychology of Religion.*

Strommen, M.P., Brekke, M.L., Underwager, R.C. and Johnson A.L. (1972): *A Study of Generations.* Minneapolis MN: Augsburg.

Appendix: The Rigid-Flexible Religiosity Scale (RFR-39)

No	*Scale**	Item
1	ACC1	I am convinced that my faith is the correct one
2	COM1	Life is full of conflicts, and it is important to live with the conflict
3	ASS1	For me, faith is related to creativity and phantasy
4	Q1	It might be said that I value my religios doubts and uncertainties
5	SYM1	Everything which is written in the Bible is true
6	ACC2	Everybody should believe as I do
7	COM2	My faith makes everything easy to understand
8	ASS2	According to my religious convictions, I have to think carefully before I allow myself to indulge in something I feel attracted to
9	ASS3	I feel that I ought to devote myself to other people's needs because of the demands of my religious convictions
10	SYM2	The Bible can be compared to a fable or a fairy tale which presents important things in human life in a symbolic form
11	ACC3	Other people's faith can be as correct as mine
12	COM3	I find many contradictions in my view of life, and believe it has to be that way
13	ASS4	According to my view of life I need to think carefully before I deny somehting I am attracted to
14	Q2	I do not expect my religious convictions to change in the next few years
15	SYM3	It could be written much important things about God in other books in addition to the Bible
16	ACC4	My way to believe fits me well, and I accept that other people believe otherwise
17	COM4	It is important for me that all elements of my personal faith fit together
18	ASS5	My view of life contains a set of rules which I have to live after
19	Q3	I have been driven to ask religious questions out of a growing awareness of the tensions in my world and in my relation to my world
20	ASS6	To me it is sin to act in conflict with commandments given by God
21	Q4	My religious development has emerged out of my growing sense of personal identity
22	COM5	It is important for me to maintain harmony at all times, especially in relation to those who share my faith
23	ASS7	My opinions in many areas are determined by my religious convictions
24	SYM4	The word sin can mean all evil which destroys life, both what we could be blamed for and not
25	ACC5	I should wish that everybody shared my faith because otherwise they will be lost
26	COM6	When I realize that I disagree about religious matters with someone I care about, I try to avoid thinking about it
27	ASS8	My faith makes me to do things I think I had otherwise defied
28	SYM5	Rituals are important, as they can be a symbolic representation of my life and my faith
29	ACC6	I mean that God accepts everybody if they do their best and are honest
30	COM7	I believe that God stands behind everything that happens, even the evil
31	ASS9	My faith makes me cautious
32	ACC7	I mean that all people are close to God, even if we believe we are different
33	Q5	God wasn't very important to me until I began to ask questions about the meaning of my own life
34	ASS10	My view of life makes me creative and inventive
35	SYM6	Faith can only be expressed in symbols and images

(Contd)

No	*Scale*	*Item*
36	ASS11	When I am evaluating if something is wrong morally, I am mainly considering if I am going to hurt somebody
37	Q6	Questions are far more central to my religious experience than are answers
38	ASS12	When I am going to decide whether something is morally wrong or not, I usually check whether it is in conflict with my rules of life
39	COM8	I accept that I can not know what is coming after death

* ACC=Acceptance-Nonacceptance, ASS=Assertiveness-Permissiveness, COM=Complexity-Simplicity, SYM=Symbolic-Concrete Faith, Q=Quest

CHAPTER 14

THE ROLE OF RELIGIOUS VALUES IN FUNCTIONING AND MENTAL HEALTH

Dorota Kubacka-Jasiecka, Roman Dorczak, Malgorzata Opoczynska

Psychological research on mental health, adaptation, or coping with stress has avoided for years the theme of values. Now it seems that solutions too many unresolved problems in this area can be found with the help of this idea. The system of values with which an individual identifies himself, and particular values, which he follows while realizing his aims and life tasks, specify, to a great extent, the level of individuals' maturity and mental stability.

Psychologists who have pointed out the role of integrated system of values (congruent with the whole personality) for functioning and mental health include: Allport, Bühler, Caruso, Frankl, Fromm, Horney, Maslow, and Rogers. These authors emphasize the fact that in the process of development man starts realizing higher and higher values, that his openness, his sensitivity to moral values —that transcends the individual's needs— values that are strong and give stable meaning to one's life, continually increases.

Every pathology, as these authors claim, affecting man as a whole must also affect his system of values and disturb the normal process of development. And thus we can talk about systems of values characteristic for different types of pathology: about neurotic system of values, schizophrenic system of values and systems that are characteristic for different types of psychopathy. The problem concerning interpretation of relationships remains still unresolved. Theses suggested by most of researches and concerning cause and result relations cannot be empirically confirmed or explained due to many factors, mediating and concomitant.

Religious values should play a particular role. Present in human life since the very beginning and connected with customary and cultural aspect of life, on the other hand, as *sacrum* values bearing specific supernatural moral duties and sanctions, they are claimed to be the essential determinants of our functioning and social adaptation.

As it is currently believed, religious values can be a positive factors both from the point of view of personality development and from the point of view of functioning in everyday life. Generally speaking religion can integrate and define functioning of personality, through the fulfilment of its different functions. Religion gives the answer to questions concerning the meaning of life, it "puts in order" relationships between a person and the world in which he or she lives.

Another function of religion is its role in satisfying one's need of security. Giving man the feeling of sense, sanctifying and fixing values, religion gives the feeling of stability and security, and presents from the feeling of anxiety or even threat. Generally speaking, an individual becomes more sure and reaches mental stability.

Eventually, religion gives a believer a sort of self-identification, recovering oneself in the world and defining one's position and identity. It binds an individual to a group, provides the opportunity for identification with community at the same time sanctifying the desire of being close to people.

Yet one can find another functions of religion: it is the therapeutic function. It is generally believed that through giving the sense and meaning of life religion can prevent man from noogenic neurosis.

In our researches we have decided to concentrate on the following questions:

1. the role and influence of religious values on the level of emotional and social maturation and reaching mental health,
2. the influence of personal religious values on the process of coping with stress,
3. the position and forms of functioning of religious values in the individual system of values of people with neurotic disorders.

Studies dealing with detailed topics were based on testing a group of over eighty individuals, mainly students, working youth and patients with neurotic disorders. The studies were carried out using different techniques like interviews, projective tests, questionnaires, and situational samples of behaviour. The following aspects in the studies of system of values were used: The Rokeach Value Survey and Sentence Completion Test. The level of emotional and social maturation and the level of mental health were estimated on the basis of techniques suggested by Dabrowski, the author of the conception of positive desintegration. The level of religiousness and place of religious values was described on the basis of Prezyna's Religious Scale, behavioral indicators, statements of those questioned and their self-report.

The role and influence of religious values on the level of emotional and social maturation and mental health.

The answer to the question concerning the role of religious values during an individual's maturation and acquisition of stability and mental health was sought, on the one hand, through the description of the level of development and mental health represented by people who believe in God, on the other hand, through the evaluation of so called subjective feeling of life-happiness and life-satisfaction, which is believed to be one of the most important criteria in estimating one's mental health.

The basis of our data was a psychological study of emotional and social functioning of a group of people belonging to a charismatic religious community, established in one of the Catholic churches in Cracow; and analyses of sexual and marital functioning of a group of young women closely connected with the life of church. The studies and analyses of the charismatic group were based on the conception of positive desintegration which defines mental health as the ability to develop in the direction of higher and higher hierarchy of values, aiming at the ideal of personality and group. It is the realisation of one's ability to develop through exploiting one's potential. This development proceeds through the phase of desintegration of formerly created structures and integration on the higher level of development. The phase of desintegration is accompanied by feeling of anxiety and lack of mental stability which stimulates positive changes. Due to the results of the studies one can describe members of community —people with deeply internalized religious values— as individuals representing, in most cases, the type of so called natural development. A few persons, whose level of maturation can be described as a transition through particular phases, are characterized by anxiety and presence of numerous inner conflicts. Only a few persons can be characterized by so called accelerated development, which is a sign of just acquired value of mental health.

Generally speaking, positive and stimulating for progressive changes influence of deep internalization of religious values on maturity and mental health could be noticed only in a few cases. The fact that only a few people with high level of mental health participated in the studies is a proof that this influence is not quite clear. One can also enumerate factors that slow down maturation such as increase in the susceptibility to religious authority, and sensitivity to external values, suggested by others.

Another problem is connected with the relationship between internalization of religious values and feeling of satisfaction with one's own shape of life, which is one of the basic criteria for positive mental health. The results of studies among people who work in a charismatic Catholic community can be summarized as follows:

— immature or emotionally unstable persons are characterized by considerable changeability of the feeling of happiness, which is, to a great extent, susceptible to environment and temporary moods,

— persons representing the type of accelerated development, as one can observe, accept and are satisfied with their choice of life based on religious values, but at the same time are dissatisfied with the fact that they are not so ideal as they would like to be. Ideal values connected with one's Catholic beliefs are difficult to reach —one can notice the incoherence between one's real "self" and ideal "self". This lack of coherence is the source of continuous tension and dissatisfaction,

— in studies dealing with maritial relations of believing women who live according to Catholic family ethics one could observe that in self-reports these individuals expressed a very high level of satisfaction with one's sexual and marital life. But at the same time, in data from projective techniques one can find the presence of tension, unstable feeling of security, presence of severe moral conflicts, and feeling of guilt. The dominance of pesimistic expectations and disappointment with one's shape of life, turned out to be characteristic for these group.

The influence of personal religious values on the process of coping with stress.

The studies that aimed at finding the answers to questions of whether and how believing people involve their religion in the process of coping with stress, and the studies aiming at identificationg of intermediate factors, were based on the analyses of results taken from the group of thirty students of both sexes, aged 20 to 26. The collected material was analysed in two ways: qualitative analysis which (on the basis of interview) specified the types of situations in which the individual most frequently appealed to religion and religious behaviour in the process of coping with stress; and a statistical analysis which was to determine what was the influence of such variables as: intensity of religious attitude, intensity of stress and sex on the frequency of religious behaviour in the process of coping with stress.

One third of subjects does not mention any form of religious behaviour or presence of religious values in any situation of coping with stress. The rest of the group listed such a form of behaviour in at least one difficult situation. They used religious values in coping with stress in situations such as: an examination, death of a close person, threat to one's own life or health.

In more than half of these situations the subjects mentioned a helpful role of their religious beliefs in the process of coping with difficulties. It seems that the essential characteristic of these situations is: a subjective feeling of lack of influence on these situations, feeling of loss of something or somebody or threat of such loss, feeling of weakness and helplessness, presence of fear and anxiety.

The situations in which the subjects rarely or never appeal to religion are: conflicts with parents, peers and siblings, administrative problems, loss of something etc.. Generally speaking, these are the situations in which the person can objectively influence their course and find appropriate solutions to the problem. The character of these situations and emotions connected with them (anger, irritation, malice etc.) further instrumental acting. The fact that these situations are mostly conflicts seems also to be very important. Thus, one can speculate that involvement of religious values in these situations can cause an increase in gradients of conflict and deepening of experienced difficulty. Perhaps, it is why the subjects avoid involvement of religious values in these situations.

In these studies we tried to specify in what way religious values and beliefs take part in the process of coping with stress. It was established that it could work in two ways. The first, more mature, is the change of the perception of the world. A strong and deeply rooted system of religious beliefs changes one's aaproach to difficult situations. These situations appear to be less threatening and include deeper meaning. In the second way, the influence of religion is more superficial. Religion, in some way, provides some forms of behaviour, but they are applied without ascribing deeper meaning to them. In difficult situations these forms of behaviour are simply used in the process of coping with unpleasant negative emotions. The most frequent forms of behaviour used in this way are: prayer, participation in religious services, reading the Holy Bible, a pilgrimage to places like Czestochowa. In the case of close person's death, the belief in afterlife, thanks to the fact of working through emotions, helps to view this loss from a different perspective.

The statistical analysis of the results was done to help answer questions concerning relations between indicators of the intensity of religious attitude intensity, stress, sex and the influence of religious values in the coping process. Owing to the result of correlation and regression analyses it turned out that the intensity of stress and intensity of religious attitude influence very strongly the use of religious beliefs in the process of coping with stress. The more intense is the attitude to religion and the higher the intensity of stress — then appeal to help of religion is more likely. Among women the intensity of stress has greater influence on appealing to religious values, while among men intensity of religious attitude plays the greater role.

Summing up we can conclude that people possesing internalized religious values appeal to religion as to a helpful means in coping with a difficult situations. The more pious they are (i.e. the greater intensity of religious attitude) and the greater is the experienced stress, they will do that more often. In most observed cases different forms of religious behaviour were functioning as a means of control and reduction of unpleasant and negative emotions. In few cases religious beliefs were an important factor shaping the way of perceiving and understanding the world — its elements of environment, situations, events and one's own behaviour and reactions. The religious values help in difficult situations not only by providing people with remedial methods, but they also participate as an essential factor conditioning the perception of situations as stressful ones. However generally, one can notice the domination of the image of superficial, instrumental functioning of religious values.

The position and forms of religious values and their functioning in the individual world of values of people with neurosis.

The question concerning the position and importance of religious values in life of people with neurosis was taken up in the context of wider studies dealing with neurotic individuals' hierarchy of values. Our studies show that all neurotics live at the same time in two completely different, incompatible and mutually contradctory worlds: in the world of ideal values, it means wishful, declaratory ("I want it to be like that") and in the world of real values, it means the values that really control their life ("It is so"). (See **Table 1**).

Table 1 Hierarchy of values in neurosis

Position of values in hierarchy	ideal order	real order
1	spiritual	hedonistic
2	vital	vital
3	sacrum	spiritual
4	hedonistic	sacrum

The above comparison shows how different the two orders are. The values that are declared to be most essential and worthy of realization are completely different from those applied by subjects in everyday life. It is also characteristic that they do not realize the double character of their own system of values: being unconcious of the real hierarchy of values they claim that they, in their life, follow the values of ideal hierarchy. And so the subjects declare (ideal order) that the most important for them are spiritual values such as: honest friendship, mature love, help and friendliness for others. A bit less important, but still very essential for them, are vital values such as: strength and courage in overcoming difficulties, power and control over the environment and themselves, physical strength, and health. Religious values are also thought to be important, but their role in one's life is claimed to be less important than the role of spiritual and vital values. They strongly oppose hedonistic values such as: comfortable and easy life, seizing the day, concentration on themselves. However if one looks closer at the life of the subjects and tries to analyze types of aims and tasks they want to undertake; and if one asks them about their relationship with others and attitude towards themselves, about requirements, they specify for themselves and for the surrounding world, about the types of situations in which they feel guilty and which cause them to rebel (real order), it will turn out that the most appreciated values for neurotics are not spiritual ones but the values which serve only their own "self" — hedonistic and vital values. These values are at the top of neurotic's real hierarchy of values and they strongly influence his decisions, opinions and actions. Spiritual values, if they are to be achieved, require the involvement in objects and aims being outside "self" and —as opposed to the subject's declaration— are for neurotics of minor importance in a real life. Religious values —which even do not have a high position in the ideal hierarchy— seem to be completely absent in their real life.

All the subjects believe in the existence of God and all of them agree that he is of great importance for them. However, if asked about explanation of this importance, they could only answer that they go to church, take sacraments and pray. Among few answers on the question concerning the role of God in one's life, the most frequent statements were about usefulness of God in various difficult situations, for instance: God as a companion in loneliness, God as a partner in conversation instead of an absent friend, God as a power for solving problems, God as a healer, God as an umbrella protecting from disaster. Some of the subjects added that when God did not meet their wishes and did not solve their problems — they were distracted by the questions of the kind: "Does He really exist ?"

Religious values, despite their declaratory character, play an instrumental role in neurotic's life. *Sacrum* plays the role of servant; it is to help in achieving egoistic needs, it is to protect from disaster, solve the problems. It is to guarantee them the most appreciated hedonistic and vital values.

Summing up we can claim that in this group of neurotics the religious values do not play any important role. They are of a declarative character, are abstract and separated from real life. The neurotics cannot achieve them and cannot make them an important source of control of their functioning. The religious values are not values for themselves. They become important and meaningful only while playing a certain function: so they are instrumental and serve in preserving the most appreciated values — hedonistic and vital ones.

Conclusions.

Finally, let us sum up with the following conclusions: because of the clinical character of our studies, the small number of subjects, and lack of control groups, the collected results are of hypothethical character rather than of final findings for answers to a question raised. However they seem to be interesting as a source of inspirations for future studies. The solution of methodological problems seems particularly essential. Psychological studies on religious values and attitudes, questions concerning measurement of internalization of these values, their conditioning and importance of control role in emotional and social behaviour and functioning, should take into account the influence of non-verbalized (subconsious and unconcious) mental contents as important variables. Future psychological studies in this area should be based on a comparative analysis of behavioural data (behavioral indicators measuring the level of internalization of religious values) and on projective material which is very rarely used in this area of studies.

The following suggestions are presented in connection with the questions raised at the beginning:

1. There was no relationship between the internalization of religious values and accelerated development and maturation, higher levels of mental health in the meaning of K. Dabrowski. The internalization of religious values, in term, is connected with number of factors which slow down mental maturation.
2. It seems that intermediate levels of internalization of religious values are the least useful for mental health (presence of tension caused by divergence between real "self" and ideal "self", fear, defense through

denial, presence of conflict and feeling of guilt). Internalization of religious values eliminates so called feeling of hapiness as a criteria in estimating mental health.

3. Religious values are more frequently present in the declarative order of values — in ideal "self" than in a real one (low level of internalization of religious values). At the same time they have only a limited influence on emotional and social functioning. The higher the level of internalization, the greater the influence of religious values.
4. Religious values play, most frequently, an instrumental role serving essential non-religious values — hedonistic values, need of security, or need of support.
5. Religious values play an important role in coping with stress by reducing tension. The intensity of influence of religious values, at the same time, depends on the level of internalization of religous values and on the perception of stressful situations as leading to helplessness and lack of control. It is worth mentioning that the first factor plays more important role for men and the second for women.
6. The presence of neurotic behaviour is connected with a comparatively low position of religious values in two settings — ideal (a bit higher) and real. Religious values do not play an important role for themselves — they become essential only when given instrumental functions by neurotics.

To sum up: The results at this stage do not allow a formulation of the relationship between religious beliefs, religious values, and achieved level of mental health. Some of the data suggest that the lack of suitable internalization of religious values and beliefs can influence negatively mental development and health. The key role seems to be played by the notion of the power of internalized values, which specifies their direct influence on behaviour. Achieving objective indicators of power, measurement and description, seems to be an important task of waiting researchers in this area.

CHAPTER 15
HOW COUNSELORS CAN HELP PEOPLE BECOME MORE SPIRITUAL THROUGH RELIGIOUS ASSESSMENT

H. Newton Malony

In an earlier essay, the question of how religious assessment could be used in counseling was considered (Malony, 1989). Of primary concern in that publication was to determine the ways in which persons' religion impacted: the diagnosis of symptoms, the evaluation of underlying personality strengths and weaknesses, and the resolution of problems. In the present essay it will be proposed that religious assessment can be applied to two additional aspects of counseling. These are: (a) efforts to achieve a spiritual understanding of emotional problems, and (b) efforts to help people grow spiritually. Both of these are goals that go beyond symptom reduction. They are therapeutic possibilities which many believe are positively related to mental health. However, a spiritual understanding of problems and growth in spirituality have not always been considered appropriate counseling goals. Yet, at least one survey found that a significant number of professionals report these concerns as relevant in their counseling (Shafranske & Malony, 1990).

In providing a foundation for discussing the place of spiritual issues in counseling, the following topics will be considered:
— the goals of counseling,
— the meanings of "spirituality", and
— the assessment of religious functioning.

The thesis of this essay is that counselors who help people grow in their faith and become more spiritual may be doing what is not only possible but preferable if they would guide their counselees toward mental health.

The Goals of Counseling
First, consider these questions: "What are the goals of counseling?" and "Should counselors try to increase their clients' spirituality?" In answer to the first question, one way to describe the goal of counseling is to say that counselors assist persons in adjusting to the environment(s) in which they choose to live. Almost all clients present their problems as

difficulties in adjustment. Of course, "adjustment" is a broad term which is not self-defining. Adjustment can imply surrender to the inevitable at one extreme or calculated, successful manipulation of life events at the other. Typically, clients report experiences of failure, of frustration, of fear, of anxiety, of misunderstanding, of misperception, or of disapproval in their attempts to adjust to their environment(s). Thus, helping persons to cope with these difficulties and to find ways to meet their needs to adjust and function could be considered the overarching goal of counseling.

Let us turn to the issue of whether counselors should try to increase spirituality in their clients. One way to answer this question might be to say "If clients want help in the spiritual area, counselors should give it." From this point of view, spirituality should be no different from family relations, vocational confusion, emotional control, or reality perception. These are all problems that arise as persons attempt to adjust to the differing environments of their lives — family, work, relationships, culture, values, religion, etc. As the above definition of counseling suggests, if clients choose to live in a spiritual environment, then counselors should not hesitate to help them when they have problems in adjusting to it.

That spirituality is, indeed, one of the arenas in which persons might experience adjustment problems can be seen in Sarbin's (1970) five- fold taxonomy of life environments. Sarbin's five life environments are: the physical, the situational, the interpersonal, the valuational, and the transcendental.

Adjusting to the *physical* environment means finding a favorable relationship to one's body and one's geographical setting. Adjusting to the *situational* environment means finding a successful role to play in one's society.

Adjusting to the *interpersonal* environment means finding mutually satisfying relationships with other persons.

Adjusting to the *valuational* environment means finding an adequate relationship with the rules and ideals of one's culture.

Finally, adjusting to the *transcendental* environment means finding meaning in life in relation to the unseen, eternal reality which lies behind the material world.

If Sarbin is correct, problems in adjustment can occur in one or more of life's environments, and counseling which helps persons cope in any or all of them is appropriate. So, once again the answer to the question of whether counselors should try to increase spirituality among their clients is "yes," if the transcendent is the life environment in which they are having problems. As Strupp, Hadley, and Gomes-Schartz (1977) concluded in their book *Psychotherapy: For Better or Worse*, goals are negotiated between clients and counselors. There is no inherent reason that increasing spirituality cannot become part of counseling contracts, which are worked out between those who counsel and those who come for help.

However, the issue of dealing with spiritual concerns in counseling is more complex than the above discussion implies. The "should" in the question of whether counselors ought to try to increase spirituality in clients might be interpreted by some counselors as a mandate quite apart from whether their clients requested spiritual help or not. Much has been written about whether spiritual considerations or religious answers should be foisted on persons without their request or interest (cf. Malony, 1983). The weight of professional opinion seems to imply that these concerns should not be imposed on clients unless they are explicitly part of the counseling contract. The above discussion on life-environments would seem to support this position.

However, there is an alternative point of view which might provoke a reconsideration of this issue. This alternative viewpoint has concluded (a) that dealing with the transcendent environment is inevitable (Sarbin, 1970), (b) that most adjustment problems are essentially spiritual problems (Tillich, 1952), and (c) that finding a meaning and purpose that transcend empirical reality can transform adjustment in all the other areas of life (Malony, 1983). When these presumptions are affirmed, increasing spirituality ceases to be a counseling option and becomes, instead, a necessity. A further discussion of these ideas may make this way of looking at spirituality more understandable.

Sarbin implies that every human being has to reach some sort of adjustment to all five of the realities of life (1970). If this is true, adjustment to transcendent reality is not optional. Sarbin also implies that the quality of adjustment, i.e., its satisfaction or its failure, varies from environment to environment. Thus, were we able to chart clients' life adjustments, we would have to give them scores on *all* five environments and their five scores would not necessarily be the same. For example, they might be well adjusted situationally but be poorly adjusted interpersonally. Furthermore, we might find that what they identified as the problem which brought them to counseling might be their lowest adjustment score but that their scores on one or more of the other environments might be close behind. For example, they might come to counseling because of a marriage problem but have recently been fired from their work as well. Both adjustment scores would be low. Adjustment in both the interpersonal and situational environments would be troublesome. Thus, their adjustment to other environments might be almost as frustrating to clients as the problem for which they sought help. Therefore, surveying how well clients were doing in their adjustment in all five of the life-environments might be as necessary as taking a good life-history during the intake procedure. Intentionally provoking a discussion of spiritual issues might become an obligatory feature of good counseling. To ignore spiritual issues could become a matter of dereliction from this point of view.

Tillich (1952) is only one among many who have asserted the possibility that there is a spiritual core to most adjustment problems (cf. Bergin, 1980). In his well-known book *The Courage to Be*, he distinguished neurotic from basic anxiety but suggested that, in the final analysis, all neurotic anxiety was grounded in basic anxiety. If neurotic anxiety be made synonymous with problems in adjusting to the physical, the situational, the interpersonal, and the valuational environments, then basic anxiety could be said to be their depth or spiritual cause. Therefore, becoming more spiritual may become the very essence of true problem solving and adjustment.

To elaborate this point, neurotic anxieties might be thought of as adjustment difficulties in the physical, interpersonal, situational, and valuational environments of life. Neurotic anxiety is that kind of anxiety one experiences when relationships with others, one's status and accomplishments, one's satisfactions with culture, one's perceptions of what others expect, and one's physical health all erode and are threatened by circumstance and the passage of time. Basic anxieties, on the other hand, have less to do with interpersonal role performance and more to do with solitary reflection late at night when no one else is around. It is then that one wonders about who one is apart from daily existence. Such questions as from whence one came and one's eternal destiny are normal. Basic anxiety is the universal urge to find a meaning which transcends bodily changes, daily experience, monetary wealth, achievement reputation, interpersonal relationships and the passage of time.

Much anxiety over daily problems could be looked upon as a frantic cover-up for these basic anxieties. Basic anxieties pertain to adjustment to the transcendent environment. There is some warrant for assuming that the essence of many adjustment problems in the physical, the interpersonal, the situational, and the valuational environments is due to problems in relating to the transcendent environment. It may be fanciful to think that counseling can ever be confined to solving difficulties in daily living. It may be impossible to separate "how" one lives from "why" one lives. Although the line may be indirect between the adjustment problem for which clients seek help and the state of their spirituality, if one assumes there is an inner spiritual core to those adjustment problems, then attending to this core becomes a counseling mandate. Therefore, dealing with spiritual issues could become synonymous with the well known counseling process of seeking the cause beneath the symptoms.

Yet a third contention about the relationship between adjustment to the five life environments and the centrality of adjustment to transcendent reality has been addressed by Malony (1983). He contends that the interrelationship of these adjustments in determining total mental health is only additive up to a point. By this he concludes that while one can add up the scores for adjustments to the physical (P), the interpersonal (I), the vocational (V_1), and the valuational (V_2) environments, this sum must be multiplied by the score for adjustment to the transcendent reality rather than simply added to it. This formula, $(P + I + V_1 + V_2)\,xT =$ Mental Health, reflects the viewpoint that spiritual issues are more important to mental health than all the other issues of life combined.

Of course, this is an unproved assumption. Yet, if Tillich and others are found to be correct, then the centrality of spirituality to mental health would be demonstrated. It further implies that adjustment in the more mundane areas of health, vocation, relationships, and values are intricately related to, and even profoundly determined by, spiritual adjustment.

It also implies that an increase in spirituality is positively related to an increase in emotional well being, a presumption which has, not, been universally affirmed (cf. Batson & Ventis, 1982). In fact, spirituality and mental health have been assumed by some to be qualitatively distinct and evenly diametrically opposed (Ellis). Nevertheless, Malony, Sarbin, and Tillich are among those who are convinced otherwise. They would see an increase in spirituality as a prime determinant of mental health. Spirituality is hereby assumed to be practically and intricately involved in day-to-day well-being. Spirituality is not other worldly, as many have presumed. Helping clients grow in faith and deepen their spirituality would thereby become an unavoidable goal in counseling.

The Meaning of Spirituality

Since the foregoing discussion has proposed that the goals of counseling should include helping persons become more spiritual, a more extensive understanding of this spiritual ideal is in order. In an absolute sense, to be spiritual implies that one has achieved a satisfactory adjustment to the transcendent life environment. This would imply that so long as one had intentionally worked out such an adjustment, it would not matter whether that adjustment was atheistic, agnostic, or theistic — each would be considered "spiritual". The degree to which persons' relationship to transcendent reality provided meaning and purpose to their lives would be the criterion of its spirituality, regardless of whether that relationship was in accord with one of world's great religions.

However, since the method of assessment described in the next section of this essay is designed to evaluate Christian spirituality, a discussion of the meaning of "spiritual" from the viewpoint of that tradition is in order. A caution should be stated, however. All religious traditions are formalized options for adjustments to the transcendent environment. Thus, for those who choose a given religion, that religion provides an understanding of the meaning of spirituality as well as a set of beliefs and practices by which to make judgments about it. Nevertheless, these understandings and criteria do not exhaust the options in spite of the fact that they are presented as otherwise. Other options are available although not all options are common within a given culture.

Each religious tradition perceives the meaning of life in a unique fashion. From the viewpoint of the Christian faith, human beings are children of Almighty God. They are made in God's image and are put on earth to serve God in their daily lives. The Westminster Catechism states the issue plainly when it responds to the question "What is the chief end of man?" with the answer "The chief end of man is to glorify God and to serve Him forever." Further, this tradition affirms that by the mighty act of God in Jesus Christ, humans have been redeemed from their inclination toward self-centered living and have been restored to the image of God in which they were created.

To be spiritual from a Christian point of view implies affirmation of these beliefs. To become more spiritual implies a style of daily living which reflects these affirmations. One statement of Christian spirituality is as follows:

Mature Christians are those who have identity, integrity, and inspiration. They have "identity" in that their self-understanding is that they are children of God-created by God and destined to live according to a divine plan. They have "integrity" in that their daily lives are lived in the awareness that they have been redeemed by God's grace from the guilt of sin and that they can freely respond to God's will in the present. They have "inspiration" in that they live with the sense that God is available to sustain, comfort, encourage, and direct their lives on a daily basis. These dimensions of maturity relate to belief in God the Father, God the Son, and God the Holy Spirit. They pertain to the Christian doctrines of creation, redemption, and sanctification. They provide the foundation for practical daily living. (Malony, 1985, p. 28)

A recent cartoon illustrated this spiritual goal for life from a Christian point of view. It showed an army recruiter sitting beside a channeler.

The sign above the recruiter repeated the familiar maxim of the Army, "Be all that you can be". The sign above the channeler spoke to the conviction that persons return to earth again and again in new roles. It stated, "Be all that you have been". Christian spirituality encompasses both. It is the sine qua non of all that persons can be as well as all that they have always been in the mind and purposes of God. This is the meaning of life and the purpose for living which the Christian faith provides as an adjustment answer to the transcendent environment.

The process of becoming more spiritual is just that, i.e., "a process". Being spiritual is both a state of mind at a given moment, and a trait of behavior from time to time. And both states and traits can exist to different degrees. At a given point of time, persons can be in a spiritual state — to a greater or lesser degree. Further, over a given span of time, persons can exhibit spiritual traits — to greater or lesser degrees. We may hope that when counselors attempt to increase Christian spirituality they will encourage a process that results in more consuming spiritual states of mind at a given time and more consistent spiritual traits of behavior over time. These same goals of increasing states of mind and traits of behavior would apply to other religious traditions as well; only the criteria of spirituality would be different.

After persons have decided to adjust to the transcendent environment in a Christian fashion, two types of spiritual processes are involved. One is *preparatory* and the other is *practical*. Preparatory spiritual processes are those in which study, contemplation, reflection, prayer, and worship are undertaken. These increase persons' spiritual awareness and resolve. Practical spiritual processes are those in which behavior, service, forgiveness, assistance, mercy, compassion and social action are undertaken. These confirm behaviorally persons' intent to approach adjustment to the other life environments in a Christian manner.

Two words for Christians who become more spiritual are "pious" and "holy". Deeply spiritual persons are those who are pious and holy. These words have negative as well as positive meanings. In a negative sense, being pious or holy means not doing certain things such as stealing, abusing, or cursing. In more conservative Christian groups this has sometimes meant not working on Sunday, not drinking, or not going to movies. In a positive sense, being pious or holy means engaging in certain activities such as Bible study, worship, prayer, unselfish giving, and action on behalf of the poor and dispossessed. What has been said of spiritual direction could also be said of counseling that attends to spiritual issues. La Place wrote that spiritual direction was "the help one person gives another to enable him to become himself in faith" (Geromel, 1983, p. 57). Since, as has been said, the Christian faith assumes that each person is a child of God who is put on earth to serve Him in some form or another, then growth in spirituality implies a greater awareness of, commitment to, and action toward the realization of that goal.

The Assessment of Spirituality

Evaluation of clients is an important part of contemporary counseling. Counselors undertake assessments of symptoms, of mental status, of personality, and of adjustment patterns in order to plan their treatments and better help their clients. These systematic evaluations should be no less true of adjustments to the transcendent environment, i.e., spirituality, than to the other life environments.

Although judgments about the spiritual state of individuals are assumed to be a regular part of Christian spiritual direction it is interesting to note that one of the standard texts in the field does not include a chapter on how such judgments are to be made (cf. Culligan, 1983). Both the fields of spiritual direction and spiritual counseling have needed a standardized method for assessing the states and traits of spirituality in the directees or clients. The construction of the Religious Status Interview (RSIv) (Malony, 1985, 1988) and the Religious Status Inventory (RSIn) (Hadlock, 1988; Massey, 1988) were attempts to meet that need.

The Religious Status Interview (RSIv) is a set of thirty-three questions designed to ascertain how Christian faith is functioning along eight dimensions: Awareness of God, Acceptance of God's Grace, Being Repentant and Responsible, Knowledge of God's Leadership, Involvement in Organized Religion, Experiencing Fellowship, Being Ethical, and Being Open in Faith. These dimensions were originally suggested by Paul Pruyser in his seminal volume *The Minister as Diagnostician* (1968). They are thought to be encompassing of the major components of functional Christian theology and ecumenical Christian spirituality. The basic assumption underlying the RSIv is that it provides an assessment of how Christian convictions are expressed, applied, and utilized in daily life rather than a set of creedal statements or denominational practices affirmed in isolation from the ways religion is applied to living.

The RSIv has been subjected to a variety of studies designed to determine whether it truly assesses Christian spirituality and whether it can reliably measure spirituality over time. The RSIv has been found to be reliable in test-retest and inter-rater situations (Davis, 1985; Hadlock, 1987; Jackson, 1987). Further, the RSIv discriminated among Christians hospitalized for psychiatric treatment and those who came to visit them

(Tilley, 1985). It also distinguished between church members considered to be spiritually mature and immature (Massey, 1987; Nelson, 1985; and Wong, 1989). Further, older Christian women experiencing less distress had higher RSIv scores than those experiencing more distress even when their amount of life-stress was statistically controlled (Atkinson, 1986). In all of these studies higher RSIv scores were in the expected direction.

Of relevance to the assumption that greater spirituality was related to mental health was the finding that higher RSIv scores were correlated with intelligence, bold venturesomeness and imaginativeness (McPherson, 1987). In this same study, negative relationships were observed between lower RSI scores and guilt proneness and anxiety.

More recently an inventory form of the RSIv has been developed (Massey, 1988). The Religious Status Inventory (RSIv) has been found to correlate highly with the Religious Status Interview (RSIn) (Hadlock, 1988). It is a 160-item questionnaire in which persons are asked to judge whether a given statement is more or less like them. Half of the items are descriptions of less spiritual responses while half are descriptions of more spiritual responses to the transcendent environment from a Christian point of view. The reliability and factor structure of the RSIn is being determined in ongoing research studies.

Of importance in the use of such measures as the RSIv and the RSIn is the question of how such assessments of spirituality can be used in the counseling process. This will be discussed in the following section.

Using Spiritual Assessment in Counseling

In an earlier publication, Malony (1989) suggested that religion "functions as one among many attitudes, or predispositions to respond in certain ways to the environment. As such, any person's religion (or spirituality) can vary as to whether it is (a) important or unimportant, (b) active or inactive, (c) good or bad, and, finally, (d) helpful or harmful in their adjustment" (Malony, 1989, p. 3).

Thus, after determining persons' spiritual state and trait(s) through such measures as the RSInterview or the RSInventory, counselors can decide to disregard, annihilate, correct, reinstate, or encourage the ways in which faith is being expressed. These become options for using spiritual assessment in counseling.

In this earlier essay, these alternatives were explained as follows: To take the DISREGARD option would be to assume that a given person's functional religion was so weak or ill-formed that it was having no impact and could not be used in his or her treatment. To take the ANNIHILATE option would be to assume that the persons' functional religion was completely destructive and needed obliterating because, as part of their pathology, it would impede their treatment. To take the CORRECT option would be to assume that parts of the person's functional religion were weak or erroneous, and should be changed, or else they would handicap treatment. The REINSTATE option would be to assume that while the person's functional religion was potentially helpful it was not consciously operative, and, therefore, should be made more explicit, self-conscious, and intentional. The ENCOURAGE option would imply that the person's functional religion was adequate, active, and a definite strength to be supported and enhanced. (Malony, 1989, p. 8)

The emphasis in this previous essay (Malony, 1989) was on the ways in which religion impacted the diagnosis of symptoms, the evaluation of underlying personality strengths and weaknesses, and the plan for treatment of presenting problems. In the present discussion, these uses of religious assessment are extended to considerations of how spiritual assessment can be utilized in (a) achieving a spiritual understanding of presenting problems and (b) inducing growth in spirituality over and beyond problem solving. In these endeavors the first two options noted above, i.e. disregard and annihilate, would seem inappropriate. The last three, i.e., correct, reinstate, and encourage, coupled with a new option, i.e., initiate, would seem appropriate. These several options will be discussed in more detail.

The possibility of taking the *initiative* in counseling toward spirituality borders on encouraging the counselor to be evangelistic. Whether counselors should evangelize or not has been a commonly discussed question. It has its roots in the issue of whether values should play a role in psychotherapy. Bergin (1980) noted that there is no such thing as "value-free" counseling. In this sense, all counselors are evangelistic. All counselors initiate. Treatment inevitably involves interpretations and recommendations. Of course, most counselors would contend that these interpretations and recommendations are grounded in extant theories of personality and therapy rather than in religious traditions such as the Christian faith. This is true.

However, what is not so readily admitted is that these non-religious theories of personality and psychotherapy often, if not always, include implicit metaphysical assumptions regarding the nature of reality (ontology), the nature of pathology (sin?), the process of healing (redemption), and an understanding of wholeness (holiness). It is possible that all one does in initiating conversation in counseling about spirituality is to make explicit some of these underlying assumptions.

For example, when the Christian theologian Paul Tillich (1952) suggested that all neurotic anxiety has its roots in basic anxiety, he was implying that most of the problems persons face in interpersonal relations are indirect expressions of their anxieties over being finite. The ultimate anxieties of knowing one will die, of feeling alienated and alone, of fearing loss of status and security, and of experiencing powerlessness can only be assuaged, in the final analysis, by answers which are metaphysical or supranatural. Tillich contended that life posed the questions to which faith was the answer. And faith is the province of religion or spirituality.

Thus, to initiate "God talk" in counseling is perfectly appropriate — even when the counselee has not brought up the issue. When counselors are convinced that these metaphysical foundations could be helpful, they should take the initiative and introduce them. This can be done through Socratic-type questioning such as "Have you ever thought that..." or "I'm wondering if..." or "What would you say if someone suggested..."

To take this approach is no different from any other treatment situation where the helper elects to utilize a treatment of "choice" rather than a treatment of "convenience" (see Malony, 1986, pp. 107-110).

If one makes the assumption that the essence of all adjustment problems is how one handles adjustment to the transcendent environment, then the major question is how such initiation should be done — not whether. In an essay entitled "God talk in psychotherapy" (Malony, 1983, pp. 269-280), a "dialogical" method was recommended. This approach was explained as follows: "The dialogue in the dialogical approach is the interaction of the pain and dilemmas brought to therapy by the client and their deeper context in the estrangement of the person from the center (or truth) of his/her existence. The goal of therapy, therefore, becomes one of gentle contextualization of the struggle of the client so that uncovering the depth meaning of a specific event becomes probable and the reception of the saving truth about God becomes possible" (Malony, 1983, p. 278).

Turning from the option of initiating to the option of *correction,* counselors can instruct clients about ways in which their spirituality might be improved. Here is where the value of such instruments as the RSIv and the RSIn can be seen. Growth in spirituality implies growth within the best of a religious tradition. A number of well-known theologians assisted in the development of the RSI. There was consensus among them that the dimensions assessed in the interview encompassed the major dimensions of functional Christian faith. Counselors can note those dimensions in which clients seem to be doing more or less well and have confidence that they are expressing criteria beyond their own personal opinions. In fact, through such instruments as these, the counselor can confidently make judgments about the correctness of the client's faith even when the counselor does not share that same belief system.

By gentle questioning, counselors can provoke insight into how more conscious development or application of given dimensions could induce more mental health. By observing ways in which there is error or deficiency, according to the rating scales of such instruments the RSIv and RSIn, counselors can assist clients in changing their faith behavior. Subsequent reflection would reveal, we may hope, increased spirituality and greater life effectiveness.

Reinstatement is yet another option in counseling toward increased spirituality. Here a correct, but dormant faith, is observed by counselors using the RSIv or the RSIn. Often, this can be seen in a faith characterized by correct beliefs, good intentions, and recognition of many shoulds and oughts. Probably persons with this type of residual, but inactive, faith have bifurcated their religion and their daily lives. Counselors can lead these individuals into connecting their problems with their faith. Counselors can also prescribe for these persons certain active ways to reinstate their spirituality. Many of the familiar procedures used by counselors in making therapeutic contracts with clients to try new behaviors or covenant with them to engage in certain activities are appropriate here.

Turning finally to the option of *encouragement* in counseling toward great spirituality, we should not be surprised that clients are routinely dependent on their counselors for reassurance. In fact, the lack of encouragement for being religious has been a cardinal characteristic of much counseling. Ellis, for example, has suggested that counselors should actively discourage religion in their clients (Ellis, 1971). Those counselors who are convinced that spirituality is important for life should be no less bold in encouraging their clients.

It has long been known that counseling behavior is shaped by the response of counselors. Where counselors, using such measures as the RSIv and the RSIn, determine that their clients have a fully functioning faith, they should express approval of it. More importantly, where counselors are convinced that becoming more spiritual means becoming more healthy and whole, they should encourage their clients to become even more spiritual than they are. Counselors should not be afraid that their clients will get too much religion or become too spiritual. Whatever problems that such a possibility entails are so rare as to allow us to conclude, contrary to William James (1902), that "saintliness" is a rare disease!

Conclusions

This essay has attempted to legitimize and explicate counseling toward spirituality. The thesis behind such a discussion is the contention that there are implicit spiritual issues in the problems people present to counselors. Further, gaining insight into the spiritual nature of problems and becoming increasingly spiritual are means for achieving greater mastery over life's difficulties and enhancing mental health. Simply adjusting to life can never be a goal for psychotherapy, as the Christian existential theorist John Finch has perennially stated (1981, 1990).

Thus, this essay has concluded that counseling toward spirituality should become the treatment of "choice". It should take precedence over any other treatment of "convenience". Moreover, counseling toward spirituality should become preferable as well as possible as a strategy for helping persons. Sensitive counselors should be encouraged not to settle for less.

A standardized procedure for assessing spirituality was detailed. Procedures for using the Religious Status Interview and Religious Status Inventory were discussed. These measures can be utilized by counselors in spiritual diagnoses of problems. They can also be utilized in assisting clients to become more spiritual. Several counselor options were noted. In addition to disregarding and attempting to annihilate grossly bad religion, counselors can initiate, correct, reinstate, and encourage the faith of their clients.

The one remaining question is when such spiritual interventions can be utilized. Here the Christian theologian Ray Anderson (1987) has suggested being sensitive to "agogic" moments in therapy. Taking a cue from the European pastoral theologian Jacob Firet (1986), Anderson defines agogic moments as those unique times in counseling when the motive power of God's love can be released through the intermediary of the counselor. This motive power of love works in the situation to release the person for healing and for holiness. The result is a transformation experience in which persons reinterpret their experience in such a way that their problems are seen in a new light and the possibility of a move toward "godly" living becomes possible.

Such agogic moments become reenactments of "kairos moments" not unlike the experience Karl Barth spoke about when he said that the Holy Spirit comes into life from time to time and "blesses the Word to the hearts of believers so that they become contemporaries of Christ Jesus". Taking advantage of agogic opportunities becomes the prime task of therapists who would counsel toward greater spirituality in their clients. As stated earlier, counseling toward greater spirituality is a preferable goal, and discerning "agogic" moments when spiritual interventions can be made becomes the prime task for those counselors who would undertake this task of increasing spirituality in their clients.

REFERENCES

Anderson, R. S. (1987). *Christian psychagogics: An approach to holistic therapy.* Unpublished manuscript, Fuller Theological Seminary, Pasadena, CA.

Atkinson, B. E. (1987). Religious maturity and psychological distress among older Christian women. *Abstracts International, 47*, 4333-B.

Batson, C. D., & Ventis, W. L. (1982). *The religious experience: A social psychologist's perspective*. New York: Oxford.

Bergin, A. E. (1980). Psychotherapy and religious values. *Journal of Consulting and Clinical Psychology*, *48*, 95-105.

Culligan, K. G. (Ed.) (1983). *Spiritual direction: Contemporary readings*. Locust Valley, NY: Living Flame Press.

Davis, S. P. (1985). *Interviewer reliability of the Religious Status Interview.* Unpublished master's thesis, Graduate School of Psychology, Fuller Theological Seminary, Pasadena, CA.

Ellis, A. (1971). *The case against religion: A psychotherapist's view*. New York: Institute for Rational Living.

Finch, J. G. (1981, 1990) Malony, H. N. (Ed.) (1981, 1990). *Toward a Christian existential psychology: The contributions of John G. Finch.* Lanham, MD: University Press of America.

Firet, J. (1986). *Dynamics of pastoring*. Grand Rapids, MI: Eerdmans.

Geromel, E. (1983). Depth psychotherapy and spiritual direction. In K. G. Culligan (Ed.). *Spiritual direction: Contemporary readings* (pp. 57-69). Locust Valley, NY: Living Flame Press.

Hadlock, M. N. (1987). *Assessing religious maturity. Inter-rater reliability of the Religious Status Interview*. Unpublished master's thesis, Graduate School of Psychology, Fuller Theological Seminary, Pasadena, CA.

Hadlock, M. N. (1988). *The cross validation of the Religious Status Inventory.* Unpublished doctoral dissertation, Graduate School of Psychology, Fuller Theological Seminary, Pasadena, CA.

Jackson, C. (1987). The *test-retest reliability of the Religious Status Interview.* Unpublished master's thesis, Graduate School of Psychology, Fuller Theological Seminary, Pasadena, CA.

James, W. (1902). *The varieties of religious experience*. New York: Scribners.

Malony, H. N. (Ed.). (1983). *Wholeness and holiness: Readings in the psychology/theology of mental health*. Grand Rapids, MI: Baker Book House.

Malony, H.N. (1985) Assessing religious Maturity. In E.M. Stern (Ed.). *Psychotherapy and The Religiosity Commited Patients* (25-33). New York: Hawaeth Press.

Malony, H. N. (1986). *Integration musings: Thoughts on being a Christian professional*. Pasadena, CA: Integration Press.

Malony, H. N. (1988). The clinical assessment of optimal religious functioning. *Review of Religious Research*, *30*(1), 2-17.

Malony, H. N. (1989). The uses of religious assessment in counseling. In L. B. Brown (Ed.), *Current psychology of religion* (pp. 3-18). New York: Springer-Verlag.

Maslow, A. H. (1954). *Motivation and personality*. New York: Harper.

Massey, D. E. (1987). *Self-designating, pastor nominating and religious maturity: A validity study of the Religious Status Interview*. Unpublished master's thesis, Graduate School of Psychology, Pasadena, CA.

Massey, D. E. (1988). *The factor analytic structure of the Religious Status Inventory*. Unpublished doctoral dissertation, Graduate School of Psychology, Fuller Theological Seminary, Pasadena, CA.

McPherson, S. E. (1987). *The relationship between religious maturity and personality traits*. Unpublished master's thesis, Graduate School of Psychology, Fuller Theological Seminary, Pasadena, CA.

Nelson, D. O. (1985). The construction and initial validation of the Religious Status Interview. *Dissertation Abstracts International,* 46, 965.

Pruyser, P. W. (1968). *The minister as diagnostician*. New York: Scribners.

Shafranske, E. P., & Malony, H. N. (1990). Clinical psychologists' religious and spiritual orientations and their practice of psychotherapy. *Psychotherapy, 27*(1), 72-78.

Sarbin, T. R. (1970). A role theory perspective for community psychology: The structure of social identity. In B. L. Kalis (Ed.), *Community psychology and mental health: Perspectives and challenges* (pp. 89-113). Scranton, PA: Chandler.

Strupp, H. H., Hadley, S. W., & Gomes-Schartz, B. (1977). *Psychotherapy: For better or worse, The problem of negative effect*. Northvale, NJ: Aronson.

Tilley, S. B. (1986). Religious maturity and mental health: Verification of the Religious Status Interview. *Dissertation Abstracts International, 46*, 2826.

Tillich, P. (1952). *The courage to be*. New Haven: Yale University Press.

Wong, G. (1989). *Religious maturity among American and overseas born Chinese Christians*. Unpublished doctoral dissertation, Graduate School of Psychology, Fuller Theological Seminary, Pasadena, CA.

SECTION 4 CASE STUDIES

CHAPTER 16
PSYCHOSIS AND RELIGION

Nils G. Holm and Pertti Järvinen

Our material consists of depth interviews over the course of a year with six patients diagnosed as schizophrenics at the Turku Mental Asylum. The project should be regarded as a case study of the role of religion among psychotics.

In the theoretical part of the research, two perspectives have been adopted: firstly, depth psychology, and secondly, a socio-psychological approach, here mainly in the form of role theory developed by Hjalmar Sundén. Depth psychology has long enjoyed an established position in the study of more serious mental cases; Sundén's role theory, on the other hand, has not —to our knowledge— been used previously in the study of psychoses. In the present report it is not possible to provide a more detailed account of the theories used. We assume that they are largely known.

On the basis of these theoretical considerations, the tasks at hand may be described as follows. First, to study the patients' early environmental conditions: this should include how they lived, which individuals formed part of the immediate family, what moves and transformations took place during the formative years of their life.

The second task was to study emotional ties, particularly with parents, siblings and other members of the immediate environment. It is here, above all, that depth psychology has its relevance.

A third important task was to see how religion had been transmitted to these people. According to Sundén's arguments based on role theory, people select roles from mythical models according to how the latter have been transmitted to them. Sundén sees religion as a confidential dialogue with "reality" and in the transmission of tradition distinguishes between three groups: the confident, the unconfident and the over-confident. Modern theories of object relations, as well as attachment theory, are quite close to the formulations which Sundén tried to give to the process of transmission. But we will not go into this in greater detail now.

Early environmental conditions

Patients' early environmental conditions proved to have been problematic in several ways. The parents were often in a state of conflict with each other: frequently, one of the parents may be said to have carried a burden of guilt within the family. Communication had been more or less broken off, and one of the parents assumed the role of the one who had failed in the child-rearing process. Often, moreover, the family as a whole had a problematic relationship with the rest of the environment. It had either joined what in political or religious terms was an extreme minority group, or else the family regarded itself as being rejected in some way. This was instrumental in the forming of insecure and unstable relations with those around them. It was easy, in other words, to make a role out of being abnormal or "bad".

In the internal family relationship the child learned submissiveness at an early age, and patients may therefore be seen as having been extremely well-behaved children. The child, in other words, became a silent symptom carrier. Symbiotic relations, above all with the mother, could be observed in some of the cases. This often led to inadequate sexual identity during a patient's teens. The father was regarded as an omnipotent figure who did not allow the son to intrude into his world, which meant that the process of separation from the parents remained incomplete. Furthermore, the mother, for her part, needed to hang on to her child in order to be able to survive.

If one considers the transmission of tradition, this was also characterized by conflicting feelings. There was often a lack of agreement between the parents over the role and function of religion within the family. A secure dialogue with "reality" or God could not therefore be developed.

To sum up, we may say that early environmental conditions were characterized by conflicting tendences. No clear and positive role identifications could therefore be made. The child was meant to be submissive, but at the same time it was expected to manage the key role in the parental conflict. It was meant to cope with life outside the family, even as it was forbidden to find roles outside the family's dynamic sphere. Furthermore, it had not acquired adequate symbols at the religious level to interact with "reality", with what occurred in life. We are thus left with something which could be described as an "inability to adapt" in new situations.

As far as the actual illness itself, or the process of fragmentation, is concerned, we may say that it occurred during the teenage period, when role conflicts became insurmountable. Fragmentation means that the patient returned to early childhood methods of satisfying its needs. This means that the the child looks for a "blessed state" experienced at an early age, i.e. the temporary "paradise" known at some time during childhood. The subject then denies impinging reality and escapes into a form of infantilism. At the actual period of onset, the patient often felt strongly subject to negative feelings, that nobody cared for him, that everyone hated him, and that there were no solutions to these problems. The sense of being unable to deal with the situation also increased feelings of guilt.

It is important to note that religion did *not* function as a release factor in the actual fragmentation of the patients. It was instead provoked by "falling in love" with another person, someone with whom it proved impossible to establish contact. The individual's sexual immaturity then became clearly evident.

Functions of religion

If one studies the concepts of God held by psychotics, one finds that these are strongly linked with the image of the father. The picture of God clearly acquired properties which the father had possessed. Usually, relations with the father lacked warmth and security, which meant that that God was regarded as a remote but unpredictable figure. It is interesting to note that distinctions between a good side and a bad side thus became muddled for the person in question. The usual dichotomy between God and the devil, together with the ability to keep this at a certain distance, had dissolved, and the individual could identify himself sometimes with God, the omnipotent, and sometimes with the devil, the force of destruction.

In many cases, subjects had lived in a world where miracles of different kinds were thought to provide help. Putting up with suffering, and even surpassing God in this respect, was something with which an individual could identify. Jesus was often seen as a maternal figure, regarded as thoroughly trusting, loving and good. The religious system was linked with sexuality. This meant that patients, in some way, needed God's permission to achieve sexual satisfaction. But everything was nevertheless drawn into a complicated and guilt-ridden pattern.

If one looks more closely at patients' ideas of omnipotence, one notes the presence of strong feelings of separation and loss. To counteract these feelings they assumed the role of an omnipotent being, at times, therefore, identifying with God. In this way such heavy losses as death and separation could be overcome by simply declaring that a miracle has occurred and that death has been defeated.

The strong feeling of sexual incapacity also led to assumptions of omnipotence. By adopting God's role the patient thought he was creating a new humanity and a new world. Sexual incapacity was thus transformed into super-potency. The male-female conflict could find an outlet here: it was difficult to decide which sex one should identify with. Identification with Jesus could then mean that one neutralized sexuality and, for example, protected the mother from the father's sexual advances.

Another area where omnipotence emerged in a way was that of suffering. All patients have experienced difficulties and suffering in their lives. On the cosmic plane they could also take on a kind of "super-suffering", and thus resolve the problem on a more total level. Patients with this propensity often sought religious associations where punishment and condemnation had a central role. It appealed to the individual at a mental level to be punished — he then knew that someone was caring for him. This often coincided with an urge to confess. Through confession one seeks punishment, through punishment one can suffer, and by suffering one can atone for one's own and perhaps other people's faults and weaknesses. This attitude was often combined with a sense of imminent global catastrophe, apocalypse, which will show how the individual is saved from his sufferings and his crisis, while the rest perish.

Generally speaking we can say that the worse the conditions of a patient were, the stronger was his need for religion. The religious reference system functioned as an escape from anxiety.

Recovery

It should be mentioned that in one case the patient recovered from his illness. In this process of recovery, religion came to play a major part. This person found a therapeutic symbiosis through contacts with friends with strong religious beliefs. Gradually the individual himself learned the Christian role repertory, and could take on and adopt roles in a meaningful way. The world of religious concepts satisfied the patient's symbiotic need, expressed in a longing for the lost father or mother. This symbiotic need was tranferred to the concept of God, who thus came to have a salutary effect. The important thing was that the person first established secure relations to individuals with a stable religious orientation. Through "symbiosis" with these people and the spiritual communion they represented, the patient established positive relations with the myth system of religion. In other words, the central religious concepts became projection screens, on which the patient played up his mental conflicts in order to to achieve distance from them. The possibility of structuring the problem thus became available, together with an opportunity for role identification with mythical figures and characters. Through this, therapeutic effects were achieved in favourable cases.

Summary

By way of summary, it may be said of the cases forming the basis of the present study that the individual's early life was chaotic and difficult. Healthy relations with other people were not developed. The patients were instead drawn into a conflict model with their parents on one side, and with the environment —the world outside— on the other. Stable and secure relations, in other words, were not developed.

And neither was religion given to these people in a satisfactory way. The religious roles did not succeed in becoming models for a dialogue with existence. At the actual onset of illness, religion did not play a central part. It was instead emotional and sexual ties which did this.

In all the cases studied, however, the religious system acquired a central significance after the onset of illness. The cosmic system of religion was allowed to provide identification models in different ways. Above all, a need was noticed in patients to adopt omnipotence roles. In this way, patients acquired "control" over their chaotic situation. No permanent system was established, however, but the individual fluctuated between omnipotence and deep despair. Suffering could also acquire cosmic dimensions.

In the single case where recovery could be observed, religious concepts played an important part. Through "symbiotically" positive contacts with individuals with a solid religious background, the patient learned role patterns which could then be adopted and identified with. In this way, a healing effect was achieved.

The combination of perspectives of depth psychology and Sundén's version of role theory proved fruitful in the present study. Depth psychology allowed the possibility of interpreting relations between the individual and his closest relatives; role theory, on the other hand, emphasized belief models as active roles in encounters with reality. The combination of the two showed that the role system of religion could absorb the difficult emotional ties present in the mind, and when active support could be given from good friends, this also functioned positively in the healing process.

REFERENCES

Holm, N.G. (1987). *Scandinavian Psychology of Religion*. Religionsvetenskapliga skrifter nr 15. Åbo Akademi.

Järvinen, P.(1991). *Psykos och religion. Psykodynamiska mekanismer och rollpsykologkoiska processer bakom religiösa föreställningar hos psykotiker*. [Psychosis and Religion. Psychodynamic mechanisms and role-psychological processes behind religious concepts among psychotics.] Åbo Akademi. University Press, ÅBO.

CHAPTER 17
TWO CASES OF "LOSS OF FAITH" IN DEPRESSED FEMALE PATIENTS AND SOME QUESTIONS CONCERNING THEORETICAL AND CLINICAL VALIDITY

Gustaf Ståhlberg

In this chapter I will present two cases of religious, depressed women, who have experienced a loss of faith during the deepest phases of their depressive disorder. These women belong to a larger sample of patients from a pilot study I made concerning the correlations between different types of religiosity and various mental disorders. Some of the negative results, which I am going to present here, are consequences of the fact that my pilot study was not tailored for studying correlations between religious and depressive experiences, and further, not designed to study the loss of faith phenomenon.

How common is depression today among Christians in Sweden? Epidemiological questions such as this can not yet be answered from empirical data, but I will mention a new psychiatric study among Christians in Norway, (see Roness, 1988 p. 140) showing that depression is the most frequent mental disorder. Depression is the most frequent disorder even among non-Christians. The rate of depressive disorders is, however, higher among the Christians than the non-Christians. Various subjective observations indicate, I believe, that the same holds for Sweden.

In the literature concerning the relationship between religion and depression, the loss of faith in depressed individuals is a rather well-known phenomenon. By "loss of faith" is meant, that the religious, depressed individual says that she knows what she believes in, even during the depressive phase. She also expects that, after the depression, she will continue to experience God as before. However, *when in the deepest phase of the depression, the individual indicates that she loses her sense of contact with God or that her sense of God's presence has either totally disappeared or greatly diminished.* This description will constitute our definition of the loss of faith phenomenon.

To my knowledge, there is no epidemiological study showing how common loss of faith is among depressed individuals. I have made a rough calculation from Gunter Hole's (1977) extensive study *(Der*

Glaube bei Depressiven) estimating that between a fifth and a third of his patients were suffering from these problems of faith.

As concerns my method of collecting much information from a single individual, I hope that my study in some degree can be compared to a case study of the classical psychoanalytic type. And as far as my use of interviews and typical quantitative methods is concerned, I believe that my study can be compared to the so called single case research studies. But in both instances I have to admit, that my data are not longitudinal in any real sense but the results of only one moment of interview and measurement.

In my opinion, one important weakness in the classical case study method is that the diagnostic assessment, the interpretation of the therapeutic process, as well as the discussion of results, are all made without real reference points or measures outside the psychiatrist's or psychologist's examination or consulting rooms. What I am saying is that today we know a good deal about the importance of the *relation* between the doctor/psychologist and the patient/client for the psychological processes going on in the examination or treatment room and the psychotherapist's interpretation of these processes. This I believe will make us question the psychiatrist's or psychotherapist's ability to be an effective healer and a serious scientist at the same time.

Another way of expressing this weakness in the case study method, more applicable to the subject of interest in this paper, is to say that conclusions concerning the role of religion or mental disorder have to be drawn without a direct comparison between the patient and some control or reference group of so called normals or between the patient and groups of patients without religious committment. This can, for instance, lead to bias in interpreting one individual's religious orientation as more "coloured" by a mental disorder than it really is or one individual's form of mental disorder as more "coloured" by a religious committment than it actually is.

Questions concerning the theoretical validity of my study lead us also to questions about the mechanisms behind the depressive symptoms. When Arieti & Bemporad (1978) presented their psychoanalytic/dynamic formulations about these mechanisms they mentioned early conflicts, traumata or deprivations, which the adult suffered as a child. These malignant experiences predisposed the adult patient to expect nourishment, recognition, and love from an external agency ("the dominant other" which sometimes will be experienced as "the tyrannical other") or to develop relationships of a clinging, dependent type. In milder depressions one can see how the depressed individual is unable or fears the gaining of pleasure and gratification from independent achievement or from himself. Instead he tries to win love through barger relationships or becomes apathetic feeling hopelessness and unable to alter his environment.

This interpersonal perspective closely resembles an object relations point of view. In accordance with this, we will be very interested in how the individuals in our study describe their parents and other important persons from their childhood memories.

In my opinion, an object relations perspective towards religious experiences is very fruitful, especially for a clinical psychological study of religiosity. This perspective is found in Ana-Maria Rizzuto's (1979) theory of God as a kind of transitional object, the "God representation". The sources of that representation are five:
i) The idealized and real mother, ii) The idealized and real parents in relation to each other, iii) The idealized and real father, iv) The child's grandiose image of himself, and v) Cultural and social circumstances, what we can call the religious tradition.

In accordance with these sources of the God representation we will search for similarities and differences in our patients' description of God on the one side and parents, important persons in childhood and her/himself on the other. Did a loss of faith in some way result from a loss of a mother or father representation? That will be one of our main questions especially to the interview material. We will also search for elements of "mature religion", free from emotive anthropomorfism, in our patients attitudes and interview answers.

From a general psychological point of view, the loss of faith can be described as changes in the depressed individual's religious attitudes. If we try to differentiate between emotional and cognitive components of the religious attitude, we can define the loss as a very strong decline in the emotional component, whereas the cognitive component changes to a very small extent. It is from one of our attitude measures, from a semantic differential, that we expect low scores in emotionally charged dimensions and high scores in cognitively charged ones.

Batson & Ventis (1982 p. 246) made a "box score analysis" concerning correlations between three different ways of being religious and measures of mental health. The three ways were 1: an extrinsic, means orientation (the individual scoring highly on this factor *uses* his faith in a self-centered way), 2: an intrinsic, end orientation (the individual scoring highly on this factor *lives* his faith, which is autonomous, self-motivating), and 3: a quest orientation (the individual scoring highly on this factor sustains complexitivity, appreciates doubts about faith and holds only preliminary points of view). A main result of their analysis was, that the extrinsic, means orientation was negatively correlated with mental health and the other orientations rather more positively than negatively correlated. In accordance with this we foresee in our study high scores on the extrinsic factors and low scores on the intrinsic, end and quest factors. From an applied, psychotherapeutic point of view it can be said, that the loss of faith has negative consequences for treatment. The loss of faith implies that the God imago or representation is kept outside the depressive process and thus can not be a "curative factor" in the psychotherapeutic work with the individual. This issue leads us to some questions concerning the clinical validity of my case study method.

From the point of view of clinical validity, scores on general factors and dimensions from my quantitative methods did not give us much guidance about how to work practically with the patient. On the positive side, however, we do find very personal interview data. On the positive side as well, by using quantitative methods we gained reference points outside the examination or treatment room. This can help us to restrain our eagerness to cure behaviours and experiences common in reference groups of so called normals. Spero (1990) provides us with a very interesting model concerning the experiences of religious patients in psychoanalytic psychotherapy. In this model one can see how the influence of projections and early object relations "colour" the God imago.

His model also implies that an "objective divine object" tries to establish contact with the individual (his self). However, this part of the model, I think, lies outside a scientific, psychological analysis. In my opinion, it is enough to speak of "mature parts" of the individual's religious committment. Perhaps my intrinsic and quest scales can function as an empirical measure of this important Christian experience.

Aims

The main goal of this study was to provide a better understanding of the loss of faith phenomenon through an intensive examination of the cases of two depressed female patients. Three aims can be added to this end:

1) To gain extensive and varied data by the use of qualitative and quantitative methods.
2) To improve the case study method by using quantitative methods, which make it possible to compare the results of the depressed individuals with the reference groups and thereby establish reference points outside the examination or treatment room.

3) To discuss this type of case study from the view point of theoretical and empirical validity.

Method

In these case studies I used five different data-collecting methods:

1. A "semi-structured" and "free" *interview*. The interviewers had a guide covering six main areas with subsequent minor questions. The interviewers were free concerning the sequence of the questions and were instructed to "follow" the interviewees in their answers and comments. The intent was to have a sort of dialogue with the interviewee. The interviews were recorded (see Ståhlberg,1988).

The six main questions covered the following subjects: what the belief meant to the believer, who was of importance for the individual's Christian development, present day committment to the congregation, how the individual experiences God (the God representation), the individual's use of the Bible, hymns and songs, and the differences in the individual's view of his belief when feeling bad and feeling good.

2. A *symptom checklist*, named SCL-90-R, which is a 90-item self-report symptom inventory, modified and validated by Derogatis, Rickels & Rock (1976). The dimensions are labeled as follows: I Somatization, II Obsessive-Compulsive, III Interpersonal sensitivity, IV Depression, V Anxiety, VI Hostility, VII Phobic anxiety, VIII Paranoid ideation, and IX Psychoticism. There are three major normative samples for the SCL-90-R. Our test persons are compared with two of them: 1002 "heterogenous psychiatric out-patients" and 974 "non-patient normals".

3. An *"existential" scale*, named The Purpose in Life Test, constructed by Crumbough & Maholick (1969). The test is aimed at testing Frankl's concepts of noogenic neurosis and existential meaning. The dimensions are labeled: P 1 Life satisfaction, P 2 Life purpose, and P 3 Goal achievement. As normative sample is used 59 non-patient normals, 34 women and 25 men, which I tested some years ago. They were active members of the Swedish lutheran church and aged 14-65 years.

4. A *"religious" Likert scale* with items from King & Hunt's (1972), Hoge's (1972) and Batson & Ventis's (1982) studies on religiosity as a multi-dimensional phenomenon, particurlarly the extrinsic, the

intrinsic, and the quest orientations. Three items are my own, covering the Swedish congregational activity. The dimensions are labeled: I Faith, II Church Involvement, III Extrinsic Emergency, IV Growth, V Knowledge, VI Extrinsic Social Relationships, VII Extrinsic Inconsequence, VIII Special Intrinsic Scale, and IX Quest Scale.

My scale (1978) has earlier passed through some tests, using a factor analysis method (factors VIII and IX are not results from my own factor analysis). As normative sample is used the same 59 non-patient normals, which answered the Purpose in Life Test (Ståhlberg,1988).

5. A *Semantic differential test*, which Thorleif Pettersson and I (1974) constructed several years ago. We factor analysed answers from 120 university students, taking the basic course in religion and mainly between the ages 19 and 25. In the factor analyses we got six factors or dimensions, labeled AV General Evaluation, AK Activity, SR1 Traditional Christian, SV Specific Evaluative, SR2 Traditional Pietistic, and F Familiarity.

I used the four stimulus concepts: the conciliating Christ, love, the crucified Christ, and God. The normative sample was the same 59 normals, which answered the Likert scale and the Purpose in Life Test. They rated these four concepts by using 60 bipolar adjective scales.

CASE 1

From the interview we find that this woman is about 50 years old and a committed member of the Swedish lutheran church. She has grown up in a Christian home but emphasizes, that she became a Christian on her own.

For the last six months she has been suffering from her second depression, which she describes as deep and which has caused her to contact a psychiatric clinic. She says, that she has had some "discussions" with God, but that she now has decided to let religious "ruminations" wait until the depression has passed. She says, that God is not so "unmerciful" that He can not accept that. She also knows people who have been struggling very hard with religious ruminations and they have had a "frightful situation".

What she refers to as religious ruminations are connected with her relationship to her family and friends. When she is deeply depressed, she feels that she relates very poorly to her family members, friends, and fellowmen in the world. If she "draws" God into this "bad behaviour", she runs the risk of experiencing sin and guilt.

When she was relating further about God, she states that He isn't merely a "nice old uncle", but He is demanding as well: God says that you should love Him and your fellow humans as yourself. In the Bible, God does not say that you can do it if you want to, but He says you must.

When asked to describe her mother, she replies that she wasn't a saint, but "as near a saint as I can imagine". Her mother had "an inner strength" just as her grandmother and aunt. However, she tells us very little about her father. She only states that he was a believer.

And now to the quantitative measures. In **Table 1** we find some profiles. We begin at the profiles "D I" to "D IX". This data comes from the symptom checklist SCL-90-R. The profiles show our test person's mean raw scores on the nine symptom dimensions. These scores are compared to two base lines. The upper line indicates the mean raw scores of the 974 non-patient, normals, and the lower base-line the mean raw scores of the 1002 heterogenous, psychiatric outpatients.

In the SCL-90-R our test person, compared to the normals, scores highest on the dimensions Obsessive-Compulsive and Depression, followed by Somatization, Interpersonal sensitivity, Anxiety, and Paranoid ideation. She obtains her lowest scores on the dimensions Phobic anxiety and Hostility. Compared to the psychiatric outpatients our test person gets a rather similar profile. The great difference is that she has scores over the mean only in the dimensions of Somatization and Obsessive-Compulsive.

The profile "P 1" to "P 3" gives us the results from The Purpose in Life test. Base line is the mean raw scores of 59 non-patient normals, 34 women and 25 men. Our test person's mean raw scores are lower than the base line in all three dimensions and lower in Goal achievement and Life satisfaction than in Life purpose.

The dimensions "I" to "IX" represent my "religious" Likert scale. Base line is from the same 59 normals as The Purpose in Life Test. Our test person scores highest on the factor III Extrinsic Emergency. This is followed by VII Extrinsic Inconsequence, IX Quest scale, VI Extrinsic Social Relationships, and VIII Special Intrinsic scale. All scores in these dimensions are distinctly above the base line.

Table 1: Profiles showing the mean raw scores of *case 1* on the dimensions/factors of the SCL-90-R (DI Somatization, DII Obsessive-Compulsive, DIII Interpersonal sensitivity, DIV Depression, DV Anxiety, DVI Hostility, DVII Phobic anxiety, DVIII Paranoid ideation, and DIX Psychoticism. The upper base line indicates the mean raw scores of 974 "non-patient normals", the lower base line the mean raw scores of 1002 "heterogenous psychiatric outpatients")., the Purpose in Life Test (PI Life satisfaction, PII Life Purpose, PIII Goal achievement), and the "Religious" Likert scale (I Faith, II Church Involvement, III Extrinsic Emergency, IV Growth, V. Knowledge, VI Extrinsic Social Relationships, VII Extrinsic Inconsequence, VIII Special Intrinsic Scale, and IX Quest Scale). The base lines of the PIL-test and the Likert scale indicate the mean raw scores of 59 "non-patient normals", active members of the Swedish lutheran church).

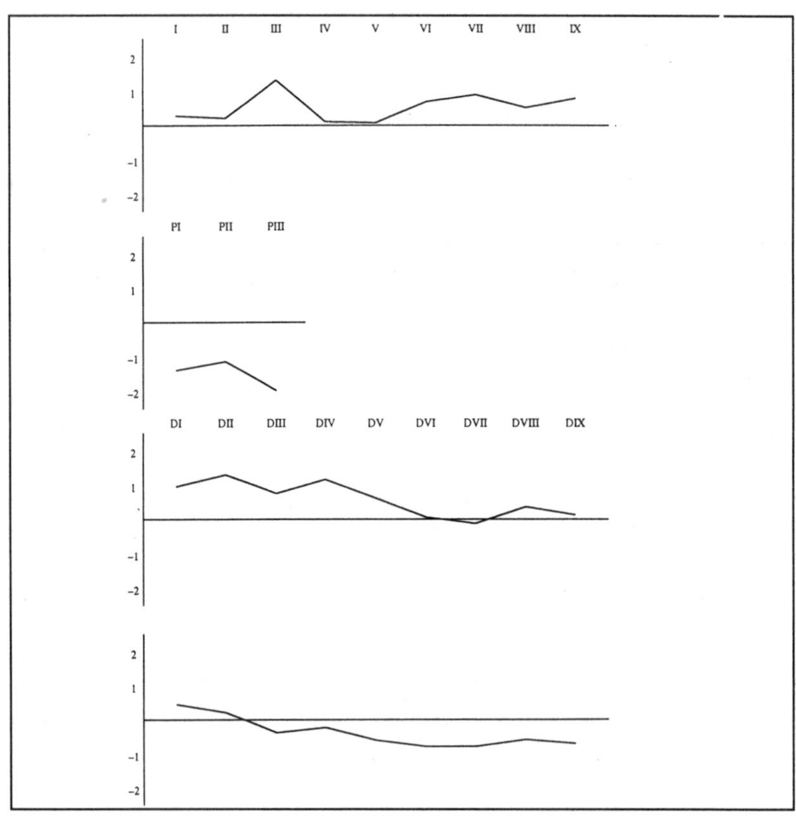

The four profiles in **Table 2** are from the semantic differential test. The base line is from the same 59 normals as before. Our test person describes Christ and Love foremost with adjectives such as "predictable", "known" and "simple" from the Familiarity dimension and God foremost with adjectives such as "brave", "converted" and "believing" from the Traditional Pietistic dimension. In the Specific Evaluative dimension we also find high scores with adjectives such as "amusing", "pleasurable" and "pleasant". And finally the test person scores high by rating the conciliating Christ and Love with adjectives such as "spiritual", "divine", "heavenly" and "holy" from the Traditional Christian dimension.

CASE 2

From the interview we find that this woman is about 40 years old. She is a committed member of the Pentecostal revival in Sweden. When she was about 18 years old, she tried to leave the congregation, but soon experienced, as she put it "that I can't manage my life without God". Thus she returned to the congregation, where her mother was a member as well.

From the interview it is impossible to ascertain how many depressive periods our interview person has suffered. However, at the time of the interview, she has contact with a psychiatric clinic. She also mentions that she is using anti-depressive drugs and that she has begun psychotherapy with a psychologist.

In the interview she also tells us about her first depression, which seems to have taken place many years ago. While suffering that depression, she experienced "that God had abandoned her". He had "disappeared", was "lost" to her. She also tells us, that she now has the same experience. Her feelings of having lost God have returned. However she now *knows* that God exists and knows from earlier situations that she will feel differently when she recovers from her depression. She also mentions that when depressed, all the frightful experiences of her childhood and youth come to mind. These frightful experiences are mostly related to her mother. When asked about the chronological order - that is if the depression or the feelings of loss come first -, she replies that the feeling of anxiety and depression comes first, followed by feelings of having been abandoned by God.

She also mentions, that when suffering her first depression she experienced a real answer from God to her prayer for help. One night, when her husbond was away on business far from home, she prayed to God for help. Her 20 year-old son came to her and gave her real

Table 2: Profiles showing the mean raw scores of *case 1* on the dimensions of the semantic differential test (AV General Evaluation, AK Activity, SR1 Traditional Christian, SV Specific Avaluative, SR2 Traditional Pietistic, and F Familarity. The base lines indicate the mean raw scores of 59 "non-patient normals", active members of the Swedish lutheran church).

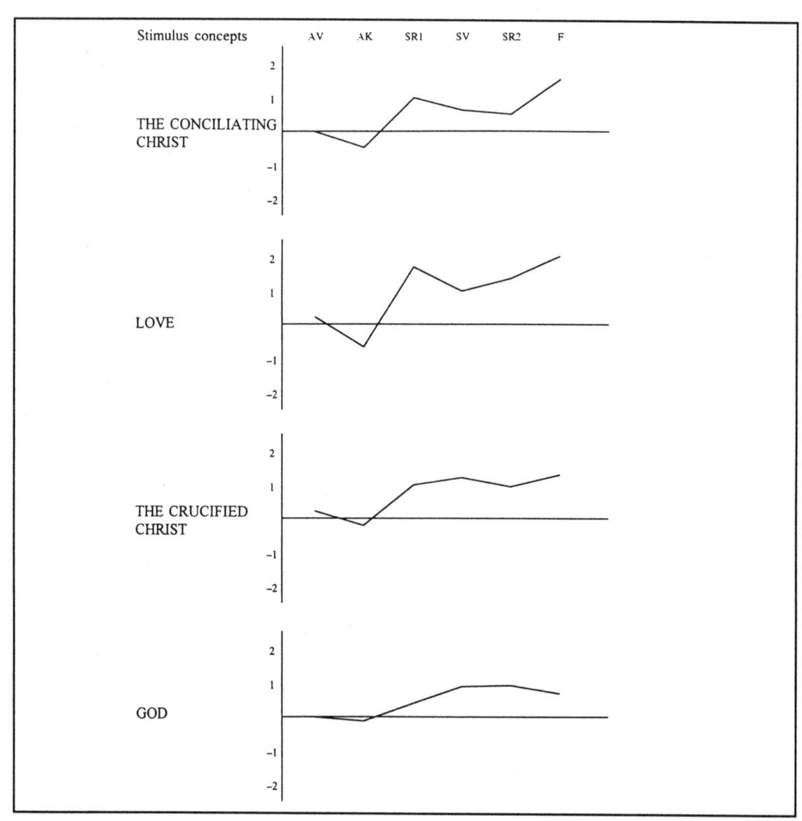

consolation. He was like a psychologist "listening and listening and listening".

When asked about her faith in God, she replies that her faith is very important to her, something she needs and that gives her security. God is also "generous". She believs that she has a more generous God than most of her fellowmen. When asked more about how she experiences God, she answers that He is like a "father", "a father-figure", who takes her hands and helps her through, and is not "judgmental".

However, when she sees and hears about people who suffer innocently, especially if they are children that are assaulted by their parents, she wants to accuse God by saying "Who are you sitting up there and doing nothing to help these innocent, suffering people". She also sometimes thinks about Noah and the flood and wonder "why didn't God annihilate everybody so that no human being would have to exist and suffer".

When asked to describe her father, she first mentions that he was not a believer, but was a "very good father and the best and finest man she ever met". He meant "everyting to her", and never made her disappointed. And now she is glad that she told her father, before he died, how much she loved him and that he never had disappointed her. And he answered "Yes, I have done my best".

The description of her mother is quite the opposite. She was very dominating and demanded that everything be perfect. Our interviewee loved music and reading books, however in her mother's eyes, that was wrong, a sin, if it was not what she called "Christian music" or "Christian books". Our interviewee also tells us that she loved Red Indian storybooks, but that her mother nagged at her and gave her feelings of guilt. When asked if she experienced guilt feelings towards God or towards her mother, she answers "both", because her mother said that it was a sin against God.

Our interviewee also states, that she is unhappy about the situation that she can not love her mother as a daughter should. She also says that when she is suffering from her depression all these experiences come back to her, but when recovered, she represses them. She says further, that she isn't bitter or angry towards any one for this situation. She knows, that her mother "did her best". But she is bitter towards what she calls "the system" that taught that everything that was amusing and fun was a sin. In accordance with this she states, that she is a suffering from an "environmental injury".

And now to the quantitative data (**tables 3 and 4**). The profiles and the base lines are the same as in Case 1. In the SCL-90-R our test person, compared to the normals, scores rather highly only on the dimensions II Obsessive-Compulsive, VIII Paranoid ideation and III Interpersonal

Table 3: Profiles showing the mean raw scores of *case 2* on the dimensions/factors of the SCL-90-R (DI Somatization, DII Obsessive-Compulsive, DIII Interpersonal sensitivity, DIV Depression, DV Anxiety, DVI Hostility, DVII Phobic anxiety, DVIII Paranoid ideation, and DIX Psychoticism. The upper base line indicates the mean raw scores of 974 "non-patient normals", the lower base line the mean raw scores of 1002 "heterogenous psychiatric outpatients"), the Purpose in Life Test (PI Life satisfaction, PII Life purpose, PIII Goal achievement) and the "Religious" Likert scale (I Faith, II Church Involvement, III Extrinsic Emergency, IV Growth, V Knowledge, VI Extrinsic Social Relationships, VII Extrinsic Inconsequence, VIII Special Intrinsic Scale, and IX Wuest Scale). The base lines of the PIL-test and the Likert scale indicate the mean raw scores of 59 "non-patient normals" active members of the Swedish lutheran church).

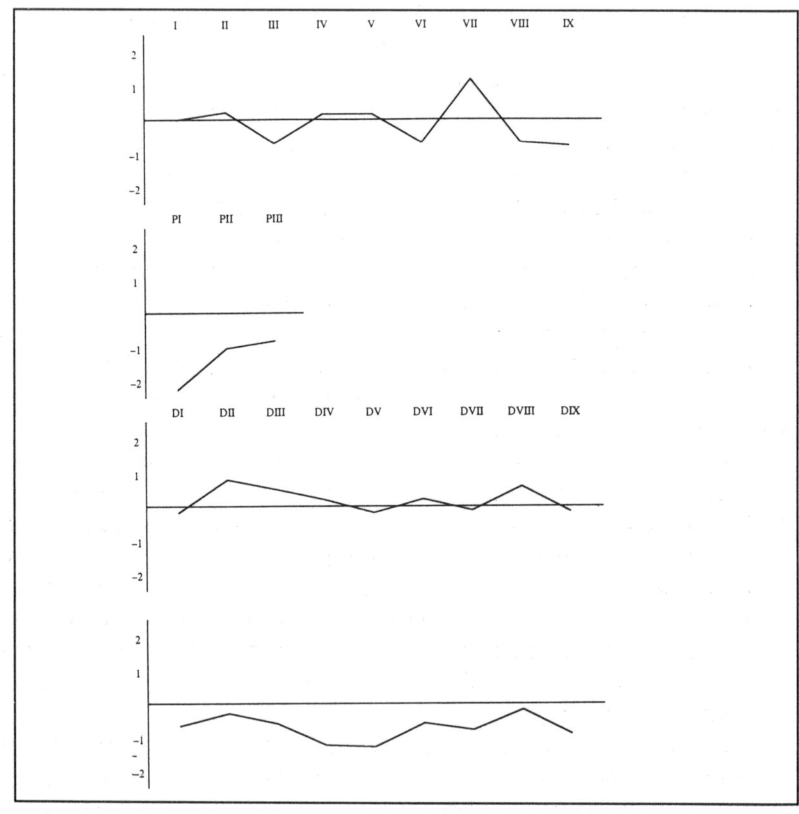

Table 4: Profiles showing the mean raw scores of *case 2* on the dimensions of the semantic differential test (AV General Evaluation, AK Activity, SR1 Traditional Christian, SV Specific Evaluative, SR2 Traditional Pietistic, and F Familiarity. The base lines indicate the mean raw scores of 59 "non-patient normals", active members of the Swedish lutheran church).

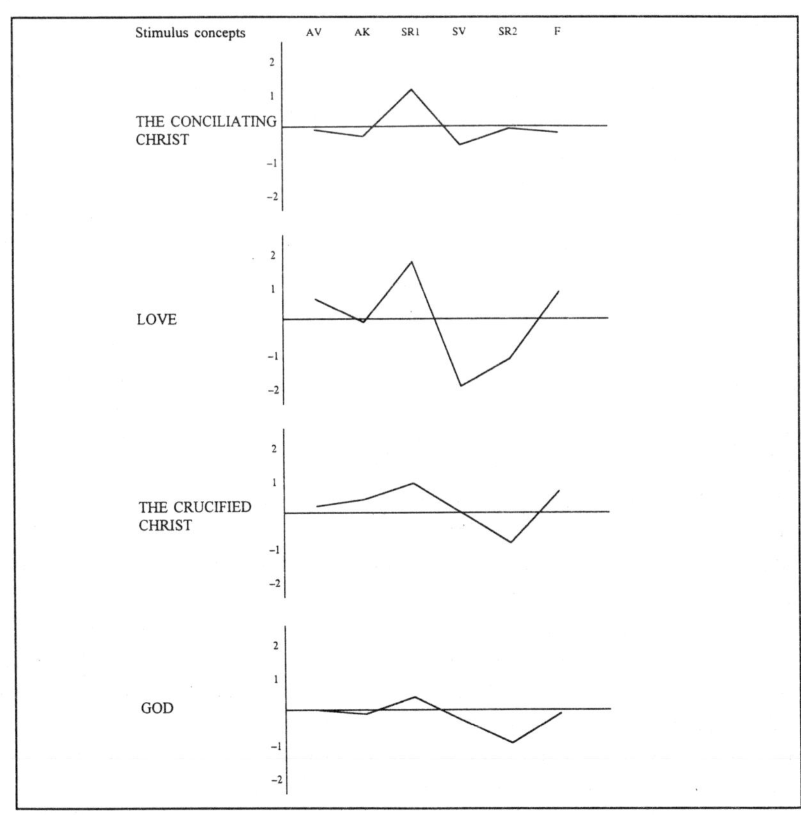

sensitivity. On the rest of the dimensions she scores near the base line. The comparison with the patients results, in a broad sense, the same kind of profile, but with the distinct difference that all scores are below the base line.

In accordance with the Purpose in Life Test profile, our test person scores distinctly lower on Life saticfaction than on the other two dimensons. In my Likert scale she scores highly only on dimension VII Extrinsic Inconsequence. Her lowest scores are on III Extrinsic Emergency, IX Quest Scale, VIII Special Intrinsic Scale, and VI Extrinsic Social Relationships.

In the semantic differential our test person scores highest on the Traditional Christian dimension (the most typical adjectives of the dimensions are accounted for in Case 1) for all four stimulus concepts. When rating the conciliating Christ and Love she scores lowest on the Specific Evaluative dimension and for the crucified Christ and God her lowest score is on the Traditional Pietistic dimension. Her scores on the Familiarity dimension do not show any typical pattern.

Discussion and conclusions

From the interviews it is noted that both of our interview persons describe their parents in "black and white" terms. Our first interviewee speaks of her mother as close to sainthood, while her father is referred to as only a believer. Our second interviewee speaks very appreciatively of her father: "the best and finest man she ever met". Her mother, however, is described as the opposite: domineering, demanding and condemnatory. It is possible that we witness in these descriptions the results of certain defence mechanisms (affect isolation, reaction formation, denial, splitting, and projection). In connection with the pilot study, my colleague and I attempted on the basis of the interviews to assess what types of defence mechanisms the patients utilized. The reliability of these assessments was relatively low and other methods should therefore be used, for example a subliminal test like the DMT (Defense Mechanism Test).

As concerns the similarity and dissimilarity of the descriptions of God, parents, and other important persons, we can note, among other things, the following: Subject 1 describes her mother as close to sainthood and emphasizes that God is not a "nice old uncle" but is also demanding. Subject 2 describes her father as "everything to her" and God as a "father", who takes her hands and helps her through. Apparently off to the side of this representation of God there is a God that arouses her disappointment. It is a God that does not intervene when innocent people, especially children, suffer. Here a disappointment surfaces which probably has more to do with the mother representation.

Looking at the various quantitative methods, I find it hard to understand why both the test subjects in the SCL-90-R are presented as "healthier" than average for the patient group on nearly every dimension. It is especially difficult to understand subject 2's low scores on the dimensions of Depression, Hostility, Anxiety and Phobic anxiety. The only possible explanation I can find is that this woman had begun psychotherapy and was being treated with anti-depressives. In this context an important factor is that the SCL-90-R both limits itself to the symptom level and concerns only the relatively present state of health. This problem emphasizes the need for complete psychiatric diagnostic. For test subject 1 it can be noted that the relationship between the scores on the dimensions of Depression, Anxiety, and Hostility may indicate an inner conflict. In the interview material I have found much that has inspired me to try and measure depressive processes more from an object-relations point of view.

I find both the test subjects' results indicating lower scores in Life satisfaction than in Life purpose and all three mean scores below the base line, comprehensible from the point of view of depression. In the depressive state it is hard to find meaning and still more difficult to experience satisfaction and the feeling of having achieved one's goals in life.

Concerning my "religious" Likert scale, the highest scores on the factor of Extrinsic Emergency as well as the high scores on the factors Extrinsic Social Relationships and Extrinsic Inconsequence for the test subject 1, and the high scores on Extrinsic Inconsequence and the low scores on the scales Special Intrinsic and Quest for test subject 2, are all made comprehensible from the results reported by Batson & Ventis. Not comprehensible from their results are, however, the high scores on the Special Intrinsic and Quest scales for test subject 1 and the lowest scores on Extrinsic Emergency and the low scores on Extrinsic Social Relationships for test subject 2.

These results raise two main questions. The first concerns the nature of depressive disorders in relation to other psychopathological disorders — as further related to the special negative correlation shown between an extrinsic religious orientation and measures of mental health. This could imply, for example, that a depressed individual experiences hopelessness to such a degree that despite her need she simply cannot bear to hope for help from God. This could also imply that the depressed individual cannot bear to seek out the social situations where she can develop an "external type" of extrinsic orientation.

The second question concerns to what extent the three dimensions intrinsic, extrinsic and quest are contradictory, uncorrelated or intercorrelated. The results I have obtained strongly contradict the first two alternatives. However, it is clear that we cannot draw any general conclusions or formulate any general hypotheses from a study of only two cases.

One reason for my use of a semantic differential test is that it can be hypothesized that it is more sensitive to the emotional component of the religious attitude than a questionnaire. And it is the Familiarity and the Specific Evaluative dimensions, that I think are most emotionally charged and the Traditional Christian dimension least so. That supposition holds for both test subjects' scores on the Traditional Christian dimension, but it is not supported by the results for the Familiarity and Specific Evaluative dimensions.

On the whole, my attempt to utilize quantitative methods to establish reference points outside of the examination and treatment rooms was both encouraging and discouraging. I have gained an equal number of positive and negative indications as to the ability to measure and understand the loss of faith phenomenon by the use of quantitative methods. As I stated at the beginning of my presentation, one important reason for this is that my methods are not tailored for the study of depressive states, especially not the loss of faith phenomenon. I believe that it is also important that we discuss negative results.

As far as the clinical validity of this study is concerned, I would like to focus on two important results. Firstly, we should be careful with the assumption that we will meet a pronounced extrinsic religious orientation in depressed patients. Secondly, we should be more open to the assumption that we may find in the depressed patients we study or treat, both an intrinsic, extrinsic and quest orientation at the same time.

For the sake of continuing scientific research into the loss of faith phenomenon, I would like to pose the following questions: Is it possible to understand the loss of faith phenomen during depression as a defence maneuver in the service of religiously engaged people? The individual can utilize defences such as affect isolation, denial, splitting and projective identification. Does this defence maneuver occur as a result of fear to direct strong negative feelings such as anger and hate towards the God representation? Or does this defence maneuver result from a fear of losing the God representation together with the love object? As a result of strong negative feelings coming forth and being directed towards one or more object representations there is a risk that this/these may be lost for a shorter or longer period of time. In both of these presumed cases of defence maneuver there has been an all too great similarity between the God representation and the parent representation. In the opposite sense, the degree of "mature" religion has been too little.

REFERENCES

Arieti, S., Bemporad, J. (1978). *Severe and mild depression*. The psychotherapeutic approach. London: Tavistock Publications Ltd.

Batson, C. D., Ventis, W. L. (1982). *The religious experience*. A social-psychological perspective. New York: Oxford University Press.

Crumbaugh, J. C., Maholick, L. T. (1969). *Manual of instructions for the Purpose in Life Test*. Munster.

Derogatis, L. R., Rickels, K., Rock, A.F. (1976). The SCL-90 and the MMPI: A step in the validation of a new self-report scale. *British Journal of Psychiatry, 128*, 280-289.

Hoge, D. R. (1972). An intrinsic religious motivation scale. *Journal for the Scientific Study of Religion, 11*, 369-376.

Hole, G. (1977). *Der Glaube bei Depressiven*. Stuttgart: Ferdinand Enke Verlag.

King, M. B., Hunt, R. A. (1972). Measuring the religious variable: Replication. *Journal for the Scientific Study of Religion, 11*, 240-251.

Pettersson, T., Ståhlberg, G. (1974). *Semantisk differentialteknik i religionspsykologisk användning*. Serien Uttryck-kommunikation-religion, serie 2: Häfte IV. Uppsala.

Rizzuto, A-M. (1979). *The birth of the living God*. A psychoanalytic study. Chicago: The University of Chicago Press.

Roness, A. (1988). *Psykiatri of religion*. Oslo: Universitets forlaget.

Spero, M. H. (1990). Parallel dimensions of experience in psychoanalytic psychotherapy of the religious patient. *Psychotherapy, 27*, 53-71.

Ståhlberg, G. (1978). Measuring religious attitudes — two empirical studies. In: *Psychological studies on religious man*. Acta Universitatis Upsaliensis: Psychologia Religionum. Stockholm: Almqvist and Wiksell International.

Ståhlberg, G. (1988). *Om religiositet och dess samband med psykiska störningar*. Uppsala Universitet, Teologiska Institutionen. (Lic. diss.: "On religiosity and its relation to mental disorders").

CHAPTER 18
RELIGIOUS INVOLVEMENT AND MENTAL HEALTH: A CASE OF DEPRESSION

Krzysztof Cieslak

Statements about "healthy" behavior and religiosity in different contexts are mostly hypothetical, pre-scientific, and normative (Textor, 1988). A meta-analysis of 24 pertinent studies revealed no support for the preconception that religiousness is necessarily correlated with psychopathology; but also showed only little evidence for positive effects of religion (Bergin, 1983). It seems that most of the contradictory results are tied to the different methodologies applied and different measurement paradigms (Gorsuch, 1984; George & McNamara, 1984). Despite major changes in our religious systems in the past decades, spiritual beliefs still affect the lives of most individuals, while not often addressed in the clinical setting. This is unfortunate, because these beliefs frequently bring comfort to distressed individuals and help them to cope with illness and crisis (Clemen et al., 1981). Following Bergin's suggestion (1983, p. 180) that "...consequently generalizations about the psychological causes and consequencies of religious involvement need to be tentative and subject to further investigation," one case is presented as to illustrate some statements already made about the positive impact of religiosity on mental health.

Medical report

On the basis of hospital archival documents we can describe the history of Anna's illness. Anna, 50 years old, has two younger and two elder sisters, born in a small village. After finishing primary school at the age of 14, she left home and went to live in a boarding school. Having graduated from secondary school she entered university to study Polish philology. After five years of studies, just before completing her M.A. thesis, she started psychiatric hospital treatment because of an acute schizophrenic episode. She manifested the typical psychotic syndrome: emotional turmoil, confusion, excitement, delusions and hallucinations. Religious topics and symbols dominated her behavior. She saw the Last Judgment and hell, devils, and sang religious songs. She shouted: "God, God, what am I to do now — I did things in my own way not according to God's will. I am a sinner, I have abandoned God and I will be damned." She was very offensive and aggressive, wanting to bite the nurses and lick them immediately after that. When asked if there were devils around her, she answered that were no devils but angels. She received typical medical treatment for three months and was released from the hospital. Leaving hospital she was depressed and apathetic. She came back after two months' suffering from headaches, insomnia, feelings of guilt and she was very depressed. She had good contact with the world around her, she did not manifest clear psychotic symptoms.

Anna described her condition not as an illness, but as a state of despair caused by a sin she committed. She considered that sin as more serious than murder. She told one of her professors absolutely frankly that the whole truth about her way could be told only to God. Because of this, she was damned and she had suicidal thoughts. She regretted being cured of the previous illness and she was sure that she would never be healthy and a valuable person. Two months later she was released from hospital at the request of her relatives.

During the next six years she came back to the hospital more than a dozen times for a periods sometimes longer than six months. She manifested psychotic symptoms, syndromes of deep depression, a strong sense of illness and suicidal thoughts. She also blamed her relatives and friends for her faults and being rejected by God. She also reproached herself for not loving anybody in her life and asked who would teach her to love.

She was also examined by psychologists and the report suggested schizophrenia with depressive syndrome and anxiety. Anna gave some characteristic answers in the test of unfinished sentences (my secret ambition in life is... "nothing anymore;" future seems to me... "hopeless;" when I am older... "I don't want to live so long.")

Doctor's report

We have here the opinion of the doctor who treated Anna for more than 20 years: "Anna has been ill for more than 25 years. She was hospitalized many times from 1964 to 1970. Since 1970 her health has improved to such an extent that she hasn't been hospitalized anymore. During the 1960's she was in a very bad state with a strong component of depression and suicidal thoughts. We hesitated with diagnosis between endogenous depression or process schizophrenia. Finally, we diagnozed it as schizophrenia with a strong component of depression. In the beginning of the 1970's she 'came together' and never came back to the hospital. She received a disability pension and started to work in a firm for disabled persons. She was very well motivated for work and regularly visited her doctor. She took medication, but in very small amounts. Of course she had worse periods but not in the sense of having evident psychotic symptoms. She was depressed, had difficulties with concen-tration and falling asleep, suffering from fears and anxiety. Such a state is rather stable and has lasted since 1970. She never manifested acute psychotic symptoms anymore.

I know that in the beginning of the 1970's she joined a church group. She is very much involved in it and she says that it helps her very much, that it 'mobilizes' her. For the last ten years she has suffered from very weak signs of depression and now they are almost absent."

Patient's report

Anna has described her illness and the process of recovery in her own words: "I was really seriously ill and I 'spent' 6 years in a psychiatric hospital, returning there more than a dozen times. Since 1970, I have never come back there. I think that I am healthy now. It is possible because of my religious involvement in Neocatechumenate Community [a Roman Catholic movement which started in the 1960's and has spread all over the world. Members have two or more meetings during the week for Bible reading, celebrating Holy Mass, and sharing their personal experiences]. It has enabled me to understand and helped me to form a new attitude to many facts in my life. My depression hasn't 'attacked' me any more. I can even talk about it without any fear or anxiety. It is completely behind me. I consider it a complex problem. First of all, I felt strongly alienated from others. I knew that there existed 'better' and 'worse' people ,and I was the 'worse' person. I always was the 'worst.' I imagined that God stood in with my superiors who were so wonderful, noble, wise, an I was a complete wreck. I strongly felt that I was rejected by others. In the hospital I also felt that I was rejected by God and I had no hope of being redeemed. But when one sees that God loves him, one does not care about other loves. I don't feel it so strongly now, when somebody has a bad opinion about me. In the past, I felt it as very painful. ...But it is not that I have changed myself. Objectively, I am weaker than others, not so talented, not so strong, but I have seen that God loves me and it is vitally important for me."

"...I have seen that God is really present in my life, that God has led me and constructed the story of my life. God is above me and keeps my life in His hands. Having such an experience, I realized that it is not by chance that I belong to the Neocatechumenate Community... I can also understand better the source of my fear and anxiety; I was born during the Second World War in times of stress. My sisters remember that as a child I was always afraid of something.

Second, after having two daughters, my father wanted to have a son, who would help him on the farm. I always felt rejected by my father, and my sisters were always loved more, more appreciated. It influenced my relationships with my superiors and men in general. Paradoxically, my father was more kind to me than to my sisters! I tried very hard to please him, but I had to work hard for his love. If I behave properly, in accordance with expectations of other people, I am loved, but if not, I am rejected. I projected the above principle on God, expecting the same reaction from Him.... It doesn't mean that I haven't any problems now. They exist, but God's word comes with help... I had never known that my life was in God's hands, and I always tried to solve my problems by myself. This led to many contradictory and confusing situations. ...Now it is very important for me to differentiate between my own wisdom and God's wisdom. I should try to follow the God's wisdom. But before, I had always tried to judge God, to create Him in my own imagery. The best way is simply to accept the God's word as one hears it. I see that quite unnecessarily, I had thought so much, analyzed so much, and exerted myself."

The patient has her own rules and ways of interpreting past events: "I think that he illness started when I was a child... When I was a university student, 6 months before going to the hospital, I felt very badly, I had no one to speak to, something wrong was going on in my head. I felt lonely, needed very much for someone who would appreciate and accept me, who would be kind to me... In my mind, there recurred the situation that I tried to accept myself and to do it on my own, thus, two different personalities developed in me... The fact that I could forgive and become reconciled with others, has been vitally important for me. My depression was also caused by the fact that I had a grudge against some people, I blamed them as being responsible for my illness and going to the hospital. I bore strong resentment against them — unwarranted resentment.... It has helped me to such an extent that I have stopped returning to my unpleasant past, to my painful reflections and to my depressive thoughts. I live in the present and for the future. But I have not achieved this through my own efforts. I wouldn't be able to do this on my own. It is easy to say 'I forgive,' but to realize it is very difficult. It is God who has enabled me to do it...."

Concluding comments

It seems that the patient recovered from her illness and the state is rather stable for almost 20 years. Religious involvement (Anna attends Neocatechumenate Community meetings very regularly) undoubtedly plays a central part in the healing process and contributes in some ways to

Anna's private dialogue with existence (Holm & Jarvinen 1990). Anna's religious faith is a central and ultimate component of her life. Having in mind the Dombeck's and Karl's (1987) sugestion that "while we 'translate' a person's religious language into working languages of our professions, it is important to recognize that our tentative translation is not necessarily the reality for that person," we will try to understand and describe some of the important facts from the reports in a broader context. Bergin (1980) has proposed the spiritual alternative called "theistic realism" and a list of eight contrasts between theistic and clinical-humanistic values as they pertain to personality and change. Some of Bergin's assumptions seem to be very useful in analysing and understanding Anna's statements about her illness and her experiences:

1. acceptance and strong conviction that God is supreme, humility, acceptance of God's authority and that obedience to the will of God, are the virtues for a healing process;
2. personal identity is eternal and derived from the divine, relationships with God define one's self-worth;
3. forgiveness of others who cause distress (including parents) completes the therapeutic restoration of self;
4. acceptance of personal responsibility for one's own harmful actions, and acceptance of guilt suffering, are the keys to change.

Symbolic interactionism and hermeneutics may also help in understanding the data. The concept of the definition of situation is regarded a key and constitutive concept for symbolic interactionism. It is related to the assumption that behavior is formed actively on the basis of changeable meanings assigned to objects. Meanings are constituted by relating the concrete experience to a posessed frame of reference. The horizon of reference system may be changed, enriched with new elements belonging to the context of knowledge. This context is constituted by the subjective stock of knowledge of a person's social biography and the social stock of knowledge (objective ideas, beliefs, norms, etc.) with which the subjective stock of knowledge overlaps to some degree. The stock of knowledge, which is the source of typifications, constructs provinces of meanings — "multiple realities" or "worlds" of everyday life (the reality of work, past time, religious experience etc.). Originally, the problem of contextual character of meaning belongs to the current of hermeneutic reflection (Halas, 1985).

In Anna's statements, we could easily find many examples of the "private" meanings and "private" significances she attaches to the facts and situations in her life (e.g., her own vision of illness, understanding of the relations with father and God, presentation of the contributors to the positive nature of her relations with other people, etc.). These statements are offered after many years of having the religious experien-ces. They have required Anna to have an active attitude, to be active in religious dimension of her life. The "effects" are in accordance with Glueck's (1988, p. 110) hypothesis that: "the more demanding religion is for its adherents, the more health and spirituality will be seen as distinct."

The case of Anna could be also understood as a result of the process of conversion and therapeutic effect of her involvement in the Neo-catechumenate Community. A review of concepts made by Kilbourne and Richardson (1984, p. 247) led them to conclude that a conceptual comparison of new religions and psychotherapy in general, indicated a number of significant commonalities. Some of them are clearly appearent in Anna's statements:

1. elements of the underlying deep structure; e.g., special supporting relationship between the client and adherent religious group; a special setting imbued with powerful symbols of expertise, help, hope and healing;
2. successful religious conversions and successful psychotherapeutic treatments strengthen the person's self-concept and facilitate the person's psychological and social integration ; e.g., a powerful set of positive self-attributions — positive new identity and sense of life's meaning;
3. adopting the standards of the system (and living according to it), which one uses to explain situations and events, makes a sense out of it, and makes a sense of self. It seems that the above constructions should be considered a special set of theistic, and not humanistic constructs, that have been differentiated by Bergin.

REFERENCES

Bergin, A. E. (1980). Psychotherapy and religious values. *Journal of Consulting and Clinical Psychology, 48*, 95-105.

Bergin, A. E. (1983). Religiosity and mental health: A critical reevaluation and meta-analysis. *Professional Psychology: Research and Practice, 14*, 170-184.

Clemen, S. A., Eigsti, D. G. & McGuire, S. L. (1981). *Comprehensive family and community health nursing*. New York: McGraw-Hill.

Dombeck, M. & Karl, J. (1987). Spiritual issues in mental health care. *Journal of Religion and Health*, 26, 183-197.

George, A. S. & McNamara, P.H. (1984). Religion, race and psychological well-being. *Journal for the Scientific Study of Religion, 23*, 351-363.

Glueck, N. (1988). Religion and health: A theological reflection. *Journal of Religion and Health, 27*, 109-118.

Gorsuch, R. L. (1984). Measurement: The boon and bane of investigating religion. *American Psychologist, 39*, 228-236.

Halas, E. (1985). The contextual character of meaning and the definition of the situation. In *Studies in symbolic interactionism*, vol. 6, pp. 149-165. Greenwich CT: JAI Press.

Holm, N. G. & Jarvinen, P. (1993). *Psychosis and religion*. In this volume.

Kilbourne, B. & Richardson, J.T. (1984). Psychotherapy and new religions in a pluralistic society. *American Psychologist, 39*, 237-251.

Textor, M. R. (1989). The "healthy" family. *Journal of Family Therapy, 2*, 59-75.